GREAT AMERICAN
BEER COOKBOOK

D0943638

By
Candy
Schermerhorn

Brewers Publications, Boulder, Colorado USA

Great American Beer Cookbook
By Candy Schermerhorn
Edited by Kathy McClurg
Copyright ©1993
by Candy Schermerhorn

ISBN 0-937381-38-1
Printed in the United States
of America
10 9 8 7 6 5 4 3 2 1

Published by
Brewers Publications,
a division of the
Association of Brewers Inc.
PO Box 1679, Boulder, Colorado
80306-1679 USA
Tel. (303) 447-0816
FAX (303) 447-2825

Direct all inquiries and orders to
the above address.

Production coordinators:
Elizabeth Gold and Tim Sposato
Art direction by Marilyn Cohen
Photographs by Michael Lichter,
Michael Lichter Photography
Food styling by Diane Grove
Illustrations by Amber Sky Illustrators
Photographed table settings courtesy of
Peppercorn Gourmet Goods Inc.,
Boulder, Colorado

CONTENTS

FOREWORD
BY MICHAEL JACKSON

The notion that wine is the only drink to accompany food, or to be used in the kitchen as an ingredient, was always foolish and snobbish, and fortunately is now in retreat. Diners and cooks are rediscovering beer in each of those roles.

In some European nations beer has always had a role in the kitchen, but even there it was taken for granted, or half forgotten for several decades in the face of wine's lofty claims. There is more to cooking with beer than Carbonnade Flamande (Belgian beef stew). In America for years beer was lucky if it achieved a small part in batter or soup, and that was about it.

Today what the French and Belgians call cuisine à la bière is gaining ground on both sides of the Atlantic. It could be argued that the most interesting beer kitchen is now in North America.

One reason is that America is still a melting pot — or perhaps a cauldron — and that is a good piece of equipment to have in any kitchen. European nations borrow from one another's traditions more than they once did, but not with the ease that Americans take up ideas from elsewhere.

Another reason is that the renaissance in specialty beers is more vigorous in America than anywhere else. Again, European countries do not drink each other's beers to the extent that the United States imports theirs. More important, the European — initially British — revival in small breweries and specialty beers has been taken up on an even grander scale in the New World.

While the national beers in the United States and Canada concentrate on beer as a simple refresher, the new microbreweries often make specialty styles with more defined characters: Pilseners and Dortmunders; ales, porters, and stouts; wheat beers and brews with fruits or spices.

When I wrote my first *Simon & Schuster Pocket Guide to Beer* in the early 1980s there were only 50-some brewing companies in North America. Today there are more than 400. Many are brewpubs — taverns or restaurants that make beer on the premises. The more enterprising of these also use beer in their kitchen.

Millions of Americans still are unaware of this renaissance. There are far more brewpubs and microbreweries in the north than in the south, the coasts are better served than middle America, and there are pockets of concentration in Chicago, Colorado, Northern California, and the Northwest. Not all brewpubs use their products in their cooking or create dishes that go especially well with beer, but a growing number do. Among my personal favorites are Zip City in New York, Dock Street in Philadelphia, Goose Island in Chicago, and Gordon Biersch in San Francisco.

Take several hundred brewpubs from Quebec to Florida, from Colorado to Minnesota, from Arizona to British Columbia and you have an extraordinary range of beers and dishes being offered in North America today. Against this background, and with her own blend of enthusiasm, imagination, and skill, Candy Schermerhorn has compiled the entertaining range of recipes that follows. If a brewpub can feature beer cuisine, so can the home cook.

Why the wine-versus-beer snobbism in the first place? Both beverages have a long history. Wine dates back to the beginning of civilization, but so does beer. There is a serious academic theory that humankind first settled in organized communities to grow grain from which to brew — that civilization began with beer.

Wine can be very complex in flavor, but so can beer. In a glass of either there can be hundreds of naturally occurring flavor and aroma compounds. Wine manifests itself in a great variety of styles, but so does beer. Some

drinkers know no wine but Chablis, and even more have encountered no beer but the fizzy golden stuff that is an international and very distant derivation of Pilsener.

Perhaps the snobbism is because the grape — soft, colorful, and juicy — grows in sunny lands alongside such similarly sensuous fruits and vegetables as the olive, tomato, and pepper, making for a fine cuisine.

Beer is made from barley that has been malted (sometimes also from wheat or other grains) and aromatized with the flower of the hop vine. It is true that the grain — harder than the grape, less colorful, and spikier — thrives in cooler climes alongside potatoes and beef cattle. Maybe this led to the idea that beer goes only with meat and potatoes. Perhaps this notion was furthered by the knowledge that wine has little food value but beer can be quite nutritious. In Germany beer still is regarded as liquid bread.

Grains may be less obviously sensuous, but they give us some delicious products: pasta, polenta, and bread, along with beer. A truly fresh beer can have all the malty, grainy aromas of bread straight from the oven.

Then there are the hops. They, too, grow in cooler climes, often alongside cherries and apples, and rarely very far from grapes. The hop is a distant relation of cannabis and full of grassy, piny, floral, earthy aromas not too distant from coriander, which also is occasionally used in beer, or mint.

Wine and beer (especially the stronger and fuller-flavored examples) can have a hint of meaty yeast aromas, but they are surely more appetizing in the complex of a brew, especially if consumed with, or added to, soups or stews.

The snobbism began in Europe. The early imperial rulers were from wine-growing regions: Rome, Burgundy, Spain. Did that make wine an elite drink? I find that hard to accept. In the south of Europe everyone drinks wine, not just the aristocrat but also the peasant. The idea makes even less sense in supposedly egalitarian America. I am told that truckers drink beer — so what? What is wrong with being a trucker? In any case, truckers in France drink wine; does that make wine less acceptable?

In modern times the Northern European brewing nations were more powerful and their citizens had the money to take vacations in the southern sun and lazily drink wine with the foods of the region. To the Northerners, wine came to be associated with unhurried meals in romantic places.

For the Southerners it is the other way round. "Wine is for peasants," a young mover-and-shaker in Milan once told me. "Sophisticated people drink beer." Today the Italians and French are great admirers of German, Belgian, and British beer, not to mention le rosbif, the roast beef of England and Scotland.

Drink and food have always been especially interesting where the wine and beer regions interlock: where Moravia meets Bohemia, where the grainy and grapy parts of Bavaria and Rhineland encounter one another, and especially in Northern France where the Champagne region blurs into Alsace on one side and Flanders on the other. Northern France and Belgium have a cuisine that counterpoints Gallic flair and Teutonic heartiness, and beers to match.

In these regions beer still is served with meals and used in the preparation of many traditional dishes, though without any fuss or snobbism. Parisian chefs have known the value of John Barleycorn since Edouard Manet's model, Emile Bellot, held monthly banquets featuring dishes made with beer in the 1870s. Manet's painting, "The Bar at the Folies Bergeres" (1882) gave equal prominence to bottles of Champagne and what is clearly identifiable as Bass Pale Ale. In his classic *Le Guide Culinaire*, in 1903, Auguste Escoffier, founding chef at the Ritz in Paris, set out several dishes made with beer.

I suspect the grape's greatest advances at the expense of the grain came before and after the two world wars, though even in the 1950s the great Belgian chef Raoul Morleghem was using beer in cooking for various heads of state. His work was the basis for a book of 300 recipes compiled by more than 20 Belgian chefs. The Belgians call this style of cooking cuisine à la bière, and several restaurants in Brussels, Antwerp, and elsewhere make it their specialty.

In 1960, a group of French devotees founded the order of the Chôpe d'Or (golden tankard) to further "the gastronomic appreciation of beer." Their events have attracted great chefs like Paul Bocuse, the Troisgros brothers, and Emile Jung.

In 1984, four Belgian chefs with six Michelin stars between them prepared a luncheon featuring ten beers at the Pierre Hotel in New York City. As the speaker my job was to discuss the character of the beers and their suitability to accompany, or flavor, the dishes. I believe that event introduced the revival of cuisine à la bière to the New World. One of those chefs, Pierre Fonteyne, later cooked on my television series, "The Beer Hunter," on the Discovery Channel.

In the mid-1980s I was invited by Charlie Papazian, founder of the Association of Brewers, to "design" a series of meals in which beer was used as both an accompaniment and an ingredient. I worked with local chefs to present these meals at Association conferences in Boston, Chicago, Denver, San Francisco, and other cities.

Today New York restaurants such as the Brasserie, the American Festival Cafe, Windows on the World, and Nosmo King frequently feature beer cuisine. So do similar establishments in other cities.

The Europeans who settled the United States and Canada brought with them their own dishes and their own beers. The dishes were adapted to local circumstances in America, and to the foods of the new country's regions. To some extent so were the beers, but the ethnic and regional variety of brewing in the United States was virtually destroyed by Prohibition. Before Prohibition, beer was a part of the social and gastronomic culture. After Repeal, and with the growth of mass marketing and national television advertising, it gradually became a bland, canned convenience product.

Ethnic and regional differences in food also diminished, accelerated by two world wars. Depending upon her ethnicity, grandma made borscht, or kassler rippchen, or pasta, but after World War II her children wanted to be good Americans and eat TV dinners. The food of the 1950s was almost as bland and uniform in some European countries as it was in the United States. Today we are all confident enough in our nationalities to rediscover our ethnic origins. It is not disloyal to the Stars and Stripes to eat couscous or chicken molé, or to rediscover the local specialties of Louisiana or Arizona.

With the rediscovery of ethnic and regional foods has come, first in Britain and then throughout the traditional brewing nations but especially in the United States, a similar delight in classic styles of beers. Between imports and American products, especially those made by brewpubs and microbrewers, the consumer in some American cities can find a greater variety of beer styles than is available anywhere in the world.

Why this renaissance in beer? It began in Britain in the 1970s as a consumer reaction against mass marketing. There also was a strong element of conservation: a last-gasp preservation and then a revival of brewing traditions. The notion that "Small is Beautiful," set out in the 1973 book of that name by British economist E.F. Schumacher, has been an inspiration. Small brewers can more easily produce limited runs of specialty beers. Another factor has been increased travel and leisure. Many of the new American small brewers were first excited by the beers they tasted as tourists or students, or during their military service in the British Isles, Belgium, or Germany.

Without this renewed variety, cooking with beer could not have extended much beyond the odd bread, batter, or soup. With this range of beers, a new world is open to the cook.

It is tempting to argue that in either Europe or the United States the dishes of the warm south go best with wine and those of the cool north with beer. This is to forget that American melting pot.

Americans sometimes propose a philosophy that "anything goes." I cannot always accept this — I think pastrami belongs on rye and not in risotto, for example — but the openmindedness of the "New American Cuisine" has brought forth some wonderful combinations. One of the best beer meals I ever ate was in the New World, albeit not in America but in Australia. It matched a bittersweet stout with the caramelized flavors of sun-dried tomatoes in a focaccia, the fruity tartness of wheat beer with eggplant in a beer batter, and the richness of bockbier with a beer-marinated kangaroo ragout. While South and North flirt in Europe, they have married in the New World, and that has created a New Beer Cuisine.

My personal guidelines say that an intense dry porter or stout goes with shellfish or crustaceans; a flowery crisp Pilsener lager with fish; a sweeter Munich pale or smooth Dortmunder lager with chicken; a spicy, malty Vienna-style or Oktoberfest with pastas, pizzas, pork, and spicy dishes; and English-style brown ale with nutty salads; a fruity English-style ale with red meat; a richer Scottish or Belgian ale with game; an acidic wheat beer with fruit desserts; and a dark bockbier, or sweet or strong stout with creamy desserts, cakes, and chocolate.

I like to use beer to moisten breads, pastries, and puddings; to marinate (and thus tenderize as well as flavor) meats; to season and spice both savory and sweet sauces; as a cooking liquid; and as an ingredient in salad dressings (try a really tart framboise in a raspberry vinaigrette). Professional chefs often worry that beer will make their dishes too bitter. This is a danger when sauces are made by reduction, concentrating the flavors of the beers, but it can be overstated. When sampling the creations of professionals I have more often felt they used insufficient beer.

Some people are astonished by the whole notion of cuisine à la bière and others have been surprised by eclecticism of my own approach in articles, books, and the dinners I have hosted.

They have many pleasant surprises in store when they come to grips with Candy Schermerhorn's *Great American Beer Cookbook*.

Michael Jackson is the world's leading writer on beer. Some of the questions raised here are more extensively explored in his book, Michael Jackson's Beer Companion *(Running Press, 1993). Previous works include* The New World Guide to Beer *(Running Press, 1988),* The Simon and Schuster Pocket Guide to Beer *(Simon & Schuster, 1988), and* The Great Beers of Belgium *(M.M. Communications — CODA, 1992), available from the Association of Brewers. He also writes on whiskies, especially single-malt Scotches.*

Jackson is an occasional contributor to the food pages of The Washington Post *and a columnist for* The Independent of London*. He has lectured at Cornell University in Ithaca, New York, and the Suntory Food Business School in Tokyo. He is a consultant to Restaurants Unlimited of Seattle, Washington.*

INTRODUCTION
BY CANDY SCHERMERHORN

I sometimes feel like the proverbial mad scientist, entering my laboratory and concocting edible potions that bring to life previously unknown dishes which embrace both beer and food.

As I studiously measure the mystical potion of beer into the victuals, I am struck by how the addition of beer seems to breathe animation into the food's very essence, lifting it from the deathbed of the mundane to a vibrancy it might never have attained.

Picture a caramel sauce joined with ale that emerges with animated complexity. Or a lifeless omelet stirred into a resurgence of character by a mere trickle of chili beer. And the alliance of chocolate, stout, and whiskey that begets desserts of such spirit they live forever in the minds and palates of those who taste them.

Of course, it can be pondered that these flavors have lived before, perhaps buried in some long-forgotten tomes dissolved into the dust of their surrounding kitchens. Even so, when you encountered your first exhilarating taste of freshly brewed beer was it any less spectacular because others before you had tasted it? Of course not!

If the flavors contained in this book have existed before and we are merely rediscovering them, then so be it. Considering the momentous influence beer has had on humankind throughout the ages, I certainly believe this is not the first time the culinary possibilities of brew have been studied and researched.

You see, when cooking with beer every kitchen becomes an experimental lab focused on the infinite combinations of food and beer. Just as the eccentric scientist discreetly doles out treasured vials of elixirof-life, so the cook holds the bottle of prized brew, adding it lovingly to each new dish.

And as the meticulous scientist looks over his or her notes to see if anything was missed, so the cook should look over the recipe and ask if an opportunity to expand the flavor of the dish is being passed up, or if any procedure should be altered to intensify the character.

My hope is that by using the suggestions and recipes for cooking with the classic beer styles from the pages of this "laboratory journal," you too will gleefully concoct delectable fare content with the knowledge that for beer lovers, it doesn't get any better (unless, according to my husband, you are cooking for the Swedish bikini team).

I have always been adamant that cooking is an adventure and recipes are only the suggested itinerary for that experience. They will supply you with a place to begin your culinary quest and a general direction in which to head.

The purpose of this book is not to require you to follow a particular cooking style (mine), but rather to make you aware of culinary possibilities gleaned from the addition of beer.

For the uninitiated, many of the dishes that incorporate beer will be startling. Why, whoever heard of adding beer to everything from chocolate cake to omelets? To these people I say welcome. Come and be charmed by the subtle and delectable nuances the addition of our most prized beverage will give to your daily fare.

For many others, this style of cooking will come as no revelation, for they have been tipping the bottle into their dishes for years. Kudos to you adventurous souls. Please visit the pages of this book and search out the new or different that you might care to experience.

Whichever you are, I hope you will feel free to substitute ingredients and follow your instincts.

Each recipe includes specific beer styles that will harmonize with a particular dish. If you are new to experiencing the wide world of beers, you may be surprised to learn that there are dozens of classic beer styles to choose from, and each will add its distinctive characteristics.

The styles suggested reflect personal preferences gleaned from extensive sampling and research. I suppose this is where I tell you that it was a tough job, but somebody had to do it!

If I could share only two pieces of advice to assist you on your culinary adventure in cooking with beer, they would be:

1. Recognize that beer should uplift and enhance the flavor of the final dish, not overshadow it.

Flavors should be balanced and harmonious, each supporting the essential qualities of the other.

Breaking this advice down to its simplest elements: pair lighter-bodied beers with delicately flavored foods and heavier-bodied beers with the more intensely flavored foods.

This is not to say that you should never pair opposites, merely that you should do so cautiously.

2. The amount of beer required in a recipe is of little or no consequence.

No specific guidelines dictate how much beer entitles a dish to be considered "beer cuisine." The only important consideration is how the addition of beer transforms the flavor of a dish, heightening and enhancing the final flavor.

Many dishes require only a few tablespoons of beer to augment their flavor. To add more simply for the sake of quantity would be folly. Naturally, there will always be those who are more generous than others with their beer additions, but please do so only for the sake of flavor.

Last but not least, remember that these recipes were composed with the knowledge that you might be a homebrewer with an overabundance of brown ale, or your experimenting may be confined by the limited stock of your supplier's shelves. For whatever reason, if you do not have the particular beer called for, use what is available and within your budget.

After all, the true experience lies in understanding real beer, the food it enhances, and ultimately, the feasting upon both with delightful enthusiasm.

CHAPTER 1
COOKING BASICS

This chapter was written in the hope that even those who rarely venture into the kitchen would be enticed to do so by the prospect of cooking with the fine beers

of the world. The following should help to allay any kitchen apprehension, covering everything from stuffing poultry to working with a sugar syrup. It is also excellent reading for those who simply want to review the basics or garner specific cooking information.

USE QUALITY INGREDIENTS

Does the belief "use the best to make the best" apply to life's numerous escapades in the kitchen? It most certainly does. The best recipe in the world cannot transform inferior ingredients into fine food. High-quality meats and cheeses, impeccable herbs and spices, the freshest produce and, of course, premium beer will always show through in the final dish, elevating it from adequate to exceptional.

This does not mean you must shop at only the most expensive store in town, simply that you must be aware of what is and is not suitably fresh. For example, dried spices and herbs still brimming with their original essence are worth searching out or even ordering by mail, but you need not drive extra miles to purchase bones for stock from the most expensive butcher.

RECOGNIZE THE PROPERTIES OF YOUR INGREDIENTS

When purchasing ingredients, substitute or vary them whenever you wish, taking care to recognize the characteristics needed for that substitution. For instance, using common long-grain white rice instead of short-grain Arborio rice in a risotto would spell certain disaster. Arborio rice absorbs more liquid, does not disintegrate or become gummy with stirring, and has a creamy consistency, the opposite characteristics of long-grain white rice. Yet substituting the rich flavor of fontinella cheese in place of Parmesan in that same risotto would be a successful variation.

READ THE RECIPE THROUGH BEFORE BEGINNING

I wish I could go back and fix all the flops I had because I did not read the recipe through before starting. Dishes that required overnight refrigeration were started two hours before they were supposed to be served, cookies that should have aged for two weeks were baked the day before Christmas, and cakes were begun before realizing I did not own the appropriate pans. These mistakes could have been avoided with a simple read-through of the recipe before beginning. So many of us live by the maxim, "If all else fails, read the directions," but trust me, cooking is not an area where this philosophy works.

ASSEMBLE ALL INGREDIENTS BEFORE BEGINNING

Of course, most recipes instruct us to have all ingredients and equipment assembled before beginning. Many of us have a tendency to scorn that little pearl of wisdom, but sooner or later it catches up with us, usually when we are expecting guests. Timing is critical for many recipes, from stir-frying to cakes, so protect your investment — assemble your ingredients and your equipment.

DO NOT MISS AN OPPORTUNITY TO ADD FLAVOR

If I could impress only one new thought into everyone's cooking technique it would be always look for new opportunities to add flavor. Brown each item separately to retain individual flavors, replace the customary cheese in a sauce with a less common variety, roast garlic before adding to a sauce, or, of course, substitute beer for other liquids. Watch carefully and soon you will realize how many dishes can honestly benefit from a bit of creative substitution or addition.

One last note, do not be intimidated by recipes that have a long list of ingredients. Upon reading the recipe you will often find the actual preparation to be quite simple, it merely contains a wide variety of spices, herbs, etc. If the recipe requires separate steps, these are numbered so as not to be overwhelming.

The following are basic cooking hints of interest if you are new to the kitchen, or merely want to bone up (no pun intended) on cooking skills.

HIGH ALTITUDE COOKING

When cooking at altitudes above 3,000 feet, adjust recipes to compensate for the decreased atmospheric pressure. The following are "rule-of-thumb" suggestions.

Baking

Increase oven temperature by 25 degrees because foods take longer to absorb heat at high elevations.

To compensate for liquids evaporating faster, increase the liquid called for by 2 tablespoons for cooking at 3,000 to 5,000 feet, 3 tablespoons for 5,000 to 10,000 feet.

Because of diminished atmospheric pressure which causes the leavening to overexpand, decrease the leavening called for by 1/8 teaspoon for 3,000 to 5,000 feet, 1/4 teaspoon for 5,000 to 10,000 feet, and 1/2 teaspoon for elevations higher than 10,000 feet. To strengthen the structure at elevations of 10,000 feet and above, add an additional egg and increase each cup of flour by 1 to 2 tablespoons.

Always decrease the time that eggs or egg batters are beaten, especially when working with recipes that derive most or all their leavening from eggs. Underbeating allows the structure formed by the eggs to overexpand at elevated levels without collapsing.

Because the sweetness of sugar is intensified at high altitudes, decrease the total amount of sugar used by 1 tablespoon for 3,000 to 5,000 feet, 2 tablespoons for 5,000 to 7,000 feet, and 3 tablespoons for 7,000 to 10,000 feet.

At high altitudes it is essential that pans be buttered and floured generously to avoid sticking. This applies even to the non-stick baking pans.

All other cooking

Because it takes longer for food to absorb heat at high altitudes, be prepared to increase cooking time on just about everything.

These modifications are based on information found in *California Culinary Academy — Cakes & Pastries*. (Ortho Books, 1985).

BEANS

When cooking with beans (legumes) of any type, it is always advisable to rinse in a colander and put them into the pot one handful at a time. Poke through them and make sure there are no stones or clumps of hard soil mixed in.

Beans require slow, gentle cooking. Rapid boiling leaves them tough and flavorless.

Including a ham or roast bone with beans will impart richness of flavor.

CAKES

Real homemade cakes are much easier than you may think. Cakes usually require simple ingredients, basic techniques, and a suitable pan. If you have never made a homemade cake, the following tips will help.

When flour or powdered sugar require sifting, use a mesh sieve placed over a bowl for rapid sifting.

Always sift cake flour because it is usually lumpy.

Use the egg size specified in the recipe whenever possible — it does make a difference in the overall texture.

Do not tap a filled cake pan on the counter to break up large air bubbles; this collapses half the leavening. Rather, run a knife zigzag through the batter without scraping the bottom to release large air pockets that may have formed when filling the pan.

If you have only one pan and are making a two-layer cake, prepare only half the batter at a time. If the batter sits while the first layer

cooks, it deflates and loses leavening.

To see if a cake has finished baking, insert a thin wooden pick into the center. It will come out clean when done.

Use a rack to cool the cake evenly and efficiently.

Level the top before frosting cakes by trimming off the peaks with a long-bladed serrated knife. Place one hand lightly on the top of the cake and cut using light, short strokes. Be sure to keep the knife horizontal and steady.

PIE & TART CRUSTS

Many will moan and ask if they can please buy ready-made frozen crusts. No problem, but you will be missing out on a lot of flavor. Flavor, you say? Crusts have no flavor, do they? No they don't, but yes they should. Crusts should have flavor, in fact, I firmly believe the crust should always enhance the flavor of the filling.

Adding a pinch of citrus zest to a crust used for fruit pie or adding curry powder to a crust used for spicy meat pie ensures that the pastry will be enjoyed every bit as much as the filling. The additions need not be complicated, even a mere touch of beer, vanilla, and sugar in a crust can greatly enhance the overall experience of a sweet potato pie. Try it and you will be amazed at the difference this simple addition can make.

One important key to tender pie crust is that even though you are mixing butter and flour together, you do not want them to dissolve. Delicate crust comes from tiny, separate particles of butter that expand during the baking process, providing a flaky tenderness.

To keep butter from dissolving it is critical to use icy cold ingredients. You may want to cut the butter into small pieces and freeze it, along with the flour and utensils.

Combine the chilled butter and dry ingredients using a pastry blender or food processor fitted with a steel blade. The mixture should resemble crumbly oatmeal when the butter has been cut in properly.

After combining the flour and butter, add the liquid. Be sure to add just enough to pull the crust together in a mass without leaving excess dried flour. Most instructions are so careful to keep you from adding too much water that they leave you with the impression that the dough must be very dry. This dry-dough concept creates frustrated pie makers because the dough crumbles and cracks the moment it is rolled.

After the dough pulls into a mass, quickly and gently knead exactly 12 times to give just enough structure to facilitate easy rolling without dissolving the butter. To knead, press the dough down with the palm of your hand. Stand on its edge and press again, rapidly repeat 12 times. Do not fold the dough over itself during this process.

Wrap in plastic and chill for at least 30 minutes. Unwrap and firmly pound with the rolling pin into a 3/4-inch-thick circle on a lightly floured surface. Press the edges to form a smooth-edged circle.

Roll from the middle out on a lightly floured surface. If the dough does not spread easily when you roll it then it is sticking underneath. Loosen with a long spatula, gently roll the dough up over your rolling pin, sprinkle more flour underneath, unroll it, and continue.

When the crust is the desired size, gently roll it up on the rolling pin and immediately unroll over the pan. Pick up the edges and ease the crust into the bottom of the pan. If the crust is stretched it will shrink during baking. Do not fret if the crust tears while easing it in, merely patch it with a piece of excess crust. When patching, use the unfloured side of the dough to facilitate bonding. Trim or flute the top edge.

Refrigerate a minimum of 30 minutes to allow the dough to relax, otherwise it will shrink while baking.

If baking without a filling, place a lightly buttered piece of foil, butter-side down, into the bottom of the crust. Fill with pie weights or beans and bake on the lower shelf of a 400° oven for 15 minutes. Remove beans and foil, prick with a fork, and continue baking until golden.

CANDY & SUGAR SYRUPS

It is vital when working with sugar syrups that you have a dependable candy thermometer. Using the old method of dropping a bit of syrup into ice water to see how hard it is can be tricky if you have never actually observed this method before. By the time you decide what stage the syrup is, it has continued cooking to the next stage!

Use a pan that has a capacity 6 times larger than the amount of syrup to prevent boilovers.

Use a wooden spoon so the handle stays cool.

Warm beer to room temperature before adding to a recipe.

Most syrups are based on sugar dissolved in a small amount of liquid. Although a simple procedure, dissolving the sugar correctly is critical. Place the sugar and liquid in a heavy-bottomed pan over medium-low heat. Stir constantly until the sugar has completely dissolved before turning up the heat to cook.

Once the sugar is dissolved and the heat is turned up, do not stir the syrup. Allow to cook until the desired temperature. Stirring the syrup will result in granular, crunchy sugar crystals instead of a smooth, velvety texture.

If you feel you must check to make sure the syrup is not scorching, slowly tip the pan to one side without disturbing the cooking process.

An exception to the do-not-stir rule is pecan pralines, which are supposed to be stirred during cooking for their own distinctive sugary texture.

If you have a supply of unhopped malt extract at your disposal and appreciate its earthy flavor, try substituting it in equal quantities for honey or corn syrup in your recipes.

CHEESE

The majority of us were brought up on spaghetti sprinkled with canned Parmesan or Romano and sandwiches made with processed yellow American cheese. Weary of the prepackaged cheese of our youth, our taste buds deserve an exciting variety of new flavors. French goat cheese and Brie, Greek kaseri cheese, Italian fontinella, English cheddar, fresh Parmesan and Romano, the list goes on and on. These cheeses are not only being imported, but some are produced right here in America and possess equal or superior quality. Do check to see if you have any local cheese producers. It is vital that we support the "cottage" industries flourishing in this country and this applies to local breweries, too!

The following are a few techniques to help you make the most of your cheese purchases.

When cooking cheese, always use the shortest amount of time and the lowest heat possible. This will keep it from separating and becoming stringy.

Always grate cheese that is thoroughly chilled for easy handling.

To melt cheese, grate or cut the chilled cheese into very small chunks, then warm briefly to room temperature to facilitate melting.

It is sometimes helpful to lightly toss grated cheese with a small amount of flour before adding to soup, sauce, or fondue. This not only helps thicken the dish but disburses the cheese evenly.

When stirring cheese into a hot liquid, remove the liquid from the heat and stir cheese in slowly, stirring in one direction just until the cheese is melted. Stirring in one direction will keep the cheese from breaking down and becoming stringy and tough.

To keep cheese from overcooking in a baked dish, freeze the sliced or grated cheese just prior to assembling. When baked, it takes longer for the cheese to come up to temperature, thereby increasing its cooking time.

DESSERTS

An exquisite dessert can often overshadow the impression of the entire meal. If the entrée was adequate but the dessert divine, people remember the experience as a total success, but if the dessert was merely satisfactory their assessment is promptly reduced accordingly.

Preparing an exceptional dessert is effortless if you are aware of a few hints to make it foolproof.

I cannot stress enough the rule to have all ingredients and utensils assembled before beginning. It may sound boring but you could save yourself a lot of grief.

When working with desserts, remember an extra 5 minutes spent making preparations can be invaluable. Greasing and flouring baking pans can be a pain, but if you have had a cake stick because you skipped this step, you appreciate the necessity of the details.

Sweet, unsalted butter usually is fresher than its salted counterpart because salt is a preservative. In addition, salted butter browns faster and is inappropriate in lighter cakes, cookies, or candies.

Countless baked desserts are ruined by ovens that are not calibrated. Get an oven thermometer and make any adjustments needed so your efforts are well-rewarded.

EGGS

When cooking eggs remember their worst enemy is overcooking. Eggs continue to cook briefly after they are removed from the heat so it is best to lightly undercook them; they will firm further when cooled slightly.

Separate eggs while they are cold. The yolks are much less likely to break.

If your recipe requires only whites or yolks, freeze the leftovers in a small airtight container. Defrost in the refrigerator before using.

To whip egg whites to their fullest, have them at room temperature. Whip in a copper or stainless-steel bowl with a large whisk, or a mixer. If using a stainless-steel bowl, add 1/4 teaspoon cream of tartar for every 2 egg whites. This improves the ability of the albumin (protein) to stretch and hold air without bursting. The same chemical reaction happens when egg whites are beaten in copper, making the cream of tartar unnecessary.

When adding beaten whole eggs to hot liquids (avgolomono soup, flan), stir a small amount of hot liquid into the eggs to warm them, then whisk hot mixture constantly while slowly pouring the warmed eggs in a thin stream.

FRUITS & VEGETABLES

To get the longest shelf life out of fresh parsley or cilantro, wrap the bunches loosely in moist paper towels, place in an open plastic bag, and refrigerate.

When using fresh mushrooms be sure to clean carefully. For most, wiping with a damp cloth will suffice. If they are especially dirty, use a soft mushroom brush and gently clean under running water.

To clean spinach, wash several times in fresh water to remove sand or grit. Remove the tough stem clear up into the leaf, if necessary. A salad spinner is the ideal way to dry spinach leaves for salad.

When adding salt to fresh greens or salads, use kosher or coarse salt to prevent wilting.

When adding the often misunderstood flavor of cilantro (fresh coriander), remember the more it is chopped, the harsher the flavor. The tastiest method is to wash and very coarsely chop the leaves. A more attractive method is to pluck the leaves from the stems and use whole. Even though the pieces are larger the flavor is milder.

Briefly charring or browning the outside of thickly sliced onions is a delightful method of subduing their flavor without eliminating their essence. The soft-cooked outside and crisp inside is the perfect addition to salads and hamburgers. Char thick slices by brushing lightly with oil and grilling over very high heat or browning in a heavy skillet lightly coated with oil.

American eggplants should be sliced and soaked in salted water for at least 20 minutes before rinsing and patting dry to remove bitterness. Japanese or Asian eggplants do not require this process.

Drizzle whole heads of garlic with a small amount of olive oil and herbs, bake until soft, and pop out of the skins when cool for the most sensual garlic experience ever. The buttery, silky flavor will enhance everything from salad dressings to sauces to stuffings. It is good mashed and spread on fresh bread.

Use vegetables such as acorn squash and large tomatoes as edible serving containers for complementing vegetable dishes.

Try combining fruits and vegetables such as apples and onions or carrots and pineapple for unique and stunning side dishes.

Thin-skinned vegetables and fruits require paring one slender ribbon of skin from around the middle to prevent bursting when cooking whole. Boiled new potatoes and baked apples benefit from this procedure.

Delicate-flavored Chinese napa cabbage can be torn or thinly sliced and used in place of lettuce in many salads. It is especially nice as a base for fruit salad.

To seed cucumbers, split lengthwise and scrape a spoon down the center until all the seeds have been scooped out.

MEATS

Many volumes have been devoted to the art and intricacy of cooking meats. I will hit only the areas that generate the most trouble and that apply to the recipes in this book.

When purchasing meat it is tempting to go strictly for deep red meat with no fat. Keep in mind that only marbled meats retain their juiciness. Marbling is fat, not gristle, found throughout the meat that enhances its juicy, tender, flavorful qualities.

As with seafood, it's important to pair the right cut of meat with the proper cooking method. A rib-eye steak would disintegrate with long-cooking methods and a thick chuck roast would be tough if pan-fried. Each recipe is specific about the type of meat to use with a particular cooking method.

MARINATING

A marinade has three essential ingredients. First is an acidic liquid (beer, wine, fruit juice) to flavor the meat while the acid breaks down the tissue with a tenderizing effect. The second is oil, which acts as a lubricant, aiding moisture retention during cooking. The third can be a group of ingredients for flavoring, including herbs, spices, and garlic. The basic functions of a marinade are to tenderize, add succulence and, of course, enhance flavor.

It is important to consider the type of meat and strength of the marinade. If you have a tender cornfed top-sirloin steak, it is unnecessary (and criminal) to marinate in a strong-flavored marinade for 18 hours!

If meat is to be cooked twice, as in fajitas, it is important not to overcook it during the first cooking or the final results will be tough and tasteless.

When cooking meat remember the higher the temperature the more shrinkage you get, whether grilling, pan-frying, or roasting. Steaks normally are not cooked long enough for this to apply, but a larger cut such as a roast will shrink to nothing and expel flavorsome juices as its structure constricts.

When preparing raw pork remember to follow the same safety precautions you would when handling poultry.

Most methods of cooking meat are pretty straightforward. It's interesting to note, however, that roasting still seems to be the method that draws the most questions. The following should help answer them.

ROASTING

Roasting is a dry-heat cooking process, meaning the meat must be elevated on a rack in a shallow pan to allow even heat circulation and drain off the juices. This applies to all roasted meats.

Good old-fashioned basting still is the unbeatable method of keeping meat moist and infusing it with flavorful herbs and pan juices. Use a glass or metal bulb baster. The plastic ones tend to melt if the tip comes in contact with the hot pan.

Basic roasting method for large cuts of meat (7 or more pounds) such as a standing rib roast: warming the meat for 60 to 75 minutes at room temperature facilitates uniform roasting. If not marinating, steep the roast in an acidic liquid (beer or wine) during this warming period. Season and place fat-side up on rack in a shallow pan.

Place in a preheated 400° oven for 35 minutes. Lower temperature to 300° to 325° and continue, basting frequently with pan juices. Use a meat thermometer or an instant-read cooking thermometer to check the internal temperature.

After removing from the oven, cover it with foil and allow to rest about 1 1/2 minutes per pound before carving and serving. This allows the meat fibers to relax and retain the juices when carved.

An alternative method for cooking a large piece of beef is explained on page 122 in the recipe for Portered Roast Beast.

Smaller cuts such as briskets and chuck roasts: These cuts can be roasted but need help with internal moisture because they are tougher and tend to dry out. Searing first and roasting on a rack in a covered pan will give a roasted flavor yet retain the all-important moisture.

Heat a skillet on high and pour in 2 to 3 tablespoons of olive or peanut oil. Quickly sear both sides on medium high until dark brown and crusty (if marinated, wipe the surface dry first). Place on a greased rack inside a roasting pan. Cover with foil or lid.

Roast in a preheated 300° to 325° oven and baste often with the juices until quite tender. Roasting time will vary according to thickness and cut.

Internal temperatures for roasted beef: 125° to 130° for rare beef, 140° to 145° for medium.

Internal temperature for roasted pork: 170° to 175°.

ROASTING MEAT WITH VEGETABLES

When roasting vegetables along with meat, parboil root vegetables (potatoes, carrots, turnips) just until tender.

Potatoes should have a small strip of skin cut from around the middle to prevent bursting. Remember that small new potatoes parboil in only 5 minutes while full-sized potatoes need 10 to 12 minutes.

Small, tender carrots do not require parboiling.

Large onions should be halved or quartered. Insert a toothpick into each quarter to keep them together. Small onions can be roasted whole.

All vegetables should be arranged around the meat for the last hour of cooking only. Baste every 10 to 15 minutes with pan juices.

BRAISING

Braising is done by searing meat first, adding a small amount of liquid (beer of course!) along with such flavorings as spices, herbs, garlic, onions, or tomatoes, covering the pan and either baking or simmering on stove top over very low heat until fork tender. Braising at a high temperature will result in tough, stringy meat.

POULTRY

Poultry is adaptable to many types of cooking methods and requires only a few hard and fast rules. When purchasing, look for full, compact birds with creamy-colored skin. Precut poultry is more expensive but convenient when a recipe calls for 8 chicken breasts.

Be sure to check the freshness dates on the package.

No section on poultry would be complete without a reminder to observe absolute cleanliness when handling. Anything that comes in contact with raw poultry, including your hands and utensils, can transfer salmonella contamination if present in the meat. Lots of hot soapy water and the following suggestions will keep you on the safe side.

Cover the faucet handle with a piece of plastic wrap so when finished the handle is not contaminated.

Have all equipment and ingredients assembled and measured before beginning (trussing thread, foil to cover the cavity, herbed butter to tuck under the skin) to minimize any possible contamination.

Keep raw poultry in a pan or bowl in the refrigerator so the store package does not leak and contaminate other foods.

ROASTING WHOLE POULTRY

For preparation ideas, see Perfectly Roasted Chicken recipe on page 161.

Truss and set on a greased roasting rack, breast-side down. Place in preheated 425° oven for 35 minutes. Baste and turn breast-side up.

Baste and roast an additional 30 to 40 minutes, or until a meat thermometer registers 160° when inserted into the thickest part of the thigh, or until the juices run clear when you puncture the skin at a thigh joint.

Remove to a heated platter, cover and allow to rest about 1 1/2 minutes for every pound. Just as in beef, this permits the meat fibers to relax and retain juices when carved.

The pan juices can be made into sauce or gravy during this resting period, if desired.

When stuffing a whole bird, lightly stuff the cavity. Stuffing will expand, absorbing flavors and juices while retaining a fluffy, light texture. Overstuffing creates a loss of flavor and leaves the stuffing gummy.

Place a small piece of foil over the cavity to keep stuffing moist and hold in those flavorful juices.

Internal temperature for unstuffed poultry: 160° to 170°.

Internal temperature for stuffed poultry: 175° to 180°.

When sautéing poultry in butter use half unsalted butter and half peanut or canola oil, especially if your cookware is thin and scorches easily. The oil allows you to cook at a higher temperature for a longer period of time without overbrowning the butter. This is especially helpful when sautéing larger pieces, such as stuffed chicken breasts, which require longer cooking.

Lightly coat pieces of poultry to be sautéed with seasoned flour to seal and retain the juices.

Most fried poultry is coated or battered, exceptions being the Buffalo wing recipes on pages 164 through 166. Be sure to pat skin completely dry before frying to minimize splattering.

When stir-frying thin strips of poultry, make sure the pan is hot enough to seal juices in the meat. Stir constantly just until cooked so the juices do not collect and boil the meat.

Poaching is one of the fastest and simplest methods of cooking chicken. Slowly boil 1 1/2 inches of water, beer, or other liquid lightly seasoned with your favorite herbs, garlic, or shallots, a squeeze of lemon or lime juice, and a pinch of freshly ground black pepper. Add skinless, boneless chicken pieces and cook, removing any scum that forms. Lower to a slow simmer and cook until meat no longer shows any pink when a small sharp knife is inserted into the thickest part. Remove and drain.

QUICK BREADS

When leavened with baking soda, make sure the box has not sat on your shelf for eons. Fresh baking soda will provide a higher degree of leavening. Make sure that recipes using baking soda include an acidic ingredient such as buttermilk or sour cream, needed to activate leavening properties.

Sift baking soda and baking powder to make sure there will be no unsightly (or unappetizing) lumps in your baked goods.

If you must substitute baking soda for baking powder, (or vice versa) 1/4 teaspoon of baking soda equals about 1 teaspoon of baking powder.

Most quick breads (biscuits, muffins) will call for the following procedure:

Thoroughly mix all dried ingredients.

Cut shortening into dry ingredients using a pastry blender or food processor fitted with a steel blade. The only exception is when using liquid oil to add it with the liquid ingredients.

Mix all liquid ingredients thoroughly in a separate bowl. Add the liquids to the dry ingredients all at once to cut down the amount of stirring.

The more a batter is stirred or mixed, the tougher the final texture will be.

SAUCES & GRAVIES

The most important proportion to remember when making any classic sauce or gravy is 2 - 2 - 1; 2 tablespoons fat, 2 tablespoons flour, 1 cup hot liquid.

The 2 tablespoons of fat can be the pan drippings of a roast, butter, margarine, or oil. The 2 tablespoons of flour should be plain flour. The 1 cup of hot liquid can be beer, broth, milk, skimmed pan juices, or a combination.

It is very important to use hot liquid to avoid lumps. If you prefer a thinner sauce, use the proportion of 1 - 1 - 1 (1 tablespoon fat, 1 tablespoon flour, and 1 cup hot liquid). For a thicker sauce use 3 - 3 - 1.

To make roux: Most sauces or gravies are thickened with roux that consists of equal portions of flour cooked in fat. Melt the fat in a heavy skillet and whisk in the flour. Stir while the flour cooks to avoid scorching. Cook until the desired golden color has been achieved, usually 5 to 10 minutes. Exceptions are for white sauce cook only 3 to 4 minutes, and for Southern-style sauces cook until mahogany to ebony in color.

To make sauce or gravy: Slowly pour hot liquid into cooked roux, whisking constantly. Continue cooking and stirring until thickened completely. Remove from heat.

If you are not using a heavy-bottomed pan when making sauce or gravy, lower heat and cook slowly to prevent scorching.

Some sauces are made without a thickening ingredient by reducing the liquid on medium-high to a concentrated state. An example is the Raspberry Sauce on page 250. You will need to lower the heat as the sauce reduces to avoid scorching.

SEAFOOD

A growing number of people want to include more seafood in their diet but are in a quandary about how to purchase it, what to purchase, and how to prepare it. The following will give a quick overview.

PURCHASING FISH

When purchasing seafood, be sure to use a type of fish that suits your method of cooking. For instance, if you sauté thin, skinless fillets of orange roughy they will often crumble when removed from the pan. A slightly thicker fillet of red snapper with the skin still attached would be more appropriate. A better use for thin fillets might be to wrap them around a savory filling and bake in parchment.

Try to locate a reliable source for quality fresh seafood. If unavailable, remember that frozen tastes better than unhealthy. If you have any doubts, it's better to buy frozen than to chance that the "fresh" you bought on Monday may be the same fish displayed in the case last Thursday.

When buying whole fish check for bright, clear, bulging eyes plus clean, reddish-pink gills.

Scales should be shiny and lay flat, not raised on end.

Flesh should be firm and spring back when pressed.

Fish should have a clean, fresh odor — no fishy smell. Do not hesitate to ask to smell the fish before purchasing.

Purchase about 1/2 pound of fish per person.

COOKING FISH

Cook as soon after purchasing as possible. If a busy schedule has kept you from cooking the fish you bought three days ago, remind yourself that throwing away a few dollars of fish is much cheaper than a trip to the emergency room.

It is now well-known that the most common mistake when cooking fish and shellfish is overcooking, which causes seafood to become tough, dry, and tasteless.

Fish should be cooked according to the rule of 10 minutes per inch of thickness.

Shellfish (shrimp, lobster, crawfish) should be cooked just until the color turns bright.

MARINATING

Marinate shellfish or firm fish fillets to add flavor and moisture.

A basic marinade combines 1 cup beer, 2 to 4 tablespoons oil, 2 to 3 tablespoons citrus juice (lime is a favorite), and 1 to 2 teaspoons of your favorite herbs or spices. Marinate in refrigerator for 2 hours before sautéing, grilling, or baking.

STEAMING

Steaming maintains delicate flavors and texture and allows fish to be cooked without fat.

When steaming, use a vessel that has plenty of room for the steam to circulate. Elevate the fish well above the liquid.

An exotic steaming liquid is 1 cup full-flavored beer (porter, dunkelweizen, India pale ale) with 1 teaspoon freshly grated ginger, 1 mashed clove garlic, 3 tablespoons soy sauce, 1/2 teaspoon cracked pepper and 1/2 teaspoon dark sesame oil.

POACHING

Poaching is a popular method of cooking fish, adding a delicate flavor and enhancing the texture.

A simple combination of 1 cup beer (German light lager, American light lager, weissbier or pale ale), 1/2 cup milk, and 1 teaspoon herbs (thyme is a favorite) produces a superb poaching liquid.

Have the liquid at a full simmer before you gently slide the fish into the pan and begin timing according to the 10-minutes-per-inch-of-thickness rule. Use a slotted spatula to remove.

If poaching a whole fish, wrap in cheese-cloth to make it easier to handle.

BOILING

My all-time favorite is to boil crawfish, shrimp, or crab in lots of American light lager doused liberally with Cajun spices. Drain as soon as they turn pink and bring out the industrial-strength napkins, herbed butter, and Louisiana hot pepper sauce. What a feast!

GRILLING OR SMOKING

Grilling imparts an outdoor essence that is simply incredible.

When grilling fish, generously oil the grill. Sprinkle flour lightly over the fish and place it on the hot grill. While grilling, the fish should be brushed with a beer marinade, flavored oil, or melted herbed butter to keep it moist.

Smoking gives a truly intense, woodsy flavor that is legendary. Use either plain fish or fish that has first been soaked in brine and dried (Dilled Smoky Salmon on page 101). Either can be smoked on an indoor stove-top Cameron smoker (page 26) or an outdoor smoker.

BROILING

Nearly foolproof, broiling is excellent for preparing fish when time is short.

Fish that is 3/4 to 1 inch thick is best for broiling because thinner cuts dry out. Adjust the broiler rack so the top of the fish is 2 to 4 inches from the heat source. Oil the broiler pan, brush the fish with a beer marinade, flavored oil, or herbed butter, and broil until lightly browned. Turn, baste, and continue broiling for the allotted time.

If fish is frozen, adjust the broiler rack to a low position for uniform cooking and allow 20 minutes per inch of thickness.

Split fish should be placed skin-side down on a greased pan and basted with herbed butter or marinade. Do not turn split fish.

Whole fish is oiled and dusted with seasoned flour. Large fish should be broiled 6

inches from the heat, small fish 3 inches away. Turn when lightly browned and continue cooking for the allotted time.

PAN-FRYING

A standard method of cooking, whether in the kitchen or sitting stream-side with a string of fat trout.

Fish cooked by this method holds its shape much better if dipped in beer or buttermilk then coated with seasoned flour or cornmeal.

Heat a pan on medium-high and add 1/4 inch melted butter or oil. Add the coated fish and fry until golden on one side, turn and continue pan-frying using the 10-minutes-per-inch-of-thickness rule.

SAUTÉING

Giving a more delicate flavor, this method lends itself to adding a simple but elegant beer sauce made right in the pan.

Sautéing uses the same cooking method as pan-frying with less butter or oil. If you use a good non-stick pan, it is possible to sauté fish with only 2 or 3 tablespoons of oil (herbed butter is delicious).

To make sauce, transfer cooked fish to a hot plate. Sprinkle freshly chopped Italian (flat-leafed) parsley, finely chopped shallots, and light herbs into the pan along with a few tablespoons of weissbier or European Pilsener. Shake and heat through before pouring over fish.

DEEP-FRYING

Is there anything that says "Friday night" like a good ol' fish fry? Try beer in your favorite batter frying recipe for crunchier results.

Fish cooked in this manner must first be battered either by dipping in egg or buttermilk and then into seasoned flour, corn meal, or bread crumbs, or by rolling in seasoned flour before dipping in beer batter.

Heat oil to 375°. Carefully slip in the battered fish and time according to the thickness of the fish.

Use a thermometer to gauge the temperature. Oil that is too cool will result in greasy, soggy, undercooked fish. Oil that is too hot will result in dry, overbrowned, tasteless fish.

MICROWAVING

Microwaving fish in its own juices gives a flavor and texture similar to poaching. This is one method where the 10-minutes-per-inch rule does not apply, because microwave cooking is dependent on shape, moisture content, density, amount of food, and wattage.

As a general rule, one pound of fish will take roughly 5 minutes to cook.

EXCEPTIONS

Exceptions to the 10-minutes-per-inch rule are:

If you are cooking a rolled stuffed fillet, measure thickness after it has been stuffed.

If you are cooking fish wrapped in paper or foil, allow an extra 5 minutes for the heat to penetrate the wrapping.

Fish can be cooked frozen. The key is to allow 20 minutes per inch of thickness.

WOK COOKING

Wok cooking is an Asian technique that has gained popularity worldwide. This wholesome, rapid method of cooking preserves color, flavor, and texture. Certain basics will help you turn out flawless dishes each and every time.

Cut food into small, uniform pieces to provide more cooking surface, quicker and more efficient cooking.

To slice meat thinly, partially freeze before cutting.

Stir-frying means just that — constant stirring while cooking over very high heat. This ensures that the moisture released by the food is constantly in contact with the hot surface, causing it to evaporate immediately. If the food is not constantly stirred, it will simmer rather than stir-"fry."

Never cook more than 1 pound of meat or vegetables at a time. This allows space in the wok to stir and move the food and helps the wok to retain heat.

Stir-frying requires very high heat, so use oil with a high flame point such as peanut or canola.

Traditionally, whole nuts are fried briefly in very hot oil, allowed to cool, then added at the end. Roasting nuts at 350° until golden will give similar results without additional oil.

Always serve stir-fried foods immediately. Involving family or guests in preparation and cooking brings a lovely intimacy to the meal.

BASIC STIR-FRYING ORDER

Most stir-fried dishes follow a basic cooking order.

1.

Plain or lightly marinated meat is usually stir-fried first then set aside.

2.

Firm vegetables (carrots) are stir-fried next until partially cooked.

3.

Push the vegetables aside, add sauce and thicken slightly.

4.

The more delicate ingredients (scallions) are stirred in as the sauce thickens.

5.

Return the cooked meat, toss to coat with sauce, and quickly reheat.

SOUPS

Soups and stews are based on a savory liquid that derives flavor from simmering with bones, meat, vegetables, or a combination, plus seasoning from herbs and spices. This liquid is referred to as either broth or stock.

If you are skeptical about the taste difference between store-bought and homemade, rest assured there is an immense difference. There is simply no replacement for doing it yourself.

BROTH

Broth is the result of simmering bones and vegetables in water (or in our case water and beer) until their flavor has been extracted.

One of the best-kept secrets of those who make fabulous soups is adding the brown papery skins from yellow onions to impart a richness of color and depth of flavor that is extraordinary. Another overlooked tip is to use bones that are first browned under the broiler or on the grill. This simple step adds a sumptuous intensity to broth. Try freezing leftover bones from cooked meat or roasted poultry for your next pot of soup.

To make broth, pour 4 quarts of cold water or 13 cups of water and 3 cups of a complementary beer over soup bones (chicken, beef, pork, lamb, or a combination) and bring to a simmer. Skim any foam that rises. When the foam no longer rises, add 1 clove mashed garlic, 1 large bay leaf, 8 fresh peppercorns, handful of parsley stems, 2 onion skins and 1 whole clove. Vegetables such as carrots or celery can be added.

Simmer the bones, seasonings, and onion skins for 3 to 4 hours and strain through a sturdy colander. Cool and refrigerate broth if not using right away, or prepare stock from this strained liquid.

STOCK

Stock is typically made by simmering the strained broth until it is reduced by half. Another method is to add a fresh batch of bones and seasonings to previously prepared strained broth. This is simmered an additional 4 hours and then strained, thereby doubling the intensity to equal that of stock.

Broth and stock can be refrigerated up to 2 days or frozen.

GLACÉ DE VIANDE

If you favor the quality of homemade broth and stock but have little time to make it regularly, you can make glacé de viande, a highly concentrated stock essence.

To make glacé de viande, prepare a large quantity of broth, strain and refrigerate. Remove all fat that congeals on top. Simmer until reduced in volume by 95 percent (if you start with 20 cups of broth you will reduce it to 1 cup of glacé). The glacé will congeal when chilled and can be frozen in small portions for lengthy storage. Reconstitute with water to the desired strength.

YEAST BREADS

One of the most enjoyable and delicious foods ever to come out of a kitchen is bread, but many shy away out of anxiety (a.k.a. "yeast-us anxietus"). To ease this apprehension, I have included the following bread basics to ensure consistent results.

YEAST

Dry bread yeast is dissolved in warm liquid where it rehydrates and multiplies. Yeast flourishes when its three basic needs are fulfilled — for moisture, warmth, and food (starch).

Most recipes call for yeast to be "proofed" by sprinkling over warm water and allowing it to grow. By modifying this procedure and stirring the yeast into 1/2 to 1 cup of bread flour before adding the warmed liquid, an immediate source of food (starch) is provided, ensuring "yeast success."

Because yeast is sensitive to heat, use a kitchen thermometer to guarantee the liquid is at optimum temperature. For dry yeast the liquid should be between 105° and 110° (not less than 100° or higher than 115°). For block or cake yeast the temperature should be between 85° and 90°, never lower than 80° or higher than 95°.

HIGH GLUTEN FLOUR

High-gluten flour and additional flavoring ingredients are mixed with the now flourishing yeast to form a smooth, stiff dough. It is the gluten in the grain that gives the dough its elasticity, allowing it to stretch and hold the carbon dioxide bubbles released by the yeast. High-gluten flour is marketed nationally as bread flour and contains 14 grams of protein per ounce.

Without high-gluten flour or proper kneading, the structure will break and collapse during the baking process resulting in a flat brick of bread.

KNEADING

Kneading is the process of pushing and folding the dough to develop and strengthen the gluten structure. The dough should be kneaded until it is very elastic and smooth, usually about 10 minutes to guarantee the strength of the structure formed.

Knead by pushing dough down, folding it over and turning slightly. Add only enough flour to keep from sticking to the work surface or your hands. Knead until smooth and very elastic.

When the surface begins to tear, stop folding and knead by pressing and pushing only.

RISING

Rising means to cover kneaded dough loosely and allow it to rest until doubled in bulk. It is then punched down (deflated) and shaped into a loaf. It undergoes a second rising before baking to give the loaf a fine, consistent texture.

Bread will rise at any temperature that does not kill the yeast. At 80° to 85° dough will rise quickly and give excellent results. Bread risen slowly at 50° to 55° will develop a slightly tangy (acidic) flavor. Bread also will rise in the refrigerator for 6 to 12 hours.

BAKING

Bread should be baked in a generously greased pan or on a baking stone on the lower shelf of the oven. One of the biggest complaints is an overbrowned top and soggy underside. Lowering the shelf one rung will help eliminate this problem.

To test a loaf, tap the top, checking for a hollow sound. Gently tip the loaf out of the pan to see if the bottom is golden. If pale or overly moist, bake an additional 8 to 10 minutes.

FORMING LOAVES

To shape the dough into loaves, rub an area of the counter with a few drops of oil. Pat the dough into an 8 x 10-inch rectangle that is slightly wider at the top. Starting at the narrow end, roll firmly but gently into a cylinder. Do not stretch the dough. Pinch the ends and turn under toward the seam.

To seal the seam, forcefully slam the dough onto the counter, seam-side down, two or three times. This removes air bubbles.

TROUBLESHOOTING

Here are a few of the most common problems when working with yeast dough the first few times.

1. Loaf collapses during baking.

Be sure to use bread flour or other high-gluten (protein) flour. If loaf collapses, next time try kneading an additional 5 minutes to further develop the protein structure. If this still does not work, purchase wheat gluten from a health-food or specialty store. A few teaspoons of concentrated gluten whisked into the dry flour will add a tremendous amount of structure strength.

2. Loaf is overbrowned on the top, soggy on the bottom.

Lower the oven shelf so the bottom of the loaf is closer to the heat source. If the top still browns too quickly, lay a piece of foil loosely over the top after 15 minutes of baking.

3. Loaf splits during baking.

Use a sharp, thin-bladed knife to lightly score the top of the loaf before baking. This allows the steam to escape.

4. Loaf has wide bands of open cavities when cut.

Roll the dough tighter when forming the loaf. Seal edges completely and be sure to slam it onto the counter, seam-side down, with lots of force 3 to 4 times.

5. Dough is very sticky and too soft to form a loaf.

More than likely the weather is very humid. Sprinkle flour on your work surface and knead dough lightly until firm and resilient. Cover and let rest for 20 minutes before forming into loaves.

COOKING TOOLS

When a carpenter purchases a hammer, a machinist selects a calibrated gauge, or a brewer upgrades hydrometers, the investment is made despite cost and without penitence. After all, they are investing in themselves by making purchases that reduce their margin of error and improve the quality of their working conditions.

So why is the kitchen, where a significant portion of time is spent, dismissed to the bottom of the expenditure list? Why do purchases of even the least expensive cookware evoke deep-seated feelings of remorse?

Perhaps some day there will be an answer to these questions. Meanwhile, a growing group of people avoid cooking because of negative experiences with unsuitable equipment. Many will label themselves incompetent in the kitchen and others will simply conclude that cooking is an unpleasant experience. All are unaware that the shortcomings of their equipment prompted their plight, not their culinary incompetence.

Cooking is and should always be a delightful experience filled with confidence and accomplishment. Therefore, let us elevate the kitchen to a more appropriate position and bestow upon it the same status as any other work place. Success in business and in the kitchen is directly related to the proper equipment, equipment that will facilitate your efforts, not sabotage them.

Admittedly, the risk of spending a large sum of money on equipment is intimidating. However, instructing more than 500 cooking classes in a well-equipped kitchen supply shop has given me the opportunity to extensively examine and ruthlessly test a myriad of products, taking the guesswork out of these purchases.

No matter what brand of equipment you choose, be certain that it will work for you, not against you. The following products have withstood my own unrestrained onslaught over the years and come through with flying colors:

SCAN PAN

The non-stick ceramic surface of this unique cookware is fired onto the pan at twice the speed of sound, bonding it permanently to the superheavy pressure-cast aluminum pan for a non-stick fantasy come true. Made in Denmark, Scan Pan's distinctive qualities allow you to use metal utensils and clean the pans hot from the fire — the company even recommends it — without a bit of warping.

The consistent heating qualities of Scan Pan allow me to cook delicate custards and melt fine chocolate over direct heat (no more double boilers) without curdling or scorching. Because the surface is fired on, not just coated, I can stir-fry at red-hot temperatures without damaging the exterior, a test that plastic-based coatings could not pass

An added advantage is that the entire pan, including the sturdy glass lids and the space-age handles, goes into an oven up to 500° for a versatility rarely found in cookware. Should you burn something (non-stick does not mean non-burn), you can scrub the pan with steel wool or even use fine sandpaper.

The designers of Scan Pan used kitchen sense in their designs. The large skillets and woks have handles on both sides for easy lifting when full. The 2-quart saucepan has a lip on both sides for left- or right-handed pouring. The 9 1/2-quart stockpot (one of my favorites) is shaped like an old-fashioned cauldron, effectively rolling and stirring the food as it simmers. This uncommon shape allows the pan to fit into the oven for baking or roasting.

After baking a batch of gooey pecan sticky buns and successfully turning them out of the high-sided skillet with all the "sticky" attached, one Scan Pan devotee summed it up by stating, "Scan Pan makes a mediocre cook emerge from the kitchen looking [and feeling] like a pro."

MESSERMEISTER KNIVES

Knives are, without a doubt, one of the most utilized pieces of kitchen equipment. And, as with beer, the Germans have perfected the art of making knives, combining old-world craftsmanship developed from centuries of sword making with modern technoengineering to produce a superior product.

Messermeister is the premier example of German blades forged from the highest quality Solingen steel. The durable, molded handles will not crack or shrink and are made of a unique plastic that assures your grip when your hands are wet. The fine, razor-thin blades hold an edge like no other.

Of special interest is the exact balance of these knives that makes their use practically effortless, easing the strain of lengthy use. There are a number of "quality" knives that left my hand and forearm aching, a thing of the past with Messermeister knives.

My most often used knives are the Chinese vegetable cleaver, 8- and 10-inch chefs knives, 3-inch paring knife, and flexible boning knife. Their sharpening steel is a superb piece that will keep the blades in optimum condition.

KAISER BAKEWARE

After scorching one too many cakes, I finally decided that my time was worth more than my stubborn reluctance to purchase quality bakeware. After examining one type after another I tried a Kaiser Laforme pan and fell in love. The heavy uniform baking qualities of this non-stick premium bakeware allow me to prepare even the most fragile items with confidence.

This line includes the finest springform pans available, pans that do not leak batter all over the oven and which come in a wide variety of sizes. A multitude of fanciful molds, bread, and cake pans is available with the same superior non-stick baking qualities.

CAMERON SMOKER

There are few foods that do not benefit from being cooked in the open over a fragrant wood fire, but few of us have the facilities to smoke food in this fashion. Enter the Cameron smoker, a stainless-steel, stove-top smoker that imparts that rich, woodsy essence to everything from steaks to pork to seafood, vegetables, cheeses, and brewing grains, right in your kitchen. This versatile piece of equipment can be used on electric, gas, or induction cooktop.

The smoker is uncomplicated to use. Sprinkle wood chips in the bottom of the rectangular pan, place the drip pan and rack over the top and arrange the food on the rack. Slide the lid over the top and position over a burner for cooking to juicy perfection without an ounce of added fat. The succulent, wood-laced results are indescribable.

CUISINART FOOD PROCESSOR

I do not need to explain this line except that I literally burned up three less expensive look-alike food processors in one year. It's dependable beyond measure and well-known the world over.

OXO POTATO PEELER

This fat, soft-handled utensil combines a sharp, precision edge with easy-grip handle, making it a joy to use. It makes short work of peeling potatoes and other vegetables and is perfect for arthritics who cavort in the kitchen!

DAMCO GADGETS

From their superbly designed citrus zester to their inexpensive (but indispensable) serrated vegetable knife, this entire line of sensibly priced utensils is comparable to ones that cost much more. When I discovered recently that Damco is the parent company of Messermeister, it came as no surprise that the quality of their products is far superior to any others I have tested.

PENZEYS SPICE HOUSE

For anyone who has ever searched desperately for top quality or unusual varieties of herbs and spices, the answer is just a phone call away. Since 1957, this small, family business has provided the best there is in the herb and spice world. The difference is incomparable and well worth the wait when only the finest will do. The Spice House, 1031 N. Old World Third St., Milwaukee, Wisconsin 53203.

CHAPTER 2
EGG & DAIRY

Combining eggs and cheese with beer is a pleasurable endeavor that can be as simple as preparing an omelet stuffed with fresh cheese or as sophisticated as stuffing a small Brie with beer-sautéed mushrooms and baking in puff pastry.

It is a pity that many of us have become so used to eating eggs and cheese that we have lost our perspective of what truly fascinating foods they can be. By preparing dishes that unite eggs and/or cheese with beer we give the combination a new perspective and wake up our taste buds.

Beer has a way of bringing out the best of these cherished foods. Eggs become full-flavored, tender, and delicate because of the rich taste and moisture added by the beer.

Cheese is particularly enhanced by the abundant grain and bittering qualities found in beer. Beer will cut the fatty characteristics of the richer cheeses, allowing you to taste more of the cheese essence.

The wide spectrum of food enhanced by this marriage of flavors is surprising. A ho-hum plate of vegetables can take on new sparkle when sauced with the Cheese Sauce with A Twist (page 215).

Because of the natural affinity of eggs and cheese, plus their relative low cost, they become an enticing and affordable area to explore when you next venture into the kitchen looking for a creative experience. For tips on cooking with cheese and eggs please refer to pages 14 through 16.

Rustic Strata, page 32. ▶

OMELETS

1.

Heat butter in an omelet pan or 9-inch skillet until bubbly but not brown or smoking.

2.

While the pan is heating, lightly beat eggs and beer in a small bowl with a fork. Add salt, pepper, and seasoning.

3.

Pour in eggs then shake and rotate the pan vigorously to distribute the runny egg mixture over the cooked egg until lightly set and creamy.

4.

To fill, place filling over one-third of the omelet on the side that will slide out of the pan first. Gently slide the omelet out, folding the unfilled portion over the filling. Garnish and serve.

1 1/2 tablespoons butter or margarine
2 eggs
2 teaspoons Pilsener, American light lager, or chili beer
salt to taste
freshly ground black pepper
dash of chipotle chili, Louisiana hot pepper sauce, or Homebrewed Steak Sauce, optional (page 214)

Serves 1

An omelet is a versatile, elegant, and economical meal that requires less than five minutes to prepare. Clearly, no other dish can be so transformed by the addition of a mere 2 teaspoons of beer. If you enjoy filled omelets, try some of the following variations.

FILLING VARIATIONS

SAVORY OMELET FILLINGS: fresh-snipped herbs; Beer-Glazed Onions (page 78) and sautéed mushrooms; fresh-grated cheese and a smidgen of beer mustard; chunks of goat cheese and lightly toasted nuts; slices of avocado, sour cream, and Pico de Gallo (page 221); bits of leftover meat and sprouts; strips of green chili, cheese, and sour cream. Garnish with fresh parsley, strips of red bell pepper, slices of avocado, crumbled bacon, or finely chopped scallions.

SWEET OMELET FILLINGS (for spectacular breakfasts or sophisticated desserts): fresh fruit or preserves and lightly toasted nuts; fresh crushed berries folded into whipped cream; Glazed Pineapple (page 261) and Crème Fraîche (page 35); Hot Fruit Compote (page 65); Glazed Apples for Dessert Crêpes (page 270). Sprinkle with powdered sugar and garnish with a dollop of sour cream, whipped cream, fresh berries, French vanilla ice cream, or toasted nuts.

CHILI RELLEÑO BAKE

Serves 6 to 8

This innovative casserole consists of chilies filled with a spicy sour cream and cheese mixture and smothered with beaten egg and beer before baking.

1.

Generously butter a 9 x 12-inch baking dish. Roast and gently peel the chilies, or use drained canned chilies.

2.

Heat oil and sauté onion, garlic, yellow banana chili, cumin, and pepper until golden. Stir in almonds and sour cream. Set aside to cool.

3.

Slit a 2-inch opening at the top of each chili and remove seeds and veins without tearing.

4.

Carefully stuff with a small portion of the onion and sour cream mixture and a strip of cheese. Roll each chili lightly in flour and set aside.

5.

Beat egg whites until firm peaks form. In a separate bowl, stir yolks, sour cream, beer, coriander seed, scallions, pepper, and salt. Gently fold the yolk mixture into egg whites. ▼

1 tablespoon butter
8 large, long green Anaheim or poblano chilies, fresh or canned

STUFFING
2 tablespoons olive oil
1 large yellow onion, coarsely chopped
2 large cloves garlic, finely minced
1 or 2 yellow banana chilies, finely minced
1/2 teaspoon cumin, lightly crushed
1/4 teaspoon freshly ground black pepper
1/3 cup sliced almonds, toasted
1/2 cup sour cream (or Créme Fraîche, page 35)
10 ounces Mexican, Muenster or Monterey jack cheese, cut in 4-inch strips to fit chilies

FIRST COATING
2/3 cup unbleached flour

SECOND COATING
8 extra-large eggs, separated
1/3 cup sour cream or Crème Fraîche
1/4 cup American Light Lager hot chili beer
1 teaspoon freshly ground coriander seed
2 scallions, finely minced
1/2 teaspoon pepper
1/2 teaspoon salt

TOPPING
6 ounces Mexican or Muenster cheese, thinly sliced or grated

6.

Coat each stuffed and floured chili with the egg mixture and lay in the buttered baking dish. Arrange remaining onion and sour cream mixture over the chilies and spread the remaining egg mixture evenly over the top.

7.

Bake at 350° until set and lightly browned. Arrange remaining cheese over the top and bake an additional 2 minutes or just until cheese is melted. Serve immediately with Salsa Ranchero (page 220).

VARIATIONS

❦ Relleños can be baked in individual casserole dishes or on top of the stove in a heavy-bottomed pan with a tight-fitting lid.

❦ Stuff the relleños with highly seasoned chicken, pork, or chorizo in place of onions for a hearty meal.

RUSTIC STRATA

1.

To prepare crust, generously butter a 10-inch pie plate. Slice bread into 1/4-inch-thick rounds and begin by pressing the first row of overlapping rounds onto the upper edge of the dish. Allow bread to extend beyond the edge of the dish by 1-inch to form petals. ▼

1 loaf soft Italian or French bread
1 1/2 sticks butter, softened
8 ounces Swiss, Gruyère, or Fontina cheese, grated
1 small bunch spinach, washed, stemmed, and chopped (optional)
3 large shallots, finely chopped
4 extra-large eggs
1/3 cup sour cream or Crème Fraîche (page 35)
1 cup ricotta or cottage cheese
1/3 cup Bavarian light lager
2/3 cup heavy cream
1/2 teaspoon freshly ground black pepper
2 ounces Parmesan, finely grated
1 onion, sliced thinly, lightly sautéed in 1 tablespoon butter
aluminum foil

Serves 6

A strata is similar to a quiche except the dish is lined with bread rather than pastry crust. This strata has the appearance of a flower when baked because the bread overlaps the edge of the dish. Vary the filling with assorted beers, cheeses, herbs, and fillings. Makes 1 10-inch pie.

2.

Continue overlapping and pressing until the entire dish is covered, sealing the pan with the bread. With a pastry brush, generously brush the remaining butter over the surface of the bread including the top edge.

3.

Heat oven to 350°. Place Swiss, Gruyère, or Fontina cheese, spinach, and chopped shallots in a medium bowl, set aside. In a food processor or blender, process eggs, sour cream, ricotta, beer, cream, and pepper until smooth.

4.

Combine processed mixture with the Parmesan cheese, sautéed onion, cheese, spinach, and shallots. Pour into prepared crust.

5.

Place a strip of foil around the edge to prevent the overhanging crust from overbrowning.

6.

Bake about 30 to 35 minutes or until the center is set when shaken lightly. Cool 15 minutes before slicing.

MARINATED CHEESE

Serves 6

Fresh soft cheese marinated in olive oil, smoked beer, and herbs makes a welcome addition to any buffet. This tastes absolutely incredible with chunks of fresh hot French bread.

1.

Whisk together vinegar, olive oil, beer, garlic, oregano, and pepper.

2.

Pour marinade over the cheese and olives. Cover and marinate 3 hours at room temperature and 12 to 16 hours more in the refrigerator.

1/4 cup balsamic vinegar
3/4 cup extra-virgin olive oil
1/4 cup smoked beer
4 cloves garlic, peeled and lightly mashed
2 tablespoons fresh oregano or thyme, finely chopped
1/4 teaspoon freshly ground black pepper
24 to 32 ounces soft fresh cheese, cubed (Mozzarella or Muenster)
1 can thinly sliced black olives (optional)

Rauchbier is a dark, bottom-fermented beer brewed in the Bavarian city of Bamberg. It has a roasted, smoky flavor derived from malts that are dried over open fires of moist beechwood logs.

RISOTTO

1.

Heat stock to boiling, remove from heat, cover, and set aside.

2.

In a heavy deep skillet, melt 4 tablespoons butter over medium heat. When foam subsides, add onion, basil, and saffron. Sauté until limp, stirring constantly.

3.

Add rice and stir until coated with butter and heated through. Add beer, stirring constantly, and lower heat to medium simmer.

4.

Ladle in 1 cup of hot stock, stirring frequently, and allow rice to absorb about half before ladling in another cup of stock.

5.

Continue in this fashion until all the stock has been added. Allow the rice to begin absorbing this last cup and add the remaining butter and grated Parmesan.

6.

Cook, stirring, until the rice is creamy but not wet. Season to taste and serve at once.

6 1/2 cups chicken stock
1 stick unsalted butter
2 medium onions, peeled and finely chopped
1 teaspoon dried basil
1 teaspoon saffron threads, finely crushed
2 cups Italian rice (Arborio), uncooked
1 1/2 cups weissbier or dry mead
2 cups (scant) freshly grated Parmesan cheese
salt and pepper to taste

A classic Northern Italian favorite given an innovative twist of weissbier, this creamy rice and cheese dish deserves to be the center of attention. Although not traditional, as a variation on this recipe you can use a combination of Parmesan and Fontinella to make an exceptionally flavorful risotto.

CRÈME FRAÎCHE

Makes 3 cups

2 cups heavy cream
1 cup cultured sour cream

Homemade rich soured cream is standard fare in many parts of Mexico and perfectly complements any dish calling for sour cream.

1.

Whisk together cream and sour cream in a stainless-steel or glass container. Cover and allow to stand at room temperature or in a warm spot 6 to 8 hours, or until thickened.

2.

Refrigerate to allow the crème to thicken further.

WELSH RAREBIT

Serves 4

It is said that this thick, melted cheese dish originated when the hunter came home empty-handed and the wife had to make a "rare bit" of supper. This classic recipe is more than a "bit," aided by the addition of beer.

1/4 cup unsalted butter
3/4 cup brown or pale ale
2 extra-large egg yolks
1 1/2 tablespoons Sweet-n-Hot Beer
  Mustard (page 218), or Dijon mustard
1 tablespoon Homebrewed Steak Sauce
  (page 214), or A-1 Sauce
1/2 to 1 teaspoon Louisiana hot pepper
  sauce
10 ounces quality cheddar cheese, grated
  at room temperature
2 tablespoons flour

1.

In a heavy saucepan heat butter over medium-low heat.

2.

Whisk together remaining ingredients except cheese and flour. Pour into hot butter and heat until very hot but not bubbling, stirring constantly.

▼

3.

Toss cheese with flour. Add one handful at a time to the hot beer mixture. Stir slowly and in one direction only.

4.

When smooth and glossy, remove from heat and serve with slices of fresh French bread and pickled vegetables.

WELSH BENEDICT

Serves 2 to 4

The next time you want something special for breakfast, try this combination of classic dishes!

2 English muffins
2 teaspoons butter
4 thick slices Canadian bacon
4 poached eggs kept warm in hot water
1 batch Welsh Rarebit with 1 teaspoon
   minced orange zest added

1.

Lightly toast and butter muffins. Sauté bacon briefly.

2.

Place bacon on buttered muffins, top each with a poached egg, and ladle the orange-enhanced Welsh Rarebit over the top. Garnish with thin slices of orange and serve immediately.

Ales are brewed with top-fermenting yeast and are generally more robustly flavored than lager beer. Barley wine, bitter, brown beer, porter, stout, and Trappist beers are just some of those included in the ale category. Bottom-fermented beer is a synonym for lager and top-fermented beer is a synonym for ale.

BRIE IN PUFF PASTRY

E

xquisite and unique, this Trappist ale and mushroom-enhanced Brie is surrounded by buttery puff pastry.

Serves 6 to 10

5 tablespoons butter
2 shallots, thinly sliced
1/2 cup onions, chopped
16 large white mushrooms, washed and sliced
1 teaspoon your favorite herb (thyme, fines herbs, rosemary)
1/3 cup Trappist ale (Belgian Trappist ale)
1/3 cup toasted walnuts or pecans, coarsely chopped
1 package frozen puff pastry dough, thawed
2 small Brie rounds with white skin, chilled thoroughly
baking parchment
1 egg, beaten lightly

1.

Heat 3 tablespoons butter in a heavy skillet, add shallots and onions and cook, stirring frequently, until translucent. Remove from pan.

2.

Turn heat to medium-high and add remaining butter. Sauté mushrooms and herbs, stirring constantly until softened.

3.

Add Trappist ale and sautéed onions, cooking briskly until the Trappist ale has evaporated. Remove from heat and cool. Stir in toasted nuts.

4.

Roll one piece of puff pastry into a 12 x 12-inch square on an unfloured surface by picking the pastry up and turning it after each roll.

5.

Split one Brie round horizontally with a sharp knife, place one-half on puff pastry.

6.

Spoon one-fourth of the mushroom mixture over the Brie and cover with the top half.

7.

Spoon another fourth of the mushroom mixture over the top half. Gently gather the puff pastry up over the top, sealing by pressing and slightly twisting the dough and forming ends into a flower. Repeat with second Brie round.

8.

Place on a parchment-lined baking sheet and refrigerate at least one hour, or wrap and freeze up to one month.

9.

Before baking, brush the surface with beaten egg. Bake at 350° until puffed and golden brown.

NOTE

Because this freezes so well in its pre-baked form, I like to make an extra batch to go in the freezer for unexpected company or an indulgent moment for yourself and family.

CHAPTER 3
SOUPS, STEWS, BEANS, & CHILI

O ur definitive comfort food through the centuries has been soup. Whether made from rich, meaty herb-laden stock, a delicate blend of broth and rice, or puréed garden vegetables lightly simmered in milk, soup in one form or another has nourished every culture in every country.

When you think about it, just about any circumstance can be sustained by soup. When you catch a cold you crave a healing chicken soup. When the weather turns frigid you hunger for a bowl of steaming stew. When summer's furnace makes it scorching hot you yearn for a bowl of chilled gazpacho. And when friends and family gather you serve a pot of Southwest Posole to appease their hunger and stretch the budget.

This chapter covers the varied categories of soups. Classic beef stews, Firehouse Chili and Frijoles, Boston Lagered Baked Beans, and Curried Corn are all based on the concept of soup, whether thick or thin.

Soups are invariably founded on two ingredients: liquid, usually water, and something to cook in that liquid for flavor. It stands to reason that because beer is distinctively delicious and has been such an indisputable factor in history, that it was also a common element in the soup pot.

One taste of an ale-doused Belgian Onion Soup or Cajun Tomato Soup will confirm that beer is an outstanding addition to the flavor of soup in any form. Even the lesser-known European chilled fruit soups served in the heat of summer become quite enchanting with the addition of lambic or sparkling cider.

Because many of these soups are based on broth or stock combined with beer, please review their preparation. See pages 22 and 23. ▼

Chilled Blueberry Bisque, page 64. ➤

CREATING YOUR OWN SOUP RECIPES

When adding beer to soup recipes that call for broth or stock, try the following proportions: For every 3 cups of liquid called for in the recipe, use a mixture of 1 cup of a compatible beer and 2 cups of the specified liquid.

RUSSIAN BORSCHT

T his earthy peasant soup based on beets can be made without beef by including an extra portion of cabbage.

Serves 12 to 14

1.

In a heavy deep skillet heat olive oil on medium-high and sear peppered brisket until browned and crisp on both sides. Pour in beef broth and beer, cover, and simmer slowly for 1 1/2 to 2 hours, skimming foam that rises to the top.

2.

When tender, remove brisket and cut into cubes. Set aside.

3.

In a Dutch oven, heat butter over medium and sauté onions until limp. Add leek and sauté until soft. Add garlic and parsley and sauté briefly.

4.

Add beets, potatoes, vinegar, 1 cup of liquid from brisket, bay leaf, fennel, and paprika. Cover and simmer slowly 1 hour.

5.

Add remaining liquid (5 cups) from brisket, cubed meat, and cabbage. Taste and add sugar, if desired. Simmer slowly, covered, for 30 minutes.

6.

Transfer to a warm tureen and garnish with chopped herbs. Serve with a large dollop of Créme Fraîche or sour cream.

3 tablespoons olive oil
1 1/2 pounds beef brisket rubbed with
2 teaspoons crushed pepper
6 cups beef broth
2 cups Oktoberfest beer
3 tablespoons butter or olive oil
2 large onions, coarsely chopped
1 large leek, split, washed, and coarsely chopped
2 cloves garlic, mashed with 2 teaspoons salt
1/4 cup Italian (flat-leafed) parsley, coarsely chopped
5 to 6 medium beets, peeled and julienned
6 medium red potatoes, cubed
1/3 cup balsamic vinegar
1 bay leaf
1 teaspoon crushed fennel seeds
1 1/2 tablespoons Hungarian paprika
3 cups finely shredded red cabbage
1 or more teaspoons sugar (optional)
1 cup Crème Fraîche (page 35) or sour cream
freshly minced dill, parsley, or a combination for garnish

FIREHOUSE CHILI

T his is one helluva "bowl of red," spicy and bursting with the flavors of chili and meat. Do not be put off by the length of the ingredients list, this is made from scratch and is the best you'll ever taste. Serve with a green salad, fresh tortillas or corn bread, and lots of chilled cerveza for an extraordinary feast.

Serves 10 to 12

6 long dried red chilies (or substitute
  1/2 cup mild red chili powder in step 7,
  see Note)
4 pounds beef chuck roast, with bones
4 pounds pork butt or roast, with bones
1 pound lean bacon, chopped into 1-inch
  pieces
4 large onions, chopped coarsely
3 cups light lager
1 tablespoon cumin powder
1 tablespoon freshly ground black pepper
1 1/2 to 2 tablespoons oregano, crumbled
1 tablespoon freshly ground coriander
  seeds
8 to 10 large cloves garlic, minced and
  mashed
2 tablespoons molé paste
1 to 2 teaspoons cayenne (optional)
2 tablespoons paprika
2 bay leaves
2 tablespoons hot red chili powder
1/2 cup mild red chili powder
1 cup olive oil or rendered lard
1/3 cup masa harina (corn flour, use more
  for thicker chili)
1/3 cup lard, bacon drippings, or
  margarine
salt to taste

1.
Remove stem and seeds from dried chilies. Pour 3 cups boiling water over chilies and set aside.

2.
Using a very sharp knife, cut beef and pork into 1/2-inch cubes, reserving the larger bones.

3.
Fry bacon until crisp and set aside, reserving 1/3 cup of drippings. Sauté onions in drippings until limp and golden. Remove and set aside.

4.
In a medium saucepan, heat beer to a slow simmer and remove from heat. Add cumin, pepper, oregano, coriander, garlic, molé paste, cayenne, paprika, and bay leaves. Cover and set aside.

5.
In a large deep skillet, heat half the oil over medium-high. Brown meat in small batches adding oil when needed. If there is time, brown the bones to give your chili a very rich flavor. ▼

6.

Drain water from reconstituted chilies into a blender and add the chilies one at a time, blending on medium until a thick, smooth paste is formed. Add to the steeping beer mixture and remove bay leaves.

7.

Heat a heavy skillet on medium. When hot, reduce to low and add the hot and mild chili powders (see Note), stirring constantly. Chili burns easily, so watch it carefully. When browned lightly, stir into the steeping beer mixture.

8.

In a large pot bring beer and chili mixture to a slow boil, add browned meat, bacon, bones, browned onions, and 4 cups of water. Simmer slowly, uncovered, stirring occasionally, for 3 hours. When the meat is very tender but not mushy remove the bones.

9.

In a medium skillet melt 1/3 cup fat over medium. Sprinkle masa harina over fat, whisking constantly to incorporate smoothly. Cook over medium-low for 3 minutes, allowing the masa to take on a pale golden hue.

10.

Add 2 cups of broth from the simmering chilies to the browned masa, whisking constantly to keep it smooth. Pour the mixture from the skillet into the simmering chilies and stir. Cook until thickened and adjust seasonings as needed. Allow to simmer an additional 30 minutes over very low heat.

NOTE

If your area does not have a ready supply of dried chilies, skip steps 1 and 6 and use an additional 1/2 cup of mild red chili powder in step 7 for a total of 1 cup mild chili powder.

VEGETARIAN MULTICOLORED CHILI

This full-flavored bean chili, afloat with fresh vegetables and infused with the essence of beer, is one of life's memorable delights.

1.

Rinse pinto beans thoroughly in a colander, remove any stones or rotted beans, and place in a Dutch oven. Cover with 8 cups of water and bring to a rapid boil for 5 minutes. Remove from heat, cover, and let stand one hour.

2.

Drain beans, add beer and enough additional water to cover 2 inches deep. Add garlic and bring to a slow simmer. Cover and cook until tender (1 to 1 1/2 hours). Be sure the simmer is slow to prevent scorching.

3.

Heat a heavy skillet on medium-low, remove from heat and add chili powders, stirring constantly.

4.

When lightly browned, stir chili powders into beans with pepper, oregano, cumin, coriander, cayenne, and paprika. Simmer slowly while preparing vegetables. ▼

1 pound dried pinto beans
3 cups Munich dark-style beer
6 large cloves garlic, minced and mashed
1/3 cup mild red chili powder
1/2 to 1 tablespoon hot red chili powder (or to taste)
1 teaspoon freshly ground black pepper
1 1/2 tablespoons oregano, crumbled
2 teaspoons cumin seed, toasted and ground
1/2 tablespoon coriander seeds, toasted and ground
1/2 teaspoon cayenne (optional)
2 tablespoons paprika
3 tablespoons olive oil or other vegetable oil
4 large onions, chopped coarsely
3 medium zucchini, sliced
2 green bell peppers, chopped
1 each red and yellow bell pepper (optional)
1/4 cup peanut butter
2 tablespoons molé paste or Pipian paste (optional)
6 large ripe tomatoes, chopped coarsely
1 pound fresh corn (frozen or canned if fresh is not available)

5.

In a heavy skillet heat 3 tablespoons oil on medium and sauté onions until limp. Add zucchini and bell peppers, sautéing just until limp.

6.

Stir a ladle of hot chili broth into a bowl with the peanut butter and molé paste, mix and add to chili.

7.

Add onions, zucchini, peppers, tomatoes, and corn to the beans. Simmer slowly for 25 to 30 minutes. Taste and adjust salt and seasonings.

SOUTHWEST POSOLE

1.

Lightly rinse fresh or dried hominy and set aside to drain. Brown the pork to give a fuller flavor.

2.

Rinse pinto beans and pick out any stones. Cover with water and bring to a boil. After 5 minutes, remove from heat and let stand 1 hour. Drain.

3.

Place beans, hominy, pork, pork bones, onions, garlic, and spices in a large roasting pot if you are cooking in the oven. Use a large heavy Dutch oven if you are cooking on the stove.

4.

Bring 14 to 16 cups water and beer to a boil, pour over beans and cover with a tight-fitting lid. ▼

1 pound bag fresh hominy (or dried or canned. If using canned hominy add during final 30 minutes only.)
1 1/2 pounds dried pinto beans
3 pounds pork butt, cut in bite-size pieces (save the bones)
2 large onions, coarsely chopped
6 large cloves garlic, peeled, chopped, and mashed
2 teaspoons dried oregano
1 teaspoon toasted coriander seed, ground
1 teaspoon toasted cumin seed, ground
1 to 2 teaspoons crushed hot red chili flakes (optional)
1 to 2 teaspoons freshly ground black pepper
3 cups Bavarian dark
14 to 16 cups water

Serves 12

This robust meal of beans, pork, hominy, and spices can be a mainstay of the winter season. Traditionally it is cooked in a big earthenware pot, but a large roaster or Dutch oven is fine. Don't hesitate to make this large a batch; posole gets better the second or third day and leftovers are easily frozen.

5.

Place in a preheated 350° oven for 3 to 3 1/2 hours or simmer on the stove very slowly for 1 1/2 hours, or until beans are tender. Check halfway through the cooking time and, if needed, add 2 cups hot water.

6.

When the posole is finished, the beans will be very tender but not mushy. Remove bones and add salt to taste.

NOTE

Serve with hot tortillas or corn bread. Fresh Pico de Gallo (see page 221) and a dollop of homemade Crème Fraîche (page 35) complement this perfectly.

HOT & SOUR SOUP

1.

In a wok or sauté pan heat oil on medium until hot. Add the Szechwan peppercorns, crushed chilies, garlic, and ginger, sautéing until fragrant (1 to 3 minutes). Add cabbage and stir-fry briefly. Remove from heat.

2.

Bring beer and broth to a boil and add the sautéed cabbage mixture, mushrooms, tofu, bamboo shoots, vinegar, white pepper, sesame oil, and soy sauce. Simmer 2 minutes.

3.

Stir the cornstarch mixture and add to the simmering soup. Stir until lightly thickened. Adjust seasonings to taste, adding salt, vinegar, or hot pepper as needed.

▼

2 tablespoons peanut oil or other vegetable oil
1 teaspoon Szechwan peppercorns
2 to 4 hot Thai chilies, crushed
3 large cloves garlic, thinly sliced
3/4-inch piece fresh ginger, very thinly sliced
4 cups napa cabbage, thinly sliced
3 cups Pilsener or Kölsch-style beer
4 cups chicken stock
4 large shitake mushrooms, soaked and thinly sliced
1/2 cup dried woods ear mushrooms, soaked (or 1 cup diced fresh mushrooms)
1/4 pound tofu (soybean curd), cut into 1/2-inch cubes (optional)
4 ounces bamboo shoots, julienned
1/3 cup rice vinegar
1 1/2 teaspoons freshly ground white pepper
1 tablespoon dark sesame oil
2 tablespoons light soy sauce
4 tablespoons cornstarch mixed with 1/3 cup cold water or stock
2 eggs, lightly beaten
4 scallions, finely minced
1 1/2 cups dry-roasted peanuts, unsalted

Serves 6 to 8 as a main course

An exquisite soup that combines the sharp flavors of pepper, vinegar, beer, and garlic with vegetables and peanuts. Although the ingredients list looks long, once the chopping is done it is ready to serve in less than 15 minutes!

4.

Stir soup and slowly pour in beaten eggs. Add scallions, simmer briefly, stir in peanuts, and serve immediately.

WON-TON SOUP

1.

Thoroughly combine garlic, scallions, soy sauce, sesame oil, chili, and ginger. Pour over pork, mix well and allow to stand 30 minutes.

2.

Place 1 teaspoon pork filling lengthwise just below the center of the won-ton wrapper. Lightly dampen all edges with water, roll into a cylinder, leaving a 1/2-inch edge unrolled at the top. Pinch ends closed, pull pinched ends together and overlap, pinching to seal.

3.

Place the won tons on parchment or plastic wrap, cover, and refrigerate until ready to cook.

4.

Heat stock, beer, and ground chili to a slow boil. Adjust seasonings with a few tablespoons of soy sauce or a few drops of sesame oil. ▼

WON-TON FILLING

2 cloves garlic, finely minced and mashed
2 scallions, finely minced
3 tablespoons light soy sauce
2 teaspoons dark sesame oil
1/2 teaspoon ground hot red chili (optional)
1/4 to 1/2 teaspoon finely grated fresh
  ginger (optional)
1 pound freshly ground lean pork
1 package won-ton wrappers
baking parchment or plastic wrap

SOUP

6 cups rich chicken stock cooked with
  1-inch piece of mashed fresh ginger
3 cups Pilsener
1/2 teaspoon freshly ground hot red chili
  soy sauce or sesame oil for seasoning stock
1 small bunch spinach, cleaned, stemmed,
  and finely sliced
6 scallions, cut diagonally in half-inch
  pieces

Serves 4 to 6

Juicy and piquant, these ginger-spiked pork won tons are simmered in a beer stock adrift with fresh scallions and slivered spinach. Virtually a meal unto itself!

5.

Drop the won tons into the boiling stock and simmer for 6 to 7 minutes, or until tender and cooked.

6.

Add spinach and scallions, simmering one minute. Serve immediately.

THE ULTIMATE POTATO SOUP

Serves 8 to 10

This lavish, creamy soup is not thickened with the usual flour or cornstarch (resulting in potato wallpaper paste!) but rather with grated potatoes for an intense, pure potato flavor.

1.

In a Dutch oven over medium, heat 2 tablespoons butter and sauté Canadian bacon until lightly browned and crisp. Remove and set aside.

2.

Melt 2 more tablespoons butter and sauté leeks and chopped onion until wilted. Add shallots and garlic, sautéing until fragrant (1 to 3 minutes). Remove and add to bacon.

3.

Add more butter if needed and sauté carrots until tender. Remove and add to bacon.

4.

Add broth and beer to Dutch oven and begin heating. Grate 3 potatoes and finely dice the other 2.

5.

Add potatoes, thyme, cayenne, and bacon mixture to the broth and bring to a slow boil. ▼

4 to 5 tablespoons unsalted butter
3 to 4 ounces Canadian bacon or ham, chopped coarsely
2 large leeks, split, washed, and coarsely chopped
2 medium onions, finely chopped
2 shallots, finely chopped
1 large clove garlic mashed with 1 1/2 teaspoons salt
1 large carrot, julienned
2 1/2 cups chicken broth
1 cup weissbier or Pilsener
5 medium baking potatoes, peeled, and placed in water
2 teaspoons Herbs du Provence or French thyme
1/4 to 1/2 teaspoon cayenne (optional)
1 cup half-and-half
1 cup sour cream
salt and pepper to taste
fresh Italian (flat-leafed) parsley or finely chopped scallions for garnish

6.

Cook until potatoes are tender but still hold their shape (40 to 45 minutes).

7.

Turn heat to low, stir in cream and sour cream and heat just until bubbles begin to form around the edges (4 to 5 minutes).

8.

Remove from heat, adjust salt and pepper to taste. Garnish with freshly minced Italian (flat-leafed) parsley or finely chopped scallions.

NOTE

Grate and dice the potatoes just before adding to avoid discoloration.

HAM & SPLIT PEA SOUP

1.

In a large pot bring the water, beer, and shanks to a slow boil, skimming off foam. When the foaming stops, add split peas, bay leaf, garlic, and herbs. Simmer, partially covered, for 2 1/2 hours.

2.

Heat oil on medium, sauté onions until translucent and soft, add carrots and sauté until lightly wilted. Add leeks and sauté until just soft.

3.

Add the sautéed vegetables and diced potatoes to the slowly simmering pot and continue to simmer for 1 1/2 hours. Remove hocks and discard bones and fat, returning meat to the pot. ▼

4 cups water

3 cups Munich dark beer (try a Bamburg-style smoked beer)

2 meaty, smoked pork shanks or hocks, split

12 ounces split peas

1 bay leaf

1 clove garlic, finely mashed

2 teaspoons each thyme and parsley

4 tablespoons oil or butter

2 onions, coarsely chopped

2 carrots, thickly sliced

2 leeks, split, washed, and coarsely chopped

2 medium baking potatoes, peeled and diced

salt and pepper to taste

1 pound lean kielbasa, cut into 1/4-inch-thick slices (optional)

Serves 8 to 10

Split pea soup assumes a European aura when beer is included in the ingredients. This rugged fare is fragrant with smoky ham, herbs, and vegetables simmered with earthy split peas.

4.

Adjust seasonings and add kiel-basa. Simmer an additional 15 minutes.

VARIATIONS

❧ Add cubed root vegetables such as turnips and parsnips.

❧ For authentic European flavor, include a washed split pig's foot with the shanks.

GREEK AVGOLEMONO SOUP

Serves 8

A simple, satisfying soup imbued with the lovely citrus flavors of weissbier. This soup is quite refreshing served chilled during the heat of summer.

1.

Bring stock and weissbier to a slow simmer. Add rice and cover, simmering slowly for 15 minutes. Turn the heat off and cover to keep hot.

2.

Beat four eggs and two yolks until frothy. Whisk in lemon juice.

3.

Stir 1/2 cup of hot stock into the eggs, whisking thoroughly. Slowly, stirring constantly, pour the warmed egg mixture into the hot stock.

4.

Cook over low heat 4 to 5 minutes or until the soup thickens slightly. Season and serve immediately. Garnish with the chopped mint, if desired.

6 cups rich chicken stock

2 cups weissbier (try a light weiss with or without yeast)

1/2 cup washed long-grain white rice (or basmati rice washed thoroughly and soaked 4 hours)

4 eggs

2 egg yolks

1/4 cup freshly squeezed and strained lemon juice

salt to taste

finely minced mint for garnish

FRENCH ONION SOUP

Serves 6 to 8

Rich and soothing, this soup can be the perfect start to an elegant holiday meal or a fast and filling supper.

4 1/2 cups strained beef stock in which onion skins were cooked
1 1/2 cups brown ale or bock beer
1 teaspoon thyme or your favorite herb
5 tablespoons butter
3 large white onions, thinly sliced
3 large yellow onions, thinly sliced
4 large shallots, thinly sliced
1 teaspoon salt
2 to 3 tablespoons sipping whiskey (optional)
2 tablespoons flour
Onion Soup Croutons (recipe follows)
freshly grated cheese (fontinella, kaseri, Parmesan or Romano)

ONION SOUP CROUTONS

1 large loaf French bread
1 stick unsalted butter
2 large cloves garlic, minced and mashed

1.

Heat stock, beer, and thyme until very hot, cover and set aside.

2.

Melt butter in a large heavy Dutch oven. When foam subsides, add onions, shallots, and salt, cooking uncovered over medium-low for 20 to 30 minutes, stirring frequently. Add whiskey and continue cooking.

3.

When onions have taken on a rich, caramel color, sprinkle in the flour and continue to cook, stirring, for 4 minutes.

4.

Stirring constantly, slowly pour in 2 cups of stock and cook 3 to 4 minutes. Stir in remaining stock and simmer, partially covered, for 30 minutes.

5.

Serve the soup in heat-proof bowls topped with an Onion Soup Crouton and a generous sprinkling of cheese. Run the bowl under a hot broiler just until cheese bubbles. Serve immediately.

1.

Slice the bread into 1/2-inch-thick rounds. Beat butter and garlic until smooth and fluffy. Spread thinly on one side of the slices.

2.

Using a sharp cookie cutter, cut bread into rounds that fit inside the serving dishes. Bake at 375° on a baking sheet until light golden brown. Turn, lightly browning the second side. Cool.

BOUILLABAISSE

A fragrant soup filled with seasonal seafood. Instead of classic fish stock, this uses a stock made from shellfish shells, herbs, and beer. Another recipe that appears lengthy, this actually goes together quickly once the ingredients are assembled. Remember, bouillabaisse has few hard-and-fast rules so allow creativity and budget to dictate the ingredients.

Serves 8

SHELLFISH STOCK

6 cups shrimp, lobster, or crab shells (in any combination) reserve meat for bouillabaisse

3 to 4 cups India pale ale or weissbier

4 cups water

1 bay leaf

1/2 teaspoon each dried thyme, peppercorns, fennel seed

brown papery skin from 2 large yellow onions

2 cloves garlic, mashed

BOUILLABAISSE

2/3 pound red snapper or halibut, bones removed

2/3 pound mahi-mahi, bones removed

2/3 pound sea bass or whiting, bones removed

1-pound whole langouste (spiny rock lobster) or 1 whole lobster tail (3/4 pound), (see Note) reserve shells for stock

2 pounds large shrimp, shelled and deveined, reserve shells for stock

6 large cloves garlic, mashed

1 tablespoon (scant) kosher salt

1/3 to 1/2 cup extra-virgin olive oil

2 large onions, coarsely chopped

3 leeks, split, washed, and chopped

8 Italian plum tomatoes, coarsely chopped

1 1/2 tablespoons freshly chopped basil or 1 1/2 teaspoons dried

6 to 7 cups shellfish stock

1/2 teaspoon saffron threads, ground finely

1/4 teaspoon cayenne, or to taste

1 1/2 pounds mussels, clams, or oysters in any combination

2 to 3 small crabs or 1 pound crab legs, cracked for easier eating

salt and pepper to taste

1.
Combine shells, ale, and water and bring to a boil. Lower heat to a simmer and skim the foam.

2.
When the foam subsides, add remaining stock ingredients and continue to simmer for 1 hour. Strain the stock and set aside. Refrigerate, covered tightly, if making the soup later.

1.
Cut fish and lobster into bite-size pieces.

2.
Combine garlic and salt to make a paste. Rub over lobster meat, shrimp, and fish chunks. Cover and allow to stand in the refrigerator separately for 4 to 6 hours.

3.
In a large Dutch oven heat olive oil on medium-high. Sauté onions until limp and golden. Add leeks and sauté briefly. Add plum tomatoes and fresh basil and sauté, stirring constantly until tomatoes soften slightly.

4.
Pour shellfish stock over sautéed vegetables. Stir in saffron and cayenne. Bring to a slow simmer and cook for 10 minutes. ▼

5.

Add fish chunks and simmer 3 to 4 minutes. Add shrimp, mussels, and lobster and simmer crab, until the shrimp and lobster are pink and the mussels plumped.

6.

Adjust seasonings with salt and pepper. Serve immediately with Onion Soup Croutons (page 51) or lots of fresh French bread.

NOTE

I prefer to use lobster tails in place of small whole lobsters. Although priced higher per pound, you get more meat for your money.

VARIATION

For a more traditional fish stock, add an additional 2 cups of liquid (beer, water, or a combination) and 2 to 3 pounds of non-oily fish heads and bones. Prepare in the same manner, straining carefully.

HELPFUL HINT

Like other stocks, shrimp stock freezes well. Use an airtight container to avoid perfuming the freezer.

Beer was a very important food in the Colonies, containing spent yeast that was filled with vitamins and minerals. Anthropologists say colonial farmers, much like present-day Tibetans, may have derived one-third to one-half of their daily calories from beer.

BOSTON LAGERED BAKED BEANS

1.

In a large pan soak beans overnight in cold water. Drain and cover with fresh water and ale. Bring to a boil, lower heat, and simmer slowly for 1 hour or until beans are tender.

2.

Place beans and simmering liquid in a large oven-proof pot or Dutch oven. ▼

Serves 8 to 10

This rich and satisfying rendition of Boston's famous dish – beans baked from scratch – uses ale to enrich its down-to-earth flavor.

2 pounds small dried navy beans
3 cups brown or pale ale
1/4 cup oil or bacon drippings
3 onions, coarsely diced
1/3 to 2/3 cup dried yellow mustard (to taste)
2 teaspoons freshly ground black pepper
3/4 cup pure maple syrup (or an additional 3/4 cup brown sugar)
3/4 cup dark brown sugar
1 tablespoon paprika
2 small smoked pork shanks, split, or 1 pound lean bacon
1 1/2 cups brown or pale ale

3.

In a small pan heat oil on medium, sauté onions to a deep golden caramel color, and stir into beans.

4.

Stir in remaining ingredients except pork and beer. Press the pork shanks down into the beans.

5.

Place the uncovered pot in a preheated 300° oven and bake for 3 hours. Add 1 1/2 cups ale plus enough water to just cover. Adjust seasonings as needed.

6.

Allow the beans to continue cooking, uncovered, without adding additional liquid until they are browned on top and have the desired consistency, about 3 hours.

7.

Shred meat from pork shanks and stir into beans, serve hot.

CALDO DE QUESO

1.

Open each chili, remove seeds and veins and slice into long strips. Set aside.

2.

In a large Dutch oven heat oil on medium and sauté onions until limp. Add garlic and continue sautéing for 2 minutes.

3.

Pour stock and ale over onions and bring to a slow boil. Simmer for 10 minutes. ▼

Serves 8

An incredibly scrumptious and inexpensive soup that can be made with only a moment's notice.

7 large green chilies, roasted and peeled
3 tablespoons olive or peanut oil
1 onion, coarsely chopped
3 cloves garlic, finely minced
9 cups stock (chicken, turkey, beef, or any combination)
3 cups Bavarian light or dark lager
2 cups seeded and chopped ripe tomatoes
1 large bunch scallions, washed, trimmed, and chopped
tortilla chips (unsalted) or toasted corn tortillas
3 cups Mexican cheese, grated or chopped (or Muenster or farmers cheese)
1 small bunch cilantro, rinsed and coarsely chopped (or substitute 1 tablespoon dried oregano and sauté with onions and garlic)

4.

Add chopped tomatoes, chilies, and scallions. Simmer for 5 minutes.

5.

Lightly crush tortilla chips and place a handful in each soup bowl. Sprinkle cheese and cilantro over chips and ladle the hot soup over the top. Serve immediately.

L ager beer is any beer produced by bottom-fermenting types of yeast. It is the predominant style, of brewing around the world. Most lagers are of the Pilsener style which is dry, crisp, pale, and low in alcohol. Some other styles that fall into the lager category are Münchner, Vienna, Dortmunder, bock, and doppelbock.

FRIJOLES BORRACHOS

Serves 8

The classic accompaniment to Southwestern meals, these beans are bland enough to be enjoyed with spicier foods, but still have enough body to stand alone.

4 cups dried pinto beans
8 cups water
2 12-ounce bottles of Pilsener
3 cloves garlic, peeled and mashed
1 large onion, chopped
1 teaspoon hot red chili powder
1 teaspoon freshly ground black pepper
2 teaspoons salt
1/2 to 2/3 cup margarine, lard, or bacon fat

1.

Rinse the beans thoroughly in a colander and remove stones and broken beans. Place in a large Dutch oven, cover with 8 cups water, and bring to a rapid boil for 5 minutes.

2.

Remove from heat, cover, and allow to stand for 1 hour. This will reduce some of the gas-producing qualities. ▼

3.

Drain, add beer, cover with fresh water plus 2 more cups. Add garlic, onion, chili, pepper, and salt. Partially cover the pan, bring to a slow simmer, and cook until tender and most of the liquid has been absorbed (1 to 1 1/2 hours). Be sure the simmer is slow to prevent scorching. Beans may be used for frying immediately or cooled and refrigerated up to 3 days before using.

4.

Any number of methods can be used to mash the beans. A potato masher is the most basic and provides excellent results, but an electric mixer or food processor also works.

5.

To refry, melt 1/4 to 1/3 cup of margarine over medium-low in a heavy 10- to 12-inch skillet, add half the mashed beans and stir constantly, simmering and reducing the liquid until beans acquire a fried consistency (from almost runny to thick). Repeat with remaining beans. Taste and adjust salt.

NOTES

❧ Remember that cooking time will vary because some beans will be younger and more tender than others.

❧ Lard or bacon fat give a meatier taste.

❧ Do not be tempted to overfill the skillet; you will get better results frying beans in smaller batches.

❧ If the beans are cooked but lots of liquid remains, simply discard the excess. Do not overcook the beans to get rid of the extra liquid.

VARIATIONS

❧ Fry 1/2 pound bacon, crumble, and add to beans at the end of frying to give a nice meaty flavor.

❧ Fry 1 1/2 pounds of chorizo or ground beef in a separate pan, drain, and add to beans after frying to use for filling tostadas, Chimichangas (see page 136), tacos, and burritos.

❧ In a small sauté pan, melt 4 tablespoons margarine over medium-low, add 3 tablespoons mild red chili powder and 2 teaspoons of hot red chili powder and sauté, stirring constantly, until chili turns a rich brown color (only a minute or so because chili scorches easily.) Add to beans while frying for a fabulous batch of red chili refried beans.

❧ Add grated cheese to beans at the end of frying. Remove pan from heat and stir gently, just until cheese is marbled throughout.

In the American Colonies lobster was considered a poor man's food because it was easy to go out and simply pick up a few.

LOBSTER & BRIE SOUP

Serves 8

One of the most luscious soups ever to grace a table, this spectacular Brie-laced soup will receive accolades every time it is served.

3/4-pound lobster tail or 1 pound lobster claws
1 1/2 cups weissbier
3 1/2 cups water
1 teaspoon thyme, finely crushed
3 cups half-and-half
4 tablespoons butter
3 shallots, finely minced
3 cups heavy cream
1/2 pound Brie cheese, with skin, cut into 6 chunks
freshly ground black pepper to taste
paprika for garnish

1.

Shell the lobster reserving shell for stock. Split tail meat lengthwise, and refrigerate.

2.

To make stock, combine weissbier, water, thyme, and lobster shell. Bring to a slow boil, cover, and simmer 40 minutes.

3.

Strain then simmer to reduce broth to 2 1/2 cups. Add half-and-half and continue simmering until reduced by half again. Cover and set aside.

4.

In a heavy skillet, heat butter on medium. When foam subsides, add shallots and sauté for 1 minute. Add lobster meat and sauté briefly until the lobster turns pink. Remove and cool. Pull meat into long shreds.

5.

Add heavy cream and Brie to the reduced broth, stirring constantly over medium-low heat. When the cheese is almost melted, add shredded lobster and shallot mixture, and pepper to taste, simmer gently for 2 minutes. Garnish with paprika and serve immediately.

SHRIMP OR CRAWFISH BISQUE

Serves 10

Rich and elegant, this bisque is imbued with the essence of shellfish, roasted garlic, and cream.

1 1/2 cups American Pilsener
3 1/2 cups water
2 shallots, finely minced
2 teaspoons French thyme
2 bay leaves
3 cloves roasted garlic (recipe follows)
2 tablespoons commercially available crab boil
1/2 teaspoon whole black peppercorns
juice of 1/2 lemon
3 parsley sprigs
1 tablespoon salt
3 pounds shrimp or crawfish with shells
5 cups half-and-half
6 tablespoons butter
1 onion, coarsely chopped
3 shallots, coarsely chopped
1 teaspoon paprika
1/2 teaspoon cayenne
8 cloves roasted garlic (recipe follows)
2 cups heavy cream
paprika and finely minced scallions for garnish

1.
To make stock, combine beer, water, shallots, thyme, bay leaves, 3 roasted garlic cloves, crab boil, peppercorns, lemon juice, parsley sprigs, and salt. Cover, bring to a slow boil, and simmer 40 minutes.

2.
Bring back to a full boil, add shrimp and cook until just pink, or add crawfish and cook 10 minutes. Remove shellfish, cool, and peel, separating the shells from the tail meat.

3.
Return the shells to the simmering stock. Skim foam, cover, and simmer 45 minutes. Strain then simmer to reduce stock to 3 cups.

4.
Add the half-and-half and gently reduce again by one-half.

5.
Meanwhile, heat butter in sauté pan on medium heat. Sauté onion and shallots until wilted and transparent. Add the paprika and cayenne and sauté an additional 2 minutes.

6.
Place sautéd onions and shallots, roasted garlic, and shellfish meat in a food processor. Process until smooth, adding heavy cream if too thick.

7.
Add the puréed shellfish mixture and heavy cream to the reduced stock mixture. Adjust salt and gently heat on medium-low for 8 to 10 minutes, or until heated through. Serve garnished with paprika and finely minced scallions. ▼

1.

On a small baking pan, drizzle olive oil over the garlic cloves and toss with thyme. Bake at 300° until the cloves are soft and golden, about 35 to 45 minutes.

2.

Cool, pop out of the skins and spread on French or Italian bread. Reserve any extra roasted garlic for salad dressings.

ROASTED GARLIC

1 large head garlic, unpeeled and separated into cloves

2 tablespoons extra-virgin olive oil

1 teaspoon crushed dried thyme

ALBONDIGAS SOUP

1.

In a small saucepan bring water to a rapid boil, add oil and rice. Cover and simmer on low for 15 minutes. Remove from heat and let stand 10 minutes. Fluff with fork and cool.

2.

In a large bowl combine ground meat, garlic, cumin, oregano, coriander, chili, and eggs and mix thoroughly. Stir in cooled rice.

3.

Using a scoop, form the meat mixture into 1 1/2-inch balls and refrigerate until ready to cook.

4.

Bring stock and beer to a slow simmer on medium. ▼

Serves 8 to 12

A hearty Mexican soup of rich stock, vegetables, and spicy rice-studded meatballs, the addition of beer lends an earthy flavor that is positively irresistible.

3/4 cup water

1/2 cup uncooked long-grain white rice

1 tablespoon oil or margarine

3 pounds lean ground beef or half beef and half pork (my favorite)

5 cloves garlic, chopped and crushed

1 teaspoon freshly ground cumin

2 tablespoons dried crushed oregano

2 teaspoons freshly ground coriander seeds

1 teaspoon finely ground red chili pepper

2 eggs

4 quarts beef stock

4 cups Bavarian dark or light lager

1/3 cup olive oil

3 medium onions, coarsely chopped

2 tablespoons fresh oregano or 1 tablespoon dried

3 large ribs celery, sliced

3 carrots, sliced thinly

5 freshly roasted green chilies, cut into strips

salt and pepper to taste

scallion and parsley for garnish, finely chopped

5.

In a sauté pan, heat 3 tablespoons oil and sauté onions until golden. Add oregano and sauté briefly until fragrant (1 to 3 minutes). Remove and set aside.

6.

Add remaining oil and sauté celery and carrots.

7.

Stir onions, celery, carrots, and chilies into the simmering stock. Begin adding meatballs, one at a time, to the bubbling liquid, making sure they are evenly distributed.

8.

Cover and lower heat, simmer until meatballs are cooked through (about 40 minutes). Season with salt and pepper and garnish with chopped scallion and parsley.

VELVET CORN SOUP

Serves 4 to 6

If you happen to have the stock and corn on hand, this light, soothing soup can be prepared in a flash.

6 ears corn, freshly shucked (or 5 cups frozen corn)
2 tablespoons cornstarch
2 teaspoons dark sesame oil
2 tablespoons mirin (sweet cooking wine)
2 tablespoons Bavarian light lager
3 extra-large egg whites
1/2 cup half-and-half
4 cups rich Chinese chicken stock (recipe follows)
1 teaspoon salt
2/3 cup ham or Canadian bacon, julienned

1.

Using a sharp knife, cut corn off the cob, making sure to cut close to the cob in a bowl so any milk can be added to the soup. Set aside.

2.

Combine cornstarch, sesame oil, mirin, and 2 tablespoons lager, stirring to form a smooth paste. Set aside.

3.

Beat egg whites until very frothy. Slowly add half-and-half, continuing to whisk until fully incorporated.

4.

Bring chicken stock and salt to a full boil. Stir in corn. As soon as the mixture returns to a boil, stir the cornstarch mixture and slowly pour into the stock.

5.

Lower heat and continue to cook until soup is thickened and stock becomes clear (about 10 minutes).

6.

Remove pan from heat and stir soup in a circular direction briefly. Pour egg white mixture into the hot, swirling soup.

7.

Transfer to a warmed tureen and garnish with chopped ham or serve immediately in individual bowls, garnishing each with a bit of ham. ▼

1.

Combine wings, water and beer. Simmer and skim foam.

2.

Add remaining ingredients and simmer 4 hours. Strain and reduce over heat by half.

CHINESE CHICKEN STOCK

3 pounds chicken wings

7 cups water

3 cups Bavarian light lager

5 tablespoons soy sauce

2 cloves mashed garlic

brown papery skin from 1 yellow onion

1-inch piece fresh ginger sliced

1/2 teaspoon whole peppercorns

FLEMISH STEW

1.

Heat oil in heavy Dutch oven over medium-high. Dredge meat in seasoned flour and brown in small batches. Remove from Dutch oven and set aside.

2.

Add butter and when the foam subsides add onions and salt, cooking uncovered on medium-low until limp and golden.

3.

Sprinkle flour and thyme over onions, stirring and cooking an additional 4 minutes.

4.

While stirring constantly, slowly add stock, ale, meat, and diced vegetables to the onions. Cover and simmer slowly for 1 1/2 hours.

1/3 cup olive oil or other vegetable oil

3 pounds boneless beef, cut in 1-inch cubes

1 1/2 cups flour mixed with 1 teaspoon each pepper, salt, and paprika

5 tablespoons butter

5 large onions, thinly sliced

1 teaspoon salt

2 tablespoons flour

2 teaspoons thyme

5 cups beef stock made with onion skins (see page 13)

3 cups Belgian ale

4 large shallots, thinly sliced

2 cups peeled white potato, diced

2 cups peeled turnip, diced

Serves 6 to 8

This simple, hearty, and satisfying soup is a great hit any time of year. Serve with a salad and hot crusty rolls.

MINESTRONE

The classic Italian soup, thick with vegetables and pasta, has as many recipes as it does cooks. This version has a richness that transcends others from the addition of fine German Pilsener.

1/4 to 1/2 cup olive oil
1 large onion, coarsely chopped
4 ribs celery, coarsely chopped
2 large carrots, coarsely chopped or sliced
4 large cloves garlic, coarsely chopped and mashed
2 teaspoons dried basil or 2 tablespoons fresh chopped basil
1 teaspoon dried oregano or 1 tablespoon fresh chopped oregano
3/4 cup Italian (flat-leafed) parsley, coarsely chopped
8 to 10 cups rich broth made with 2 to 3 cups German Pilsener, hot
3 cups cooked fava, great northern, marrow, or navy beans
4 medium white potatoes, scrubbed and cubed
2 cups fresh green beans, cleaned and snapped into 2-inch lengths
2 cups zucchini, thickly sliced
1 pound fresh tomatoes, peeled and chopped
salt and pepper to taste
1 cup shells, stars, or rice-shaped pasta
1/2 cup fresh peas
1 to 2 cups cabbage, thinly sliced
freshly grated Parmesan cheese or homemade pesto for garnish

1.

In heavy kettle heat olive oil on medium, add onion, celery, and carrots, sautéing until limp. Add garlic, basil, oregano, and half the parsley, sautéing briefly until fragrant (1 to 3 minutes).

2.

Stir in broth, then add beans and potatoes. Simmer slowly for 30 to 40 minutes or until potatoes are tender.

3.

Add green beans, zucchini, tomatoes, salt and pepper, simmer until vegetables are tender (10 to 15 minutes).

4.

Add pasta, remaining parsley, peas, and cabbage. Simmer until pasta is cooked. Serve with a spoonful of freshly grated cheese or Pesto (page 216) floating on top.

JAMBALAYA

Serves 6

Jambalaya is a marvelous Creole-Cajun dish of rice, vegetables, meat, and/or seafood. There are many versions, some using sausage, all using lots of spices. Adding a good Southern sausage lends authenticity to this dish. The sausage can be Andouille, a smoky French-style tripe sausage, or Chaurice, a garlicky French-style pork sausage. Because these are not always available, I have included a flavorsome homemade version here.

1/2 to 2/3 cup olive oil or freshly rendered lard
3 large onions, coarsely chopped
5 celery stalks, coarsely chopped
2 bell peppers, coarsely chopped
1/2 cup chopped parsley
5 cloves garlic, thinly sliced
1 to 2 teaspoons freshly crushed red pepper flakes (optional)
2/3 pound ham, cut into chunks
1 1/2 pounds Chaurice Sausage (page 64), cut into chunks, or other smoked sausage
1/3 to 1/2 cup olive oil or freshly rendered lard
3 cups uncooked long-grain white rice
4 large tomatoes, coarsely chopped
4 cups stock (beef, pork, or chicken)
1 1/2 cups American light lager
1 pound large shrimp, shelled and deveined
14 thin scallions, chopped
1/2 cup chopped parsley

1.
In a large skillet heat oil on medium-high, add onion and sauté until transparent. Add celery, bell pepper, parsley, garlic, pepper flakes, and sauté until fragrant and wilted (about 5 minutes).

2.
Add ham and sausage and cook 5 minutes. Remove from heat and set aside.

3.
Heat 1/3 cup olive oil in a large heavy pot or Dutch oven. Add uncooked rice and sauté until pale golden brown.

4.
Add sautéed vegetables and meat, tomatoes, stock, and beer. Stir, cover, and simmer over medium. Lower heat and simmer 20 minutes.

5.
Lift the lid and quickly stir in shrimp. Replace lid and simmer 15 minutes.

6.
Remove from heat and let stand 10 minutes. Stir in chopped scallions and parsley. ▼

1.

Mix together the first 11 ingredients in a large bowl, steep for 15 minutes.

2.

Add the parsley, pork, and fat to the steeped spices, mixing thoroughly. Refrigerate 2 to 12 hours.

3.

Form the meat into long cylinders, wrap in cheesecloth and tie securely, or stuff into casings according to directions on a sausage stuffer.

4.

Slowly smoke on a grill or stovetop smoker until completely cooked and smoky. Cool and refrigerate.

CHAURICE SAUSAGE
(MAKES 3 POUNDS)

1 cup finely grated or puréed onion
1 to 1 1/2 tablespoons salt
1 tablespoon thyme
1 tablespoon freshly ground red chili flakes
1 to 2 teaspoons freshly crushed hot red chilies
1 to 2 teaspoons cayenne
1 teaspoon ground allspice
1 teaspoon freshly ground black pepper
1 teaspoon sugar
7 cloves garlic, finely minced and mashed
1/4 cup Scotch ale or dark bock
2/3 cup finely chopped parsley
3 pounds lean boneless ground pork
1/4 pound ground pork fat

CHILLED BLUEBERRY BISQUE

1.

Combine ingredients except Crème Fraîche in a large saucepan. Bring to a slow boil, lower heat, and simmer 10 minutes.

2.

Strain the soup or simply remove spices. Refrigerate and serve swirled with Crème Fraîche or Crème Chantilly.

Serves 6

This striking chilled soup of berries, sparkling cider, spices, and cream can brighten any summer meal.

1 1/2 cups sparkling cider
1/2 cup fruity white wine or blush wine
zest of one lemon, finely minced
3 cups fresh or frozen blueberries
1/3 cup blueberry preserves
1/4 cup sugar mixed with 2 level tablespoons cornstarch
2 to 3 tablespoons berry syrup (optional)
1 cinnamon stick
3 whole allspice
2 whole cloves
1/2 to 1 cup lightly sweetened Crème Fraîche (page 35) or Crème Chantilly (lightly sweetened cream whipped to a soft mound.)

HOT FRUIT COMPOTE

Serves 8 to 10

1.

In a glass or stainless-steel bowl combine cherries and blackberries in the kriek. Refrigerate and marinate overnight.

2.

In a large saucepan, combine peach beer, canned pineapple juice, brown sugar, cinnamon sticks, cloves, allspice, anise seed, orange zest, and orange juice. Bring to a rapid boil, lower heat, and simmer uncovered 45 minutes.

3.

Remove cinnamon and allspice, add pear and apple chunks, and simmer 10 minutes or until tender. Add pineapple chunks, dried apricots, and raisins, including any remaining liqueur.

4.

Drain liquid from marinating berries and mix with cornstarch, whisking until there are no lumps. Stirring constantly, add the cornstarch mixture to the hot fruit and stir until slightly thickened.

5.

Add berries and stir gently until just heated. Remove from heat and serve warm with Crème Fraîche (see col. 3).

1 pound frozen cherries
1 pound frozen blackberries or raspberries
1 1/2 cups kriek or framboise beer
3 cups peach beer, mead, or cider
1 1/2 cups brown sugar
2 thick cinnamon sticks
4 whole cloves
6 whole allspice
1/4 teaspoon whole anise seed
1 tablespoon orange zest, finely chopped
1 orange, juiced
3 each Bosc pears and tart apples, peeled, cored, and diced
1 can pineapple chunks, reserve juice
1 cup dried apricots, chopped, soaked in 1/4 cup Grand Marnier
1 cup golden raisins, soaked in apricot brandy
1/2 cup cornstarch
fresh mint leaves for garnish

A splendid holiday dish, this compote is a marvelous combination of marinated fruits, spices, beer, and brandy simmered gently to create a blend of luscious fruit flavors. Serve warm christened with a dollop of Crème Fraîche or ladle over French vanilla ice cream.

VEGETARIAN BROTH

An excellent vegetable-based broth.

1.

Combine all ingredients in simmering water and cook 3 1/2 to 4 hours or until flavor has been extracted. Long simmering will leave the vegetables flavorless but provide an excellent broth. Strain and simmer to reduce by half.

3 large white potatoes, unpeeled and cubed
1 onion, chopped
3 to 4 brown papery skins of yellow onions
1/2 cup pearled barley
2 cups cabbage
1 cup celery ribs and tops
1/2 bunch Italian (flat-leafed) parsley
3 cloves garlic
1/2 teaspoon peppercorns
salt substitute to taste
1 large or 2 small bay leaves
1 teaspoon each dried thyme, basil, and oregano
4 quarts water

In a great many cultures magical and religious significance is accorded to both honey and bees without which mead (honey wine) could not be made.

APRICOT-ALMOND BISQUE

Serves 4 to 6

This is an easy-to-prepare recipe of fresh apricots, honey, beer, and Crème Fraîche puréed to create a silken concoction that is an incomparable dessert soup. Caloriewise, this is quite decadent, but you can substitute yogurt that has been strained to a thicker consistency for the Crème Fraîche. This makes a splendid base for apricot ice cream.

4 cups ripe fresh apricots or canned drained apricots
2 tablespoons lemon or lime juice
1/2 to 1 cup honey (to taste)
3/4 cup Crème Fraîche, sour cream, or yogurt
1/2 cup mead or cider
1/2 teaspoon almond extract
1/2 teaspoon salt
1 cup raw almonds, toasted dark golden
3/4 cup Crème Fraîche, stirred until smooth (page 35)

1.
In a food processor fitted with a steel blade, process the first 7 ingredients until smooth. Refrigerate until ready to serve.

2.
Crush or chop almonds coarsely.

3.
Ladle soup into a bowl, swirl in a generous dollop of Crème Fraîche and top with a sprinkling of crushed almonds.

Mead has a reputation for aphrodisiac qualities *because of the warm feeling it generates in the drinker and its association with honeymoons.*

CHAPTER 4
SALADS & VEGETABLES

Fruits and vegetables are such an inherent part of our life these days because of their healthy attributes. Scarcely a day goes by that some new benefit is not

Hopefully that day is here for you because no food are so imbued with the excitement of life as fruits and vegetables. They are forever refreshing when eaten plain and fresh, but life is made up of variety and so should our feasting be on these colorful treasures.

Adding beer to their preparation may be easier than you think. You can simply drizzle a bit of beer and herbs over vegetables and microwave till tender, or add a dash of brown ale to glazed carrots to bring out their hidden sweetness. For the more adventurous, crowning a potpourri of dark greens, grilled red onions, and smoked duck with a tart cherry and bock dressing can be an exquisite dining pleasure.

The following recipes are but a glimpse of the feasible once you begin adding the delightful flavor of malt and hops to your vegetable cooking repertoire. For vegetarians who have not yet sampled the glories of cooking with beer, Vegetarian Multicolored Chili (page 44) and Spicy Vegetarian Stir Fry (page 83) are an excellent place to start.

CREATING YOUR OWN RECIPES

Steam or sauté vegetables by adding beer (pale ale, Bavarian dark, or herb beer) along with fragrant herbs and shallots. ▼

discovered. And yet it seems this area of cooking is one we often dismiss with a shrug and say, "someday when I have time."

Spinach Salad with Sweet-Sour Amber Dressing, page 75. ➤

Make fruit sauces or dressings by substituting all or part of the liquid with a compatible beer (fruity lambics, fruit beers, meads, spiced beers, and still or sparkling ciders).

VIBRANT GARDEN ANTIPASTO

Astunning array of colors, this garlicky salad of smoked provolone, roasted peppers, fresh tomatoes, sautéed mushrooms, and charred onions is bound with a roasted garlic and smoked beer dressing.

Serves 4

1.

To roast garlic, toss cloves with dried oregano in 1 tablespoon olive oil and on a small baking pan roast until very soft at 300° in oven or toaster oven. Cool slightly and pop garlic out of skins.

2.

To sauté mushrooms, heat a heavy skillet on medium-high. Pour in 1 tablespoon olive oil and quickly sauté mushrooms until limp. Remove and set aside.

3.

Heat remaining 3 tablespoons olive oil on high. When hot, add thickly sliced onion and sear until darkly browned. Remove and chop coarsely.

4.

To make dressing, mash roasted garlic with kosher salt. Whisk together garlic, 1 1/4 cup olive oil, balsamic vinegar, beer, pepper, chili flakes, and basil.

5.

Pour on enough dressing to coat olives, charred onions, sautéed mushrooms, and peppers and toss thoroughly. Set aside at room temperature for 2 hours.

6.

When ready to serve, add provolone, tomatoes, and parsley to the salad. Coat thoroughly with remaining dressing and and toss gently.

ROASTED GARLIC (FOR DRESSING)

8 cloves garlic, unpeeled
1/2 tablespoon dried oregano
1 tablespoon olive oil

SAUTÉED MUSHROOMS AND CHARRED ONIONS (FOR SALAD)

4 tablespoons extra-virgin olive oil
3 cups thickly sliced mushrooms, button or crimini
1 large red onion, sliced 3/4 inch thick

DRESSING

8 cloves roasted garlic (see step 1)
1/2 teaspoon kosher salt
1 1/4 cups extra-virgin olive oil
2 tablespoons balsamic vinegar
1/4 cup smoked beer
1/2 teaspoon freshly ground black pepper, or to taste
1/4 teaspoon freshly crushed red chili flakes
1 tablespoon fresh chopped basil or 1 teaspoon dried

SALAD

1 cup pitted black olives
1 each red, green, and yellow bell pepper, roasted and peeled
1 pound smoked provolone or fresh Mozzarella, cut in 1/2-inch cubes
sautéed mushrooms (see step 2)
2 large ripe tomatoes, seeded and diced
1/2 cup Italian (flat-leafed) parsley, coarsely chopped

VARIATION

Add slivers of lean ham, hard salami, capicola (spicy Italian ham), and lean pepperoni for a hearty meat-lovers salad.

THAI BEEF SALAD

Fiery and piquant, this salad of dark greens, mushrooms, peanuts, and spicy beef is perfect for those days when you long for fare that is zesty but not overly heavy.

1.

In a bowl stir beef, beer, garlic, soy sauce, and sesame oil and let stand for 45 minutes.

2.

In a wok, heat 1/4 cup of canola oil on medium-high. Drain the meat and stir-fry in three small batches just until cooked. Remove and set aside.

3.

Prepare the chili oil dressing by heating 1/3 cup of canola oil over medium heat. Remove wok from heat and stir in ground chilies or curry paste, Szechwan peppercorns, and sesame seeds, stirring for 1 minute. Allow to cool completely.

4.

Add soy sauce, porter, sesame oil, and sugar to the cooled chili oil. Toss meat into this mixture and allow to stand while you prepare the greens.

5.

Arrange spinach and red-leaf lettuce on individual plates or a platter. Toss carrots and slivered green onions together and sprinkle over arranged greens. ▼

SPICY BEEF

1 pound top sirloin, sliced thinly against
  the grain
1/2 cup porter
2 cloves garlic, finely minced
1 tablespoon dark soy sauce
1 teaspoon dark sesame oil
1/4 cup canola oil

CHILI OIL DRESSING

1/3 cup canola oil (approximate)
3 ground hot Thai chilies, or 2 teaspoons
  Thai red curry paste
6 Szechwan peppercorns
2 tablespoon sesame seeds
2 tablespoons light soy sauce
2 tablespoons porter
1 1/2 teaspoons dark sesame oil
1 teaspoon sugar

SALAD

1 bunch spinach, cleaned, stemmed, and
  torn
1 bunch red-leaf lettuce, cleaned,
  stemmed, and torn
1 carrot, julienned and tossed in 1 teaspoon
  fresh lime juice
1 bunch green onions, sliced thinly and
  tops cut into 2-inch lengths
1 can baby corn, drained and patted dry
1 small can water chestnuts, drained and
  sliced
1 small can straw mushrooms, drained
1/2 small bunch cilantro, leaves only
1/4 cup peanuts or almond slivers, toasted

6.

Drain meat and reserve the chili oil dressing. Place meat on the greens and arrange corn, water chestnuts, and mushrooms on top.

7.

Garnish with cilantro and toasted nuts (see page 284). Pour any remaining chili oil dressing over the salad, if desired.

SMOKED MEAT SALAD

Serves 4

A unique combination of greens, red onions, fresh mushrooms, and lightly smoked meat, this salad is adorned with a sweet-hot-tart dressing of sour cherries and chipotle chilies.

1.

On an outdoor grill or indoor stove-top Cameron smoker, slowly smoke meat with fruitwood chips (cherry or apple) until just cooked through so the meat retains its moistness.

2.

While the meat is smoking, combine cherry preserves, porter, 1/4 cup olive oil, soy sauce, sesame oil, garlic, and chili. Set aside.

3.

Cut or pull the smoked meat into strips. Set aside.

4.

Heat a heavy skillet on high. When very hot add 1 tablespoon oil and sauté mushrooms until just softened. Remove and set aside. Repeat with all the meat, just searing the outside. ▼

1 pound boneless meat: chicken, turkey, duck, beef, or pork
1/3 cup tart cherry preserves
1/4 cup porter
1/4 cup olive oil
2 tablespoons dark soy sauce
1 1/2 teaspoons dark sesame oil
1 clove garlic, finely minced and mashed
1 chipotle chili (see Note), seeded and finely minced
2 tablespoons olive oil or other vegetable oil
1 cup sliced mushrooms: button, shitake, or crimini
1 large red onion, sliced 3/4 inch thick
8 cups salad greens, leaf lettuce, radicchio, arugula, etc.
1 1/2 cups Italian (flat-leafed) parsley
1 cup spiced walnuts or pecans (see page 74)

NOTE

Found in the grocery's Mexican food section, smoked jalapenos (chipotle chilies) are available canned and dried. If using dried chipotles, rehydrate in a bowl of hot water for 2 hours before using in this recipe.

5.

Heat remaining oil on high. When hot, add the thickly sliced onion. Quickly sear each side until darkly browned. Remove and chop coarsely.

6.

Arrange greens, mushrooms, and charred onions on individual plates or a large platter. Place smoked meat on top. Ladle a small amount of dressing over the salad and top with spiced nuts (recipe follows). Serve immediately.

SPICED WALNUTS OR PECANS

Makes 2 cups

An elegant addition to any salad.

3 tablespoons melted butter
1/2 teaspoon each ground cumin and cinnamon
1 small clove garlic, finely minced and mashed
1/3 teaspoon cayenne
1 pound large shelled pecan or walnut halves
baking parchment

1.

Combine butter and spices, mixing thoroughly. Pour over nuts and toss gently until coated.

2.

Spread on a parchment-lined baking sheet and bake at 350° for 12 to 14 minutes. Remove and cool.

SPINACH SALAD WITH SWEET-SOUR AMBER DRESSING

Serves 6

Delightfully vivid and enticing, this spinach salad is an ideal blend of sharp flavors and crisp textures.

3 bunches spinach, washed, stemmed, and torn into small pieces

1 small red onion, sliced thinly

1 small can water chestnuts, drained and sliced thinly

1 can baby corn, drained and patted dry

1 can mandarin oranges, drained (or sectioned sweet grapefruit)

1/4 cup fried shallots (see Note)

1/2 cup fresh pomegranate seeds or lightly broken raspberries

lots of fresh homemade croutons

1 batch Eureka Dressing (page 229)

1.
Assemble spinach, onion, and water chestnuts on salad plates.

2.
Arrange corn and mandarin oranges on top. Sprinkle with fried shallots, pomegranate seeds, and croutons.

3.
Top with dressing just before serving.

NOTE

Most oriental stores carry jars of wonderful fried shallots, a product of Malaysia, at a minimal price.

According to ancient Assyrian records, Noah is described as carrying jars of beer, wine and brandy aboard the ark.

GRILLED EGGPLANT WITH TAMARIND-BEER SAUCE

Serves 4

This fabulous eggplant dish is exceptional served with fresh pasta. Don't be timid about experimenting if you are unfamiliar with tamarind. Its unique, piquant flavor is well worth trying.

2 medium eggplants
4 cups water with 1/4 cup salt
1/4 cup flavored oil (see Notes)

TAMARIND-BEER
SAUCE

1/4 cup olive oil
2 red bell peppers, seeded, and coarsely
    chopped
1/2 small onion, finely chopped
2 shallots, finely chopped
3 cloves garlic, finely chopped and mashed
1/3 cup Tamarind-Beer Syrup (page 85)
    mixed with 2 tablespoons honey
1-inch piece of ginger, sliced thinly
1/2 teaspoon Thai red curry paste

1.

Cut stem end off eggplants. Slice into 1-inch rounds and place in salted water. Soak for 15 minutes to remove any bitterness.

2.

Drain and pat dry with paper towels. Brush on both sides with flavored oil and let stand while heating the grill and preparing the sauce.

3.

In a large heavy skillet heat 1/4 cup olive oil over medium-low. When hot, add red bell pepper, onion, shallots, and garlic, cooking just until soft and transparent (do not brown).

4.

Add the Tamarind-Beer Syrup, ginger, and curry paste. Continue to cook until thick and chunky. Remove from heat and cover.

5.

Grill sliced eggplant on medium-high until golden and soft when pierced with a fork.

6.

Serve immediately with the Tamarind-Beer Sauce.

NOTES

 Flavored oil can be made by heating oil on low and adding one of the following — mashed garlic, shallot, dried chili pod, or annatto seed. Cover and set aside for a few hours.

 Eggplant can be broiled instead of grilled. If using the small Japanese or Thai eggplants, soaking in salted water to remove bitterness is unnecessary. Simply score with a knife and grill whole.

RED PEPPER SAUCE

Makes 4 cups

1.

In a small baking pan toss garlic cloves with the 2 tablespoons olive oil. Bake at 350° until soft and golden. Cool and peel.

2.

Heat ale until hot. Add bouillon cube and stir until dissolved.

3.

In a food processor mix roasted garlic, red bell peppers, olive oil, basil, vinegar, cayenne, and beer-bouillon mixture until smooth. Season to taste with salt, pepper, and Louisiana hot pepper sauce.

4.

When ready to serve heat just until hot.

10 large cloves garlic, unpeeled
2 tablespoons olive oil
1/2 cup brown ale
1 cube chicken bouillon
5 red bell peppers, roasted, peeled, and
   seeded
1/4 to 1/3 cup extra-virgin olive oil
1/4 cup fresh basil, finely minced
2 tablespoons balsamic vinegar
1/8 to 1/4 teaspoon fresh cayenne, ground
Louisiana hot pepper sauce, salt and
   pepper, to taste

One of the finest and fastest sauces you will ever encounter, this is great on pasta, topping grilled chicken, or ladled over steamed vegetables. A perfect alternative to tomatoes for a red sauce on Italian foods.

BEER-GLAZED ONIONS

Serves 2

4 tablespoons olive oil or butter
4 large yellow onions, sliced 1/4 inch thick
1/2 teaspoon each salt and pepper
pinch of cayenne (optional)
1/4 cup porter, bock, Oktoberfest, or other
   full-flavored beer

1.
Heat oil on medium in a large sauté pan. Add onions, salt, pepper, and cayenne, stirring constantly.

2.
Continue cooking until onions reach a golden caramel color.

3.
Pour in the beer and cook an additional 3 to 4 minutes. Serve hot.

One of my culinary heroes, James Beard, inspired these onions. He used bourbon instead of beer. For fun, try a splash of each (boilermaker onions?) These are marvelous served alongside steak, sausage, or other grilled meats, added to hot sandwiches, or as a filling for vegetable tacos or burritos.

Bock beers, originating in Germany, were traditionally very strong, dark, full-bodied malty beers, brewed in winter for spring consumption. Pale-colored bock beers also are brewed today.

APPLE- & ONION- FILLED SQUASH

A piquant beer sauce glazes lightly sautéed apples, onions, mushrooms, and spinach. Baked acorn squash halves charmingly serve as edible bowls.

Serves 4

2 small acorn squash
8 tablespoons butter or margarine
1/2 teaspoon cinnamon
2/3 cup Bavarian light lager
1/4 to 1/3 cup sugar (to taste, a balance of sweet and bitter)
2 tablespoons cornstarch
2 medium onions, peeled and thinly sliced
4 large shitake mushrooms, soaked for 1 hour and thinly sliced
4 small tart green apples, peeled, cored, and thinly sliced
2 cups spinach, washed, stemmed, and thinly sliced

1.

Split squash lengthwise and remove seeds and strings. Place 1 tablespoon butter in each half and sprinkle with cinnamon. Bake at 350° until tender, about 35 to 40 minutes.

2.

Mix beer, sugar, and cornstarch in a small bowl and set aside.

3.

Heat remaining butter in a large sauté pan until foam subsides. Toss in onion and mushrooms and cook just until the onion begins to wilt.

4.

Stir the beer mixture and pour over onions, stirring constantly. When the sauce begins to thicken add apple slices and cook until slightly soft and clear. Remove from heat.

5.

When ready to serve, toss spinach into hot apple mixture and immediately spoon into the baked squash halves.

BEER-GLAZED CARROTS

Serves 4 to 6

The lowly carrot often is forgotten as an elegant and appetizing vegetable. This recipe should bring carrots back into vogue and give them the top billing they deserve.

1 tablespoon butter
1 tablespoon vegetable oil
6 medium carrots, scrubbed and julienned
1 tablespoon sugar
1 scant teaspoon ground ginger (optional)
1/4 cup bock or Munich-style beer
freshly ground black pepper, to taste

1.
Heat butter and oil in a sauté pan on medium-low. Add carrots and sauté slowly for 10 minutes.

2.
Sprinkle with sugar, ginger, beer, and pepper and continue cooking for 20 to 25 minutes, stirring occasionally. The carrots will be lightly glazed, golden, and limp.

VARIATION

For an attractive and scrumptious combination, use half carrots and half parsnips. Slow cooking brings out the sweetness of the parsnips and accents the carrots perfectly. Remember to peel and core the parsnips because they are tougher than carrots.

In 1789 George Washington announced a version of a "Buy American" policy. He announced he would only drink porter brewed in America.

BOILED NEW POTATOES

Serves 4

Simmer new potatoes in beer and salt, then serve with herbed mustard sauce for an unusual and delicious twist on a classic side dish.

16 small new potatoes
2 cups pale ale or light lager
2 cups water
2 teaspoons salt

1.

Cut a small ribbon of skin from around each potato to prevent bursting while boiling.

2.

Bring beer, water, and salt to a boil. Add potatoes and simmer, uncovered, until tender. Drain and serve hot drizzled with Mustard Sauce (page 217) or herbed butter.

CURRIED CORN

Serves 4

This lovely mixture of corn, onions, ale, and curry is quick to prepare and makes a unique side dish.

3 tablespoons butter
1 small onion, coarsely chopped
1 clove garlic, minced
1 red or green bell pepper, thinly sliced
  and chopped
3 tablespoons India pale ale
1 to 2 tablespoons high-quality curry powder
1 tablespoon brown sugar
pinch cayenne, to taste
1/4 teaspoon black pepper
1 pound fresh, frozen, or canned corn,
  drained

1.

Melt butter in a large skillet. Sauté onion just until it begins to soften, add garlic and bell pepper, remove from heat.

2.

Stir in beer, curry powder, brown sugar, and spices. Return to heat and cook, stirring frequently, 3 minutes. ▼

3.

Add corn and mix well, cooking an additional 3 minutes. Serve hot.

HELPFUL HINT

High-quality curry powder is not found in a small can in the spice section of your grocery store. Curry powder is a pungent blend of aromatic spices that, whenever possible, should be freshly ground or purchased from a Middle Eastern or East Indian grocery store (see page 282). Once you have tasted a superior curry powder, all others will taste like sawdust!

RENOWNED COLESLAW

Serves 6 to 8

Everyone who has ever tasted this swears it's the finest coleslaw ever to pass their lips. It goes with so many dishes that I had to include it!

1.

Combine cabbage, carrots, and onion. In a separate bowl whisk together mayonnaise, vinegar, sugar, cumin, celery seed, and mustard. Add salt and pepper to taste.

2.

Pour dressing over cabbage, toss, and refrigerate for 1 hour before serving.

1 large head green cabbage, shredded
1/4 head red cabbage, shredded
2 carrots, grated or julienned (optional)
1 large onion, finely chopped and rinsed
2 cups mayonnaise
1/2 cup malt or cider vinegar
1/3 cup sugar
1/2 teaspoon freshly ground cumin
1 teaspoon celery seed
1 to 2 teaspoons ground yellow mustard
salt and pepper to taste

SPICY VEGETARIAN STIR-FRY

Do not be put off by the long list of ingredients. This is a marvelous, spicy vegetable dish intensified with Thai curry paste and beer. The rice sticks, an oriental noodle, give it enough substance for a complete meal.

Serves 6 to 8

1.
In a small bowl combine beer, stock, cornstarch, soy sauce, vinegar, and sugar, stirring well. Set aside.

2.
Heat 3 tablespoons peanut oil in a wok over medium-high.

3.
Coat eggplant with seasoned flour, shaking off excess. Toss eggplant into wok and sauté, turning frequently, until crisp and golden. Remove and place on paper towels to drain and cool.

4.
Heat another tablespoon of oil in the wok. Add carrots and stir-fry until just wilted. Place in a large bowl. Repeat with celery, snow peas, and shallots, stir-frying each separately and adding to the bowl.

5.
Remove wok from heat to cool briefly. Lower heat to medium and add another 3 tablespoons oil, return to burner.   ▼

2/3 cup American or German light lager
1/3 cup vegetable stock (or chicken stock)
3 tablespoons cornstarch
1/4 cup light soy sauce
2 tablespoons rice vinegar
1 tablespoon sugar
6 Asian eggplants (small purple Japanese eggplant or round green Thai eggplant), split and diced into 1/2-inch cubes
1/2 cup flour mixed with 1 teaspoon pepper and 1/2 teaspoon salt
1/2 cup peanut or other vegetable oil
2 medium carrots, julienned
4 ribs celery, cut into half-inch diagonals
15 snow peas, thinly julienned
4 shallots, peeled and thinly sliced
1 to 3 teaspoons Thai curry paste (hot and garlicky)
1-inch piece fresh ginger, thinly sliced
5 cloves garlic, thinly sliced
1 small can bamboo shoots, drained
4 ounces sliced water chestnuts, diced
1 large can straw mushrooms, drained
6 cups bok choy, thinly sliced
1 block tofu, cubed
4 ounces rice sticks, soaked in water 30 minutes
8 green onions, cut into half-inch diagonals
1 small bunch mint, coarsely chopped
1 cup roasted peanuts

6.

Add curry paste, ginger, and garlic, stir-frying until fragrant (1 to 3 minutes). Add bamboo shoots, chestnuts, mushrooms, bok choy, tofu, and rice sticks, tossing and stir-frying briefly. Push up the sides of the wok.

7.

Stir the beer and cornstarch mixture and add to wok, stirring until slightly thickened. Push down the vegetables and add green onions, mint, and peanuts. Serve immediately.

VARIATIONS

❧ Add freshly rinsed bean sprouts, canned baby corn, or bitter greens.

❧ Add a variety of mushrooms — shitake, woods ears, or button — and serve with Chinese pancakes.

❧ Substitute cooked vermicelli for rice sticks.

MARINATED SKEWERED FRUIT

Serves 8 to 10

These incredible tidbits are brushed with bock beer, soy sauce, brown sugar, and butter while grilling for a terrific glaze.

1.

Combine sugar, beer, pineapple juice, soy sauce, honey, vinegar, ginger, coriander, and anise in a heavy pan and simmer uncovered for 20 minutes. Cool.

2.

Place fruit in separate bowls. Pour marinade over each and toss gently.

3.

Let stand at room temperature for 3 to 4 hours or in refrigerator for 5 to 6 hours. Drain, reserving marinade. Mix marinade with melted butter.

4.

Skewer fruit and grill, basting with the butter-marinade mixture until softened and glazed. Serve warm or at room temperature.

1 cup brown sugar
1/2 cup dark bock beer
1/2 cup pineapple juice
2/3 cup light soy sauce
1/2 cup honey
1/4 cup fruit vinegar (raspberry, blueberry)
1 teaspoon freshly grated ginger
1 teaspoon freshly ground coriander
1/2 teaspoon anise seed (optional)
1 small ripe pineapple, cut into 1-inch chunks (or canned)
2 ripe red tropical, pink-fleshed bananas or partially ripened yellow bananas, cut into chunks
10 kumquats, split, discard meat but save the peel
6 ripe apricots, quartered (or canned)
5 tablespoons melted butter

TROPICAL FRUIT SALAD WITH TAMARIND DRESSING

T

Serves 8

The beer-based tamarind syrup in the dressing has a tart-sweet quality that balances the salad beautifully. Use fruits that are in season.

FRUIT SALAD

2 ripe mangoes

3 ripe red tropical, pink-fleshed bananas or partially ripened yellow bananas

1 ripe papaya

1 small ripe pineapple or 2 cans pineapple chunks

1 can of lychee nuts, drained

1 can rambutan, drained (see Note)

DRESSING

juice of 1/2 lime

1/4 cup tamarind syrup (recipe follows)

1/4 cup coconut milk

1 teaspoon vanilla

2/3 cup toasted coconut (optional)

TAMARIND-BEER SYRUP

1 cup India pale ale

1 cup water

1 cup sugar

5 peeled tamarinds or 1/2 cup tamarind pulp

1.
Clean and cut fruit into bite-size pieces. Make sure all are drained thoroughly and combine.

2.
Combine the lime juice, tamarind syrup, coconut milk, and vanilla, stirring well. Coat fruit chunks with the mixture and chill briefly.

3.
Just before serving stir the fruit to coat well with dressing. Toss in coconut and serve.

1.
Briskly simmer beer, water, and sugar until completely dissolved. Add peeled tamarinds that have been broken into pieces and simmer 1 hour, partly covered.

2.
Stir every 10 minutes, gently mashing tamarind with the back of a spoon.   ▼

3.

Cool and strain syrup, pressing the tamarind pulp to extract as much of the flavorful liquid as possible. Discard pulp and refrigerate the syrup in a jar until ready for use. This will keep up to three weeks.

NOTE

Rambutan are pineapple-stuffed fruits that resemble lychee nuts and are available at Asian grocery stores. They can be replaced with lychee nuts from the oriental section of grocery stores.

Swaziland villagers make an alcoholic drink called umganu. It is made by mixing marula fruit, water, and sugar in bowls which are then sealed with mud. A week later the brew is ready.

The term "toast" comes from a Renaissance custom in which the host would have a two-handled drinking vessel filled with mead and a piece of toast floating in it. The host would take a sip and pass the cup among the guests. When it returned the host would honor his guests by draining the cup and swallowing the toast.

HOT POTATO SALAD

Serves 3 to 4

Ahearty side dish, this warm salad combines red and white new potatoes with bacon and beer for a memorable experience.

8 each small new red and white potatoes, scrubbed
5 strips lean bacon, coarsely chopped
1 large onion or 5 shallots, coarsely chopped
5 scallions, cut diagonally into 1-inch pieces
2 teaspoons caraway seeds
1 cup Oktoberfest beer
3 tablespoons balsamic vinegar
1/4 to 1/3 cup oil or bacon drippings
paprika, salt, and pepper to taste
1/4 cup toasted crushed walnuts

1.

Lower potatoes into boiling water to cover. Add a teaspoon of salt and boil just until tender (do not overcook). Drain, cool slightly, and quarter but do not peel. Place in a hot covered pan.

2.

In a heavy skillet cook bacon until crisp. Remove and set aside on towels to drain.

3.

Remove all but 3 tablespoons of bacon drippings. Sauté onion in drippings until golden. Add scallions and caraway seeds, sauté for 1 minute.

4.

Add beer to onions and simmer over medium-high until reduced by half. Pour in vinegar and oil and simmer briefly. Adjust seasonings.

5.

Add warm potatoes to sauce and simmer 2 minutes, turning potatoes gently. Remove from heat and place in serving bowl. Sprinkle with paprika and walnuts.

NOTE

If not serving immediately, cover and hold at room temperature. Stir before serving.

VARIATIONS

❧ Substitute 2 ounces of Canadian bacon or ham for the bacon. Substitute oil as needed in place of drippings.

❧ Replace vinegar with 1 tablespoon Mustard Sauce Dressing (page 217).

CHINESE CHICKEN SALAD

Serves 4 to 6

A hearty dinner salad with slices of marinated grilled chicken in an abundance of veggies and crispy tidbits. Looks terrific when served on individual plates with sliced grilled chicken arranged on top.

MARINADE & DRESSING

3 tablespoons dark sesame oil

2/3 cup walnut, peanut, or olive oil

1/3 cup rice vinegar

1/4 cup porter or stout

1/3 cup light soy sauce

2 large cloves garlic, minced and crushed

1/4 cup sugar

1/2 teaspoon Chinese chili oil or 1/2 teaspoon ground chili flakes (optional)

3 whole chicken breasts, skinless and boneless

SALAD INGREDIENTS

6 cups napa cabbage, rinsed and sliced thinly

1 bunch red-leaf lettuce, rinsed and torn into bite-size pieces

1 cup red cabbage, thinly sliced

3 stalks celery, sliced

1 large carrot, julienned

2 cans mandarin oranges, drained

2 cups fresh sprouts (bean, alfalfa, radish, or mixed)

8 scallions, washed and sliced diagonally

1 can thinly sliced water chestnuts, drained

1 can baby corn, drained and split in half

1/2 cup dried shitake mushrooms, soaked in water and thinly sliced

2 to 3 tablespoons sesame seeds

2 cups fried chow mein noodles

1.

Combine marinade ingredients, divide in half. Reserve half for salad dressing and marinate chicken breasts (refrigerated) in the other half 4 to 18 hours.

2.

Grill chicken, place on platter, and cover with foil. Let stand 5 minutes before slicing thinly.

3.

Toss together cabbage, lettuce, celery, and carrots. Arrange remaining ingredients including grilled chicken on top. Ladle dressing over salad and serve immediately. ▼

VARIATIONS

❧ To poach chicken instead of grill, bring 3 cups light lager, 1 teaspoon thyme, and 1 clove garlic to a slow simmer. Add chicken breasts and simmer, removing any foam, until meat shows no pink when a knife is inserted into the thickest part. Remove, drain, and slice thinly.

❧ Garnish with snow peas, sliced almonds, thinly sliced red onions, crushed ramen noodles, sliced red bell peppers, bamboo shoots, watercress, fresh grapes, or chopped apples.

❧ Use slices of leftover teriyake-marinated beef (page 121) in place of chicken.

❧ For vegetarians, add crispy cubes of fried tofu plus cubes of firm tofu marinated in dressing to add texture and substance.

SOUTHWEST FETA DRESSING

Makes 3 1/2 cups

Combining the full, hearty flavor of feta cheese with toasted cumin seeds and herbs gives this dressing an unusual and delightful flavor. Try dipping Buffalo wings (pages 164 to 166) into this dressing in place of ranch or blue cheese.

1.

Combine all ingredients in a food processor and mix until smooth.

2.

Allow to stand for 30 minutes before using. Thin with a small amount of water, if necessary.

1/2 cup yogurt

1 1/4 cup feta, drained

1 cup mayonnaise

1/2 cup sour cream (or additional yogurt for a tangy taste)

1/4 cup malt vinegar

2 tablespoons olive oil

3 large cloves garlic, finely minced

1 tablespoon finely chopped Italian (flat-leafed) parsley

1 1/2 tablespoons cumin seed, toasted and coarsely crushed

1 1/2 teaspoons each oregano, basil, and finely minced orange zest

1 teaspoon freshly ground black pepper

CARROT & JICAMA SALAD

A palate-cooling salad of ivory and orange, this goes especially well with spicy, southwest meals.

1.
Combine jicama, carrots, cilantro, and beer, tossing gently. Allow to stand 1 hour.

2.
Mix oil, vinegar, coriander seed, and garlic 15 minutes before serving. Remove garlic and pour dressing over salad.

3.
Garnish with sunflower and pomegranate seeds and serve immediately.

1 small jicama, peeled and julienned (see Note)

3 small carrots, julienned

1 tablespoon finely chopped fresh cilantro

1/4 cup American light lager or weissbier

1/2 cup olive, avocado, or nut oil

3 tablespoons fruited vinegar (orange, raspberry)

1/2 teaspoon finely ground coriander seed

2 cloves garlic, lightly mashed

salt and pepper to taste

3/4 cup shelled sunflower seeds, lightly toasted (optional)

1/2 cup pomegranate seeds (optional)

NOTE

Jicama is a large, crisp, juicy root vegetable with a slightly sweet flavor reminiscent of water chestnuts which can be substituted where jicama is not available.

BLUE CHEESE SALAD DRESSING

Makes 2 1/2 cups

1.

Combine all ingredients and refrigerate two hours before serving.

3/4 cup mayonnaise
3/4 cup sour cream
1/2 cup finely crumbled blue cheese
1/3 cup dry mead or still cider
1 shallot, finely minced
2 scallions, white only, finely minced
2 to 3 drops Louisiana hot pepper sauce
2 teaspoons balsamic vinegar

Unite the opulent flavor of blue cheese with the crisp, dry flavor of mead or still cider to make a delightful salad dressing or cooling dip for Buffalo wings (pages 164 to 166).

ALMOND CHICKEN SALAD

Serves 8

This satisfying salad is adorned with apricots, toasted almonds, and water chestnuts and dressed with Mustard Salad Dressing. It is perfect for summer suppers or casual entertaining.

2 tablespoons apricot preserves
2 teaspoons lime juice
1 1/2 cups sliced apricots, plums, or
  mandarin oranges
1/3 cup olive oil
2 cloves garlic, finely minced
1 shallot, finely minced
1 cup mayonnaise
1/4 cup lime juice
1/2 cup Mustard Salad Dressing (the honey
  version is perfect, see pages 217 and 218)
2 teaspoons each dried parsley, thyme,
  basil, tarragon, and chervil
1/2 teaspoon freshly ground pepper
3 1/2 pounds boneless, skinless chicken
  breasts, poached and cubed
1 cup celery, thinly sliced
1 cup water chestnuts, thinly sliced
5 scallions, finely minced
2 cucumbers, peeled, seeded, and
  julienned
2/3 cup slivered or sliced almonds, toasted
salt to taste
8 large leaves bib lettuce
Italian (flat-leafed) parsley for garnish

TO POACH CHICKEN

7 cups water
1 cup weissbier or pale ale
1 bay leaf
1 brown papery skin from yellow onion
1 garlic clove
6 whole peppercorns
1 teaspoon mixed fragrant herbs

1.

Heat apricot preserves and stir in lime juice. Toss fruit in this mixture, cover, and refrigerate.

2.

Whisk together oil, garlic, shallot, mayonnaise, lime juice, Mustard Salad Dressing, and herbs for dressing. Refrigerate until ready to serve.

3.

Assemble chicken, celery, chestnuts, and scallions in a bowl. Cover and refrigerate until ready to serve.

4.

Just before serving add cucumbers and sliced almonds to chicken mixture, tossing gently.

5.

Serve on plates arranged attractively with lettuce leaves. Ladle dressing over and garnish with parsley and/or additional toasted almonds or fruit slices.

1.

Simmer all ingredients except chicken for 20 minutes. ▼

2.

Slide in chicken breasts and skim off foam. Simmer just until no pink shows when a knife is inserted into thickest part (about 12 minutes).

3.

Remove and cool before cutting.

POTATO PANCAKES

Serves 6

A cross between hash-browns and traditional potato pancakes. Soaking potatoes in beer gives added flavor and crispness. Serve these crunchy pancakes with sour cream for an indulgent treat.

4 large baking potatoes, peeled
2 cups German Pilsener
1 small onion, finely minced
1 teaspoon salt
1/2 teaspoon freshly ground black pepper
1 teaspoon paprika
1 extra-large egg
1/2 cup Italian-flavored bread crumbs
1/4 cup grated hard cheese (Parmesan, Romano)
1/2 to 1 cup extra-virgin olive oil

1.

Coarsely grate or julienne potatoes, place in bowl and pour beer over. Cover and let stand 1 hour.

2.

Drain potatoes, reserving beer to use later for stew. Stir onion, salt, pepper, paprika, egg, bread crumbs, and cheese into potatoes.

3.

Heat a heavy skillet on medium until hot. Add just enough oil to lightly coat bottom of pan.

4.

Drop a few tablespoons of potato mixture into the hot pan and flatten slightly. Sauté until crisp and golden brown, turn, and brown other side. If not serving immediately, place on a heated tray.

In seventeenth century Germany a young noble would go beer riding. He loaded a cart with beer and set off for the nearest manor. The party would continue there until he refilled his barrels and set off once again, taking along those who wished to go. The beer ride continued until they ran out of beer, or places to stop.

CHAPTER 5
FISH & SEAFOOD

The selection of fresh and fresh-frozen seafood available throughout the year in this immense country of ours is an astounding achievement. The variety of

cooking methods and ingredients available to prepare this bounty of ocean, lake, and stream is infinite.

As with other dishes in this book, you will find that fish and seafood profit significantly when paired with the complex character of beer. Whether steaming fish in an exotic mixture of porter and ginger or marinating shrimp in a spirited blend of beer, garlic and chilies, you will quickly recognize the invaluable contribution beer can make in the preparation of seafood.

In Chapter 1 we explored the uncomplicated basics of preparing fish and seafood. If you have ever hesitated to prepare seafood, this chapter should alleviate your doubts and allow you to approach the kitchen with confidence when working with seafood. Once you are comfortable with these techniques you will find yourself eagerly substituting the countless varieties of fish — marinating sea scallops and sauteing them in place of shrimp, and bringing fresh-caught trout in lieu of salmon for smoking over apple and pecan chips.

When you discover just how simple it is to prepare extraordinary seafood you will experience a tremendous sensation of joy and relief. No longer will you be dependent on (or disappointed by) restaurants when you yearn for seafood prepared just the way you like it!

Scallops Escabèche, page 109. ►

HERBED MUSSELS OR CLAMS

Serves 2 to 3

Steaming in a flavorsome combination of beer, onions, and herbs is an ideal way to prepare these tasty bivalves. Simply add fresh bread, a green salad dressed with Mustard Salad Dressing (pages 217 and 218), and an Enchanted Apricot Tart (page 271) for an impeccable supper.

1.
Toss together onion, shallot, parsley, thyme, scallion, and pepper and place in a 6-quart Dutch oven.

2.
Arrange shellfish over onions and pour beer over top. Cover and steam on medium-low until the mussels open. Discard any that do not open.

3.
Remove shellfish and place on heated platter. Cover with foil. Quickly reduce cooking liquid with the vegetables by one-third. Add herbed butter, stir, and pour over warm shellfish. Serve immediately.

1 onion, coarsely chopped
1 large shallot or clove of garlic, thinly sliced
1 tablespoon chopped Italian (flat-leafed) parsley
1 teaspoon dried thyme
1 scallion, finely chopped
1/2 teaspoon freshly ground black pepper
2 1/2 quarts mussels or clams, scrubbed (mussels debearded)
1 1/4 cups weissbier or American light lager
8 tablespoons Herbed Butter (see page 228)

A typical dinner for Diamond Jim Brady would be three dozen oysters, six fresh crabs, and two barrels of turtle soup for appetizers, followed by terrapin, two ducks, and a large sirloin steak with vegetables.

CLAM CHOWDER

Serves 6 to 8

Bavarian dark lager lends subtle new flavors and depth to this classic Boston favorite.

4 tablespoons butter
4 ounces Canadian bacon or lean ham, finely chopped
2 medium onions, finely chopped
2 shallots, finely chopped
1 1/2 cups chicken stock
1 cup Bavarian dark or Oktoberfest
5 medium baking potatoes, peeled and placed in cold water
1 teaspoon dried thyme
1 1/2 pounds chopped canned clams with clam juice
2 cups light cream or milk
salt and pepper to taste
fresh Italian (flat-leafed) parsley or finely chopped scallions for garnish

1.

In a Dutch oven heat 2 tablespoons butter over medium heat. Add Canadian bacon and sauté until lightly browned. Remove and set aside.

2.

Add remaining butter and sauté onions until wilted. Add shallots and continue cooking until pale golden. Remove and set aside.

3.

Pour stock and lager into Dutch oven and place on medium-high. While the liquid is heating, grate two potatoes and cube the remaining three.

4.

Stir potatoes, thyme, Canadian bacon, and onions into liquid and bring to a slow boil. Simmer until the cubed potatoes are tender yet hold their shape (about 40 minutes).

5.

Lower heat, add clams with liquor, and slowly stir in cream. Heat just until bubbles begin to form around the edges.

6.

Remove from heat, taste, and adjust with salt and pepper. Garnish with minced Italian (flat-leafed) parsley or scallions.

GRILLED TERIYAKI FISH

Has fish become humdrum? Try this rather exotic-flavored marinade next time you grill seafood. The combination of soy sauce, porter, and seasonings elevates plain seafood to uncommon heights.

MARINADE

1/4 cup honey, warmed
1/3 cup light soy sauce or 3 tablespoons tamari sauce
1/3 cup porter, stout, or smoked beer or substitute liquid smoke for smoked beer
2 tablespoons olive or other vegetable oil
1 tablespoon sugar
1 tablespoon dark sesame oil
2 cloves garlic, finely minced and crushed
1/8 teaspoon hot red chili flakes, ground (optional)
1 teaspoon ground ginger or 1/2 teaspoon fresh ginger, chopped
1/2 teaspoon liquid smoke (optional)
freshly ground black pepper, to taste

2/3 cup flour
4 pounds mahi-mahi or other firm fish, or large shelled shrimp, or sea scallops

1.
Whisk together the first 11 ingredients and let stand at room temperature 1 hour.

2.
Brush marinade over fish and refrigerate for 2 hours before grilling.

3.
Sprinkle the fish with flour and grill, basting often with marinade.

HELPFUL HINT

Cook fish 10 minutes per inch of thickness. Cook shrimp until they turn pink and scallops until they are no longer translucent.

WHOLE STEAMED FISH

Serves 2 to 4

Steaming imparts a delicate quality and flavor to fresh fish, especially when the steam is suffused with exquisite tones of porter, ginger, garlic, and lemon grass.

1 whole fish (3 to 4 pounds), scaled and
  cleaned, or 2 pounds of fish fillets
2 cups porter
1-inch piece fresh ginger, peeled and
  sliced
2 to 3 large cloves garlic, lightly mashed
3 stalks lemon grass, the tender white area
  chopped (see Note)
napa cabbage leaves or large lettuce
  leaves (enough to line steamer)
1 tablespoon dark sesame oil
1 tablespoon peanut oil
2-inch piece fresh ginger, julienned
2 cloves garlic, thinly sliced
1/2 cup cilantro leaves

1.

Lightly score thick area of fish on both sides. Measure at the thickest part.

2.

Combine porter, sliced ginger, garlic, and lemon grass in the bottom of a steamer or wok fitted with a steamer rack. Bring to a rapid boil.

3.

Line steamer rack with cabbage or lettuce leaves. Lay fish on leaves and place above boiling liquid, cover. Steam according to the 10-minutes-per-inch-of-thickness rule.

4.

While steaming, combine dark sesame and peanut oil. Heat until very hot, cover, and set aside.

5.

When fish has finished steaming, remove and place on a warm platter. Garnish with julienned ginger and thin garlic slices. Pour hot sesame and peanut oil over fish and sprinkle with cilantro. Serve immediately.

NOTE

Lemon grass can be found in most Asian grocery stores. If not available, use 3 or 4 strips of fresh lemon zest.

VARIATIONS

❀ For spicy fish, mix freshly minced garlic, crushed hot red pepper, and light soy sauce into a paste and rub over fish before cooking.

❀ For a subtle, delicate poaching liquid, combine German Pilsener with 1 teaspoon thyme or basil and a chopped shallot.

POACHED FISH WITH LUSH SAUCE

1.

Combine milk, stock, beer, and salt. In a large shallow pan or poacher bring to a slow simmer.

2.

Gently place fillets in the pan, cover, and simmer, allowing 10 minutes per inch of thickness. Remove gently with a slotted spatula to a warm covered dish.

3.

Simmering gently, reduce poaching liquid to 3 cups, cover and set aside.

1.

In a large saucepan melt butter over medium-low until foam subsides. Sprinkle in flour, stirring briskly, to make roux.

2.

Add Canadian bacon and shallots and cook over medium-low until flour is cooked (6 to 8 minutes) but not browned.

3.

Slowly pour in the hot reduced poaching liquid, whisking vigorously until well-mixed. Continue to simmer over medium-low until sauce begins to thicken.

POACHED FISH
2 cups milk
2 cups chicken stock cooked with bay leaf, onion, thyme, and peppercorn
1 cup weissbier or American light lager
1 teaspoon salt
2 pounds turbot fillets or other firm white fish

LUSH SAUCE
8 tablespoons butter
8 tablespoons all-purpose flour
3 ounces Canadian bacon, finely minced
2 shallots, finely minced
3 cups reduced poaching liquid, hot
1 cup light or heavy cream
salt and pepper to taste
1 small bunch Italian (flat-leafed) parsley, coarsely chopped
1 small bunch fresh dill for garnish

4.

In a slow, steady stream add cream while whisking. Cook slowly until sauce thickens completely. Adjust salt and pepper.

5.

To serve place fish on a warm platter, ladle sauce over, sprinkle with parsley, and arrange dill on top. Serve immediately.

Serves 4 to 6

Poaching is a lovely method of cooking fish, but is perceived as being the domain of fancy restaurants. Not true! Poach fish in this marvelous alliance of milk, stock, and beer. Further enhance it with a sauce based on the poaching liquid and Canadian bacon for a truly elegant, sophisticated supper.

DILLED SMOKY SALMON

Serves 4

Salmon lightly brined in beer, salt, and sugar before smoking is a delicacy well worth the extra time and effort. Be sure to lock out the cat while the fish is drying!

2 pounds salmon fillets with skin, rinsed

BRINE

2 cups water
2 cups pale ale
1/2 cup coarse or kosher salt
1/2 teaspoon dried dill
1/2 cup firmly packed brown sugar
3 lightly cracked black peppercorns
1 bay leaf

1.

Heat water and beer to boiling, add salt, dill, sugar, peppercorns, and bay leaf, stirring until the sugar and salt are dissolved. Simmer 25 minutes. Allow brine to cool to room temperature.

2.

Pour over salmon and weigh fish down with a saucer. The fish should be completely immersed in brine. Refrigerate 4 to 6 hours.

3.

With cold water, lightly rinse brine from fish but do not remove all of it. To dry, thread a loop of dental floss through one end of the fillet and hang in a well-ventilated area or lay on a cooling rack elevated on 4 cans placed in front of a fan for 4 to 8 hours. The fish will acquire a glossy veneer (called pelz) that is dry to the touch.

4.

Heat smoker to low and add wood chips. Smoke the fish slowly, checking occasionally. For moist fish with a hint of smokiness, the time will be relatively short. If you like it dry and smoky, allow a longer smoking time.

VARIATION

This fish can be prepared indoors with a stove-top Cameron smoker (see page 26).

NOTE

This fish is smoked but not cured. Keep it refrigerated and use within two days.

BEER-MARINATED SHRIMP

Serves 2 to 4

A grill filled with these tantalizing shrimp and a bucket of chilled brew will please any and all appetites.

2 pounds large shrimp
1/2 cup olive oil
2/3 cup German Pilsener
3 tablespoons lemon juice
4 large cloves garlic, crushed
1/4 cup finely chopped scallion
2 tablespoons fresh basil or 2 teaspoons dried
dash or two of Louisiana hot pepper sauce (optional)
bamboo skewers, soaked in water for 1 hour

1.

Shell and clean shrimp, rinse, and pat dry. Mix oil, Pilsener, lemon juice, garlic, scallion, basil, and hot pepper sauce, add shrimp, and coat thoroughly. Cover and marinate in refrigerator 4 to 8 hours.

2.

Spear shrimp on soaked skewers and place in refrigerator until ready to cook. Barbecue or broil until the shrimp turn pink.

Pale ale is a dry, hoppy top-fermented beer. It is pale only in contrast to dark brews such as brown ale, porter, or stout. In Britain it is considered the bottled equivalent of bitter.

SOUTHWEST MARINATED SHRIMP

Serves 2 to 4

These piquant shrimp are a tasty head-clearing indulgence.

1.

Shell and clean shrimp, rinse, and pat dry.

2.

Rub shrimp with garlic and salt mixture. Let stand, covered, 2 hours in refrigerator or 1 hour at room temperature.

3.

Combine oil, lager, lime juice, shallots, coriander, cumin, cilantro, and chili and pour over marinated shrimp to coat thoroughly. Cover and marinate in the refrigerator 6 to 12 hours.

4.

Spear on soaked skewers and return to the refrigerator until ready to cook. Barbecue or broil until shrimp just turn pink.

2 pounds large shrimp
5 large cloves garlic, mashed with 1
  teaspoon kosher salt
1/2 cup olive oil
2/3 cup light lager
1/4 cup fresh lime juice
3 shallots, finely chopped
2 teaspoons each coriander and cumin
  seeds, toasted and crushed
1/2 cup fresh cilantro, coarsely chopped
1 thinly sliced serrano chili or 1/4
  teaspoon hot red chili flakes
bamboo skewers, soaked in water

AEGEAN SHRIMP IN BEER SAUCE

Serves 2 to 4

A unique sauce suffused in shrimp essence. The beer-and-shrimp-flavored stock is turned into a creamy sauce to embellish shrimp sautéed in Pesto. Serve over pasta or rice.

2 pounds medium shrimp, with shells
2 1/2 cups water
1 1/2 cups Pilsener or weissbier
2 shallots, finely chopped
2 tablespoons fresh pesto made without cheese (see page 216)
1 tablespoon olive oil
1/3 cup butter, margarine, or olive oil
1/3 cup unbleached flour
2/3 cup sour cream or Crème Fraîche (page 35)
1/4 cup freshly squeezed lemon juice
1/4 cup Pilsener, weissbier, or dry white wine
2 tablespoons minced Italian (flat-leafed) parsley
1/2 cup grated hard cheese (fontinella, kasseri, mizzithra, Parmesan, or Romano)

1.
Shell shrimp, reserving shells. To make stock, combine water, beer, shallots, and shells in a 3-quart saucepan. Bring to a slow boil, cover, and simmer 40 minutes, skimming off foam.

2.
Strain stock and reduce on medium to 2 cups. Cover and set aside.

3.
In a medium skillet heat pesto and olive oil on medium. Add the shelled shrimp and sauté, stirring constantly, until shrimp barely turn pink. Remove shrimp and pesto and set aside.

4.
Check stock to make sure it is still very hot; if not, reheat briefly.

5.
In a large saucepan or deep skillet heat 1/3 cup butter until foam subsides. Sprinkle flour over butter and cook to make roux, stirring frequently, 4 minutes.

6.
Continue whisking while slowly pouring in hot stock. Stir in sour cream, lemon juice, and beer. When thickened, lower heat and add parsley, cheese, and shrimp. Stir and serve over freshly cooked pasta or fluffy rice.

SMOKED SWORDFISH

A delightful way to prepare swordfish, the beer brine adds an extraordinary dimension of flavor that is a cut above the usual grilling.

Serves 4 to 6

2 to 3 pounds 1-inch-thick swordfish steaks, with skin

BRINE
4 cups brown ale or light bock
1/2 cup coarse or kosher salt
1/2 cup firmly packed brown sugar
1 teaspoon black peppercorns
1 teaspoon whole yellow or brown mustard seed
1 teaspoon coriander seed, crushed
8 whole allspice
2 bay leaves
1 whole clove

1.
Rinse fish lightly in cool water and pat dry with paper towel. Place in a deep bowl.

2.
Combine remaining ingredients in a pan and stir until sugar and salt are completely dissolved. Simmer 20 minutes. Allow brine to cool to room temperature.

3.
Pour brine over swordfish and weigh fish down with a saucer. The fish should be completely immersed in brine. Refrigerate 2 to 4 hours.

4.
With cold water, gently rinse brine from fish but do not remove all of it. Place on a rack in a cool, well-ventilated room until a glossy veneer (called pelz) forms that is dry to the touch, 4 to 8 hours. I place a small fan in front of the rack to keep the air circulating.

5.
Prepare smoker with chips and smoke fish over very low heat, checking occasionally until cooked through and smoky. This is not intended to be a dry fish, so remove it from the smoker while still moist.

VARIATION
This fish can be prepared indoors with a stove-top Cameron smoker (see page 26).

NOTE
This fish is smoked but not cured. Keep it refrigerated and use within two days.

HERB-BAKED SNAPPER

E

xotic and fragrant with spices and fresh parsley, this fish is baked in parchment to eliminate fat and provide the fullest flavor.

1.

Clean fish and rub with garlic salt. Let stand in refrigerator 30 minutes.

2.

Combine parsley, cumin, paprika, cayenne, lemon or lime juice, and altbier and rub over fish. Wrap each fish in parchment and place in baking pan. Let stand 15 minutes.

3.

Bake in a preheated oven at 400° using the 10-minutes-per-inch-of-thickness rule. Serve immediately.

4 pounds red snapper
5 large cloves garlic mashed with 2 teaspoons kosher salt
1/2 cup finely chopped Italian (flat-leafed) parsley
1 1/2 tablespoons cumin seeds, lightly toasted
2 1/2 tablespoons paprika
1/8 to 1/4 teaspoon cayenne, to taste
1 tablespoon lemon or lime juice
3 tablespoons altbier
baking parchment, lightly greased

English brown ale *is a dark, sweet, lightly hopped top-fermented-beer. It is flavored and colored with roasted and caramel malts. It has a low to medium alcohol content. In Britain it is sometimes called bottled mild.*

SOUTHWEST STUFFED SHRIMP

These delicious morsels of shrimp stuffed with spicy marinated cheese are elegant as an appetizer or, better yet, served in quantity as an entree.

1.

Split shrimp along back, cutting two-thirds of the way through to devein and clean.

2.

Whisk marinade ingredients together. Pour over shrimp, tossing gently. Cover and marinate in the refrigerator 2 to 6 hours.

3.

Combine the cheese marinade ingredients except bread crumbs and corn husks. Marinate in the refrigerator 2 to 6 hours.

4.

Stir bread crumbs into cheese mixture. Stuff shrimp with marinated cheese. Firmly wrap each in a soaked cornhusk and tie with long strips of torn husk to keep filling in place.

5.

Smoke, grill, or broil shrimp on medium-high until they turn pink. Serve immediately.

1 pound uncooked jumbo shrimp (12 to 16 shrimp per pound), shelled

SHRIMP MARINADE
1/2 cup olive oil
1/3 cup German Pilsener
1 tablespoon fresh lime or lemon juice
4 large cloves garlic, mashed with 1/2 teaspoon salt
1/4 cup finely chopped green onion
1/4 to 1/2 teaspoon freshly ground black pepper

CHEESE MARINADE
1/3 to 1/2 cup extra-virgin olive oil
1/4 cup balsamic vinegar
2 tablespoons German Pilsener
4 cloves garlic, peeled and lightly mashed
1 1/2 tablespoons fresh cilantro or oregano, chopped
1 teaspoon coriander seeds, toasted and crushed
1/2 teaspoon cumin seeds, toasted and crushed
1 serrano chili, thinly sliced and minced
1/4 teaspoon freshly ground black pepper
8 ounces each Queso Anejo and Queso Panela, finely cubed (or substitute Muenster and Mozarella)
1 1/2 cups fresh bread crumbs
dried cornhusks, soaked

TROPICAL MARINATED FISH

Spicy marinated fish with a unique flavor. Marvelous served in warm tortillas with Southwest Tartar Sauce (page 111).

1.
Combine the fruit nectar, pineapple juice, ale, cinnamon, tamarind, and toasted spices. Bring to a slow simmer and cook 15 minutes. Cool and strain.

2.
Stir chilies, lime juice, and olive oil into cooled marinade.

3.
Marinate fish 2 to 4 hours in the refrigerator.

4.
Drain and pat dry with a paper towel, and dredge in flour.

5.
Heat butter over medium, place fish in pan, skin-side up, and sauté according to the 10-minutes-per-inch-of-thickness rule, turning once. Serve immediately.

1 cup canned fruit nectar (apricot, peach)
1/2 cup pineapple or orange juice
1/2 cup brown ale
1 stick cinnamon
1 peeled tamarind pod
1/2 teaspoon each toasted crushed coriander and cumin seeds
1/2 teaspoon each toasted whole cloves and allspice
1 to 2 serrano chilies, sliced thinly
juice of 2 limes
1/3 cup extra-virgin olive oil
2 pounds red snapper, mahi-mahi, or other firm white fish
2 cups flour
4 to 5 tablespoons butter, olive oil, or margarine for sautéing
freshly chopped Italian (flat-leafed) parsley, or cilantro (for garnish)

VARIATION
Try grilling, broiling or baking the marinated fish.

SCALLOPS ESCABÈCHE

This captivating potpourri combines succulent bay scallops "cooked" in lime juice and beer. Tomatoes, avocados, and spices are added before serving as a refreshing seafood salad.

1 pound bay scallops
2/3 cup freshly squeezed lime juice
1/3 cup German Pilsener
2 cloves garlic, finely minced and mashed
1 serrano chili, thinly sliced and finely minced (wear rubber gloves)
1/3 cup extra-virgin olive oil
2 scallions, finely chopped
2 tablespoons coarsely chopped cilantro
2 tablespoons chopped Italian (flat-leafed) parsley
1/2 teaspoon lightly toasted coriander seeds, crushed
1/4 teaspoon each freshly ground black pepper and salt
5 plum tomatoes, chopped into 1/4-inch pieces
1 small ripe avocado, chopped into 1/3-inch pieces
1 small head leaf lettuce

GARNISH
1 cup Crème Fraîche (see page 35) or sour cream
1/2 tablespoon cumin seeds, toasted and finely crushed

1.
Combine the scallops, lime juice, and beer, stirring gently. Marinate in refrigerator 4 hours.

2.
Meanwhile, combine garlic, chili, oil, scallions, cilantro, parsley, coriander, salt, pepper, and plum tomatoes with the scallop mixture. Let stand at room temperature 3 to 4 hours. Drain and reserve 1/4 cup of marinade.

3.
Combine scallops, tomato mixture, diced avocado, and reserved marinade, tossing gently to coat.

4.
Spoon one-fourth of the scallop mixture over greens arranged on a salad plate.

5.
Combine the Crème Fraîche and toasted seeds and place a dollop on each plate. Refrigerate until served.

ZESTY FRIED CATFISH

Serves 4 to 6

Coated with a non-traditional but delicious batter, this fried catfish is light and delicate.

canola or peanut oil for pan-frying
2 pounds catfish fillets
2 cups flour for dredging
2 cups unbleached flour
1 tablespoon baking powder, sifted
2 teaspoons salt
1 teaspoon paprika
1/8 teaspoon cayenne (optional)
1 cup American light lager
1/2 cup dried milk powder
1 cup ice water
3 egg whites, beaten

1.

Heat 1 inch of oil in pan. Lightly dredge half the fillets in flour.

2.

Combine 2 cups flour, baking powder, salt, paprika, and cayenne in a bowl. Stir together beer, dried milk powder, ice water, and egg whites. Combine beer mixture with flour mixture, stirring briefly.

3.

Quickly dip fillets into batter and fry in hot oil. Dredge remaining fish while the first batch is cooking.

4.

Remove and drain on paper towels. Place in warm oven while you prepare the remaining fish. Serve as soon as possible. Try this with the Southwest Tartar Sauce (page 111) — it is dynamite!

SOUTHWEST TARTAR SAUCE

Makes 2 cups

1.
Combine ingredients and let stand 10 minutes.

1 cup sour cream, Crème Fraîche (page 35), or thickened yogurt

1 cup mayonnaise

3 finely chopped shallots

1 tablespoon lime juice

2 serrano chilies, finely minced (wear rubber gloves)

1/2 teaspoon each cumin and coriander seeds, toasted and crushed

2 tablespoons finely minced cilantro

2 tablespoons sweet pickle relish

TRADITIONAL TARTAR SAUCE

Makes 2 cups

1.
Combine ingredients and let stand 10 minutes.

2 cups mayonnaise

3 finely chopped shallots

1 tablespoon lemon or lime juice

1/4 cup sweet pickle relish or chopped dill pickle

CHAPTER 6
BEEF & PORK

Using beer to prepare meats is one of the easiest and most familiar methods of cooking with brew. Recipes abound for meaty stews enhanced with ale, ribs simmered in beer before grilling, or spicy chili bolstered by a beloved brew. Of course, you will find my version of these time-honored favorites included in the recipes that follow.

~ ❧ ~

But cooking meat with beer can go well beyond those first experiments. Infusing a classic standing rib roast with the fragrant bouquet of fine porter is delectable. Serving it with a Yorkshire pudding (an exquisite "baked gravy") made from the porter-flavored pan drippings is nothing less than jubilant.

CREATING YOUR OWN RECIPES

Marinate meat before grilling or roasting. For a simple marinade, combine 1 cup full-bodied beer (porter, Belgian strong ale, dark bock, or Scottish ale) with 1/4 cup olive oil or other vegetable oil, 2 to 3 cloves mashed garlic, 1/4 cup Homebrewed Steak Sauce (page 214) or Worcestershire Sauce and your favorite herbs and spices.

Braise meat in any combination of flavors. From brown ale mixed with soy sauce, garlic, and ginger to American lager combined with green chilies, garlic, and oregano, there is literally no limit to the possibilities.

For a first braising endeavor use a combination of brown ale, Bavarian dark, altbier, India pale ale, smoked or herb beer along with a few sprigs of your favorite fresh herb, perhaps rosemary or thyme, chopped fresh tomatoes, and garlic or onion.

Roasted meat can be marinated first, then roasted using the marinade to baste. Or omit the marinating time and simply roast and baste frequently with beer sauce. ▼

Steak Bundles, page 121.

For a beer and tomato barbecue sauce, substitute one-third of the tomato purée called for in the recipe with smoked beer, dark bock, altbier, porter, or stout. This is a richer combination than is used for poultry.

Enjoy and experiment. This is dining at its best. After all, what combination of food and drink is more scrumptious than a sizzling, juicy, beer-infused steak paired with a stein of cool Czechoslovakian Pilsener?

Before we begin, there are a few general notes on cooking and serving meat to retain the fullest flavor; please review pages 16 through 18.

THE PERFECT BEEFSTEAK

Serves 4

Few meals compare to that of a flawlessly prepared steak. A simple combination of beer, olive oil, and spices lends an intoxicating flavor further enhanced with herbed butter, creating a luscious sauce to mingle with the juices. Restaurant-prepared meat seems to pale next to these world-class steaks.

4 rib-eye steaks (or your favorite cut) wrapped with bacon

3 tablespoons coarsely ground black pepper

1/2 cup pale ale

1/4 to 1/3 cup olive oil

1/4 to 1/2 teaspoon freshly crushed hot red pepper

4 cloves garlic, finely minced

4 tablespoons herbed butter (page 228)

1.

Using the palm of your hand, press black pepper onto both sides of bacon-wrapped steaks.

2.

Combine beer, olive oil, red pepper, and garlic. Pour over and allow to stand at room temperature for 1 1/2 to 2 hours, turning once. Remove steak from marinade and pat dry with paper towels.

3.

Grill or broil over high heat and place steak on a heated platter. Cover with foil and let stand 4 to 5 minutes. Top each steak with a tablespoon of herbed butter and serve immediately.

Porterhouse steak got its name from a cut of beef made popular in a New York drinking establishment that specialized in serving porter beer.

PEPPERED STEAK

Serves 4

Hot and hearty, this robust peppered steak calls for few ingredients and is quick to prepare. Make sure your pepper is freshly crushed; anything less just won't have the same kick.

2 pounds sirloin, rib-eye, or New York steak, 1 to 1 1/2-inch thick
4 large cloves garlic, peeled and split
4 tablespoons black peppercorns, freshly crushed
1/2 cup Scotch ale
2 tablespoons canola oil mixed with 3 tablespoons olive oil
1 tablespoon kosher salt
4 tablespoons herbed butter (see page 228)

1.

Rub both sides of steak with split garlic, then press crushed peppercorns into both sides.

2.

Sprinkle ale over steaks, cover, and let stand 1 hour, or refrigerate 2 hours.

3.

Heat a large heavy pan on medium-high until very hot. Pour in oil and sprinkle salt evenly over the oil. Add steaks — do not crowd them, cook two batches, if necessary.

4.

Sear meat for about 4 to 5 minutes on the first side until dark, golden brown. Turn and continue to cook an additional 3 to 4 minutes, depending on how well-done you want your steaks.

5.

Remove from pan and place on heated platter. Cover with foil and let stand 5 minutes. Serve with 1 tablespoon herbed butter on top of each.

SMOKED BEER-N-BEEF

Serves 8 to 10

A culinary triumph, this juicy, tender beef is augmented with the flavor of a lightly smoked beer.

12 ounces smoked beer
1/2 cup olive oil
1/4 cup honey
2 teaspoons dried thyme
2 teaspoons dried oregano or basil
2 teaspoons freshly ground black pepper
1 tablespoon kosher salt
1/4 to 1/2 teaspoon cayenne
1 7- to 9-pound rolled roast
4 to 8 cloves garlic, peeled and cut in half
meat thermometer

1.
Combine beer, oil, and honey in bowl. Set aside.

2.
Combine thyme, oregano, pepper, salt, and cayenne in a small bowl. Cut slits in the roast and insert pieces of garlic that have been dipped in the beer mixture and rolled in the spice mixture.

3.
Pour beer mixture and any remaining herbs over roast, rubbing them into the surface. Cover with plastic wrap and refrigerate overnight.

4.
Let meat stand at room temperature about 2 hours before roasting.

5.
Place fat-side up on a greased roasting rack in a shallow pan and pour remaining marinade into pan.

6.
Roast in a preheated 400° oven for 35 minutes. Lower temperature to 325° and continue roasting. Baste frequently with pan juices.

7.
Use a meat thermometer to check the internal temperature. It should read 125° to 130° for rare beef, 140° to 145° for medium. Remove from oven, cover with foil, and allow to rest 10 to 15 minutes before carving.

STUFFED STEAK À LA CANDY

Serves 4

This is one of the most memorable pieces of meat you will ever taste. Rubbed with spices and beer, stuffed with beer-sautéed onions, herbs, sour cream, and cheese, this steak will earn rave reviews! The marinating rub can be used on roasts and other cuts; just remember the longer it stands the more flavorful it becomes.

3 pounds boneless top sirloin, 1 inch thick

MARINADE

2 teaspoons toasted coriander seeds, crushed coarsely

1/2 teaspoon toasted cumin seeds, crushed coarsely

2 teaspoons mild red chili powder, toasted

1/2 to 1 teaspoon hot red chili powder, toasted

1/2 teaspoon freshly ground black pepper

4 cloves garlic, crushed

3 tablespoons altbier or Oktoberfest

2 tablespoon olive oil

STEAK STUFFING

2 tablespoons olive oil

2 medium onions, coarsely chopped

1/4 cup altbier or Oktoberfest

2 large cloves garlic, finely minced

1 to 2 yellow banana chilies, finely minced

1 1/2 teaspoons dried oregano, crumbled

1/2 cup sour cream

5 ounces Muenster cheese, crumbled

toothpicks

1.

Using a sharp, thin-bladed knife cut a large pocket in the steak to about 3/4 inch from the edges.

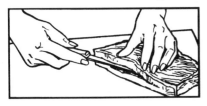

2.

Combine remaining marinade ingredients and rub generously over steak and inside pocket. Wrap and allow to stand at room temperature 1 hour, or 4 to 6 hours in the refrigerator.

1.

To make stuffing heat olive oil over medium, sauté onion until limp, add beer and cook until deep golden. Add garlic, chilies, and oregano and sauté 2 minutes. Remove from heat and cool.

2.

Stir sour cream and crumbled cheese into cooled onions. Gently stuff mixture into the pocket. Skewer edges closed with toothpicks.

3.

Grill or broil over medium-high for 10 to 12 minutes per side. Place on a heated platter, cover with foil, and let stand 4 to 5 minutes before serving. The meat will be nicely browned on the outside and medium rare in the center.

VARIATION

If you enjoy real fire-power use fresh jalapeños or chipotles, their smoked version, in place of yellow banana chili.

HELPFUL HINT

If you refrigerate meat while marinating, allow it to stand at room temperature for 1 hour before cooking.

POTENT PORTERED BEEF RIBS

Serves 6

Hearty, meaty beef ribs are taken to the supreme height of flavor with this spirited, aromatic marinade. Seared and then simmered in the marinade before slow grilling to perfection, these ribs give melt-in-your-mouth barbecue a whole new meaning.

1.

Combine marinade ingredients and allow to stand 30 minutes. Marinate ribs 4 to 24 hours in the refrigerator, turn occasionally.

2.

Wipe off excess marinade. Heat grill to very hot and sear ribs on all sides. Set aside.

3.

Place half the marinade in a large, heavy Dutch oven and bring to a slow simmer. Add browned ribs, cover, and turn heat to low. Braise 45 minutes.

4.

Place ribs on greased grill. Cover and cook slowly over very low heat, basting every 5 to 6 minutes with remaining marinade. Ribs should be very tender after 1 to 1 1/2 hours.

MARINADE

12 ounces porter
2/3 cup olive oil
1/2 cup dry sherry
1/4 cup dark soy sauce (see page 286)
1 teaspoon bottled liquid smoke
2 tablespoons dark sesame oil
1/3 cup honey
juice of 1 orange
1 tablespoon sweet paprika
5 large cloves garlic, finely chopped and mashed with 1 teaspoon kosher salt
2 small shallots, finely chopped and mashed
1 1/2 teaspoons each dried crushed thyme, marjoram, and oregano
1/2 teaspoon freshly ground black pepper
1/2 teaspoon hot red chili powder or 3 serrano chilies, finely chopped

8 pounds lean meaty beef short ribs

NOTE

After many disasters at the barbecue, I stumbled on a cookbook that taught me two very important elements of outdoor cooking. First, very low heat is critical to allow tougher cuts time to become tender. Second, when using a sweet sauce, protect meat from direct flame by covering the grill with punctured heavy-duty foil. Low heat and a foil-covered grill give you time to baste the meat over a longer period.

BEEF BEER-GUIGNONNE

This classic braised beef dish makes a sublime meal when the weather is chilly. It even tastes better prepared one day ahead, making it perfect for entertaining. Serve with a crisp salad and lots of fresh French bread.

1/4 cup fruity extra-virgin olive oil

3 pounds boneless beef rump cut into 1-inch cubes

1 cup flour mixed with 1 teaspoon each salt, pepper, and paprika

1 large leek, split, washed, and chopped coarsely

2 cloves garlic crushed with 1 teaspoon salt

2 cups porter or bier de garde (a cask-aged French beer)

1 bay leaf

1 cup beef stock

6 tablespoons butter

30 small boiling onions, blanched and peeled

2 teaspoons sugar

18 to 24 small whole mushrooms

2 tablespoons lemon juice

1/4 pound lean bacon, chopped finely

2 large ripe tomatoes, coarsely chopped

1 teaspoon French thyme

3 tablespoons Italian (flat-leafed) parsley, coarsely chopped

1.

Heat a large Dutch oven over medium. When hot, add olive oil. Dredge half the meat in seasoned flour and brown well. Remove browned meat and repeat.

2.

Add leek and sauté briefly. When it just begins to soften, add garlic and sauté only until fragrant (1 to 3 minutes). Pour in the beer and deglaze the pan (see page 282).

3.

Add the beef and bay leaf, coating thoroughly. Add stock, cover, and place in a preheated 325° oven 1 hour (see step 7).

4.

Meanwhile, melt 2 tablespoons butter in a heavy skillet. Add onions and sauté briefly. Sprinkle with sugar and continue to sauté until golden. Remove from heat.

5.

Wipe mushrooms clean and toss into lemon juice. Heat 4 tablespoons butter in a skillet on medium-high, add mushrooms and cook until slightly softened. Remove from skillet.

6.

Cook bacon until crisp. Drain off drippings and add the tomato, thyme, and parsley to the bacon. Simmer for 3 minutes and remove from heat.

7.

Remove meat from oven after 1 hour of cooking. Stir in onions, mushrooms, and tomato mixture. Cover and return to oven for an additional 35 to 45 minutes or until meat is tender but not overcooked. Serve garnished with chopped parsley.

VARIATION

Not at all traditional but every bit as delicious is Pork Beerguignonne. Simply substitute an equal amount of lean pork for the beef.

STEAK BUNDLES

1.

Combine marinade (your choice, Mustard or Teriyaki) ingredients in a glass or stainless-steel bowl. Remove 1/2 cup and set aside. Marinate meat 1 to 8 hours.

2.

Lay out a piece of meat and place one or two pieces of vegetable across the center.

3.

Roll meat around vegetables, allowing vegetables to extend out both ends. Secure with a toothpick.

4.

Grill, broil, or stir-fry just until meat loses most of its pink.

5.

Serve cradled in Belgian endive or other leaves that have been brushed with reserved marinade, or on a bed of rice.

MUSTARD MARINADE

1/2 cup olive oil
3 tablespoons balsamic vinegar
3 tablespoons German-style lager
2 cloves garlic
3 tablespoons Dijon or green peppercorn mustard
1/2 teaspoon each thyme, summer savory, and basil

TERIYAKI MARINADE

1/3 cup peanut or other vegetable oil
1/2 cup honey
1/2 cup dark soy sauce
1/4 cup Pilsener
2 tablespoons sugar
3 cloves garlic, minced and crushed
1/2 to 1 teaspoon crushed hot red chili peppers
1/2 teaspoon freshly grated ginger
1/2 teaspoon freshly ground black pepper
1 1/2 tablespoons dark toasted sesame oil

MEAT

2 pounds 1- to 1 1/2-inch thick steak, cut in 4-inch strips

VEGETABLE FILLINGS

Vegetables should be cut about 4 inches long. Experiment with your garden favorites: snow peas, canned baby corn, green onions, asparagus spears, pickled vegetables, lightly roasted peeled bell pepper, large fresh mushrooms, zucchini, and onions. You'll need about 4 to 5 cups of vegetables all together.

Serves 6 to 8

Beer-marinated strips of meat are wrapped around crisp vegetables and quickly grilled or stir-fried to create exciting appetizers. Because cooking time is short, try serving 4 or 5 of these delightful bundles on a bed of rice for effortless entertaining.

VARIATION

Use lean strips of pork for a delectable change.

PORTERED ROAST BEAST

M ost of us have had beef cravings that simply will not be appeased by anything less than a thick slice of tender, juicy standing rib. Although extravagant sounding in today's economy, a dinner for 4 at a restaurant will cost considerably more than 6 to 8 pounds of choice beef – and yours will taste far superior.

Serves 8 to 12

1 8-pound standing rib roast, choice grade, if possible
2 teaspoons dried thyme (or 2 tablespoons fresh)
2 teaspoons freshly ground black pepper
1 tablespoon kosher salt
1/3 cup olive oil
1 1/2 cups porter
plastic wrap
4 to 8 cloves garlic, peeled and halved

1.
Have butcher cut bones from roast and tie them back on for maximum flavor and easy carving.

2.
Combine thyme, pepper, salt, oil, and porter in a small bowl. Pour over roast, rubbing into surface. Cover with plastic wrap and refrigerate overnight.

3.
Bring roast to room temperature for 2 hours and cut deep slits to insert garlic pieces.

4.
Preheat oven to 375°. Place roast bone-side down on a greased rack in a shallow pan. The meat should not be placed directly in the pan.

5.
Pour remaining marinade plus 1 cup water over roast and place in oven 1 hour (1 1/2 hours for a 10 to 12 pound roast). Turn oven off and keep door closed tightly for 5 to 7 hours. No peeking!

6.
One hour before serving, reheat oven to 375°. If making Yorkshire pudding, remove pan juices and replace them with 1 cup water or porter.

7.
To cook a 7 to 8 pound roast medium-rare, roast for 45 minutes, or 1 hour for medium-well. To cook a 10 to 12 pound roast medium-rare, roast for 1 hour, or 1 hour 20 minutes for medium-well.

8.
Remove from oven, cover with foil, and let stand 15 minutes to allow juices to settle back into the meat before removing bones and carving.

NOTE
A roast this magnificent should be served au jus with Yorkshire Pudding (page 123) and/or a simple sauce of sour cream and horseradish. For a more assertive garlic flavor, insert garlic pieces before marinating overnight.

YORKSHIRE PUDDING

This lovely "baked gravy" is a delightful change of pace. Remove pan juices from roast just before you begin the second roasting of the Portered Roast Beast (page 122).

3 extra-large eggs
1/2 cup pan juices (fat removed)
1 cup milk
1 1/2 cups unbleached flour
1/2 teaspoon salt
3 tablespoons pan juices (with fat)

1.

Beat eggs until light and fluffy. Add 1/2 cup skimmed pan juices and milk, beating until frothy. Whisk in flour and salt, beating until smooth and creamy. Allow to rest 45 minutes, covered.

2.

Heat 3 tablespoons drippings (with fat) in a 7 x 11-inch roasting pan, place in preheated 400° oven until hot enough to sizzle. Whisk the batter, pour into hot drippings, and bake 20 to 25 minutes. The pudding is done when puffy and golden. Serve immediately.

Yeast is a sturdy beast. Dr. Keith Thomas recovered two bottles of porter from a ship that sank in 1825. After 168 years the yeast was still alive. Dr. Thomas cultured the yeast and created two brews from it, Flag Porter and Bottle Green.

QUICK FAJITAS

A simplified version of fajitas, this marriage of marinated meat and quickly cooked vegetables is ideal. Save time by chopping in the morning and cooking in the evening. Or put it all in sealed plastic bags for scrumptious camp fare (forget the hot dogs!). Serve with hot tortillas in place of plates or silverware and enjoy a real community supper right out of the pan.

1 1/2 cups beer (bitter, ale, or medium lager)
1/2 cup olive oil
4 large cloves garlic, mashed and finely minced
juice of 2 limes
2 teaspoons freshly ground black pepper
1 teaspoon ground coriander
1/2 teaspoon crushed hot red chili flakes
1 1/2 to 2 1/2 pounds top sirloin or sirloin tip
4 large onions, sliced
2 bell peppers, sliced
6 to 7 tablespoons olive or peanut oil for cooking
2 6-ounce cans roasted green chilies, pulled into strips

1.

Mix beer, olive oil, garlic, lime juice, black pepper, coriander, and chili flakes together. Set aside.

2.

Slice meat against the grain into 1/4- to 1/3-inch-thick strips. Place with marinade in a sturdy seal-able container. Refrigerate until ready to use.

3.

Drain meat thoroughly. Toss onions and bell peppers together. Heat a large cast-iron skillet or wok on high (get it superhot).

4.

Pour 1/4 cup oil into the hot skillet and add half the onions and peppers, tossing until lightly browned on the outside but crunchy inside. Place in a large bowl and cover with foil. Repeat with other half.

5.

While skillet is still very hot carefully add 1 tablespoon more oil and half the meat. Cook, stirring constantly, until seared. Add to the vegetables and repeat with remaining meat.

6.

Add chilies, toss, and serve with lots of hot flour tortillas.

VARIATIONS

This can be made with pork, chicken, or turkey; however, I do not recommend these meats when camping because ice chest temperatures are often questionable.

BEEF STROGANOFF

A classic of classics, this elegant dish is perfect for entertaining throughout the winter holidays. Serve over fresh pasta, boiled potatoes, or rice.

Serves 6 to 8

1.
Mix the first eight ingredients in a large bowl. Allow to steep 15 minutes.

2.
Rub mixture over steak and refrigerate 3 to 8 hours. Slice across the grain into thin strips.

3.
Heat large skillet or wok on high. Swirl with 2 tablespoons vegetable oil and add sliced onions. Sauté until browned on the outside but still crisp. Set aside.

4.
Add olive oil and brown meat in small batches, setting each aside to keep warm.

1/2 cup grated onion
1 teaspoon thyme
2 teaspoons dried parsley
1/2 teaspoon cayenne
1/2 teaspoon ground allspice
1/2 teaspoon freshly ground black pepper
1/2 teaspoon sugar
2 cloves garlic, finely minced and mashed (optional)

2 pounds top sirloin, 3/4 inch thick
2 large onions, sliced and separated into rings
1/4 cup vegetable oil
1/4 cup olive oil

1.
Heat 2 tablespoons oil in skillet over medium and sprinkle in flour, stirring to make roux. Brown flour until golden.

2.
Whisk in hot stock and beer, cooking until thickened. Stir in sour cream, paprika, and cayenne, add salt and pepper to taste, and pour over meat. Warm gently (do not boil).

SAUCE
2 tablespoons vegetable oil
2 tablespoons flour
3/4 cup hot beef stock
1/2 cup brown ale
1 1/2 cups sour cream or Crème Fraîche (see page 35)
1 1/2 tablespoons paprika
1/2 teaspoon cayenne (optional)
salt and pepper to taste

ORIENTAL BEEF STRIPS

Exceptionally delicious, these skewers of marinated beef are far superior to ones prepared with store-bought bottled sauces, and far less salty.

1.

Slice meat across grain into thin strips.

2.

Combine remaining ingredients (except skewers) and marinate meat 2 to 6 hours.

3.

Thread meat onto soaked skewers and grill or broil until just cooked. Serve immediately.

2 1/2 pounds top sirloin, 3/4 inch thick
1/3 cup honey
2/3 cup light soy sauce
2/3 cup Bavarian dark
1/4 cup sugar
1/4 cup vegetable or olive oil
3 to 4 large cloves garlic, finely minced and mashed
1/4 to 1/2 teaspoon ground hot red chili flakes, to taste
1-inch piece fresh ginger, peeled and thinly sliced
1/2 teaspoon freshly ground black pepper
1 tablespoon dark sesame oil
bamboo skewers, soaked in water for 1 hour

NOTE

When preparing these wonderful tidbits, remember you want to taste the beef, not just the seasonings. Do not marinate longer than 6 hours.

VARIATIONS

❧ Use marinade for stir-fry meats.

❧ Try on pork, duck, or chicken.

BEEF WITH SNOW PEAS

A slightly spicy, beer-enriched rendition of the classic Chinese dish. The assertive flavors of marinated meat and robust sauce are balanced nicely with the crispness of snow peas.

Serves 4

1 pound top round or sirloin steak, partly frozen
3 tablespoons light soy sauce
3 tablespoons altbier or smoked beer
2 teaspoons dark sesame oil
1-inch piece fresh ginger, peeled and mashed
1 clove garlic, mashed
1 tablespoon canola oil
1 tablespoon cornstarch
1/2 cup beef stock
1/2 cup brown ale
2 tablespoons dark soy sauce
1/2 teaspoon Chinese 5-spice powder (star anise, fennel, cinnamon, cloves and pepper or ginger)
1 1/2 tablespoons cornstarch
4 to 5 tablespoons peanut or canola oil for stir-frying
1 medium carrot, peeled and julienned
2/3 pound fresh snow peas, washed and stems removed
6 scallions, cut diagonally into 1-inch pieces

1.
Using very sharp knife, slice beef thinly against grain.

2.
Combine light soy sauce, beer, dark sesame oil, ginger, garlic, oil, and 1 tablespoon cornstarch. Pour over beef and marinate in refrigerator 2 to 4 hours.

3.
When ready to cook, combine beef stock, ale, dark soy sauce, Chinese 5-spice powder, and cornstarch.

4.
Heat wok on high and swirl with oil to coat. Stir-fry half the beef just until pink is gone. Remove from wok and set aside. Repeat with remaining beef.

5.
Add oil if necessary and stir-fry carrots 30 seconds. Add snow peas and immediately push vegetables up side of wok.

6.
Stir sauce again and pour into wok, stirring until slightly thickened.

7.
Push down vegetables, add scallions and meat, cook 1 to 2 more minutes. Serve immediately with steamed rice or Chinese noodles.

SUNDAY BRAISED POT ROAST

Serves 8 to 10

This scrumptious pot roast brings back memories of Sunday dinners and cold roast beef sandwiches. It is as full-flavored as they come.

1.

Combine beer, vinegar, olive oil, garlic, red pepper flakes, thyme, and black pepper. Pour over meat, cover and marinate 1 to 2 hours in refrigerator.

2.

Remove roast and let stand at room temperature 20 minutes.

3.

Heat heavy Dutch oven rubbed with oil on high and sprinkle in salt. Add roast and sear quickly on both sides.

4.

Pour marinade over top, add bay leaf and onion flakes, cover, and simmer slowly until tender (about 3 hours).

1 1/2 cups American or Bavarian light lager
1/3 cup red wine vinegar
1/3 cup olive oil
5 cloves garlic, mashed
1 teaspoon ground red pepper flakes
1 tablespoon dried thyme, basil, or oregano
1 tablespoon freshly ground black pepper
6 to 8 pound chuck roast
1 1/2 tablespoons kosher salt
1 bay leaf
3 tablespoon dried onion flakes

VARIATION

Surround roast with potatoes, carrots, or parsnips for the last hour of cooking.

SPICY BEEF JERKY

A spicy version of the all-time favorite. Using a sour beer adds unique depth to the flavor.

2 tablespoons kosher salt

1/2 to 1 tablespoon whole black peppercorns

1 teaspoon each coriander and cumin seeds

1 to 2 teaspoons (to taste) hot red chili flakes or 1 chopped chipotle chili

1/2 cup lambic (for sour jerky) or American light lager

1/4 cup brown sugar

3 large cloves garlic, minced and mashed

4 pounds beef, fat removed and cut in long strips with the grain

1.
Heat a heavy skillet on medium until hot. Add salt and peppercorns, toasting until fragrant (1 to 3 minutes). Toss in coriander, cumin seed, and chili flakes. Shake pan vigorously until lightly toasted.

2.
Grind toasted spices medium-fine.

3.
Combine beer, sugar, garlic, and toasted spices.

4.
Make sure every bit of fat has been removed from meat. Rub with beer mixture, coating thoroughly.

5.
Layer strips of meat in deep bowl or crock. Place a plate and heavy weight on top. Allow to stand in cool place or refrigerate 8 to 18 hours.

6.
Drain and lay strips in smoker or hang over a smoky fire. Smoke over low heat 3 to 4 hours. Lay on racks or hang in a well-ventilated place to complete drying.

NOTE
Lean brisket or flank steak is traditional but bottom round makes a good substitute. For tender, easy-chewing jerky, try top sirloin.

PIQUANT BEER-BEEF JERKY

This has a distinctive flavor provided by porter, soy sauce, black and red pepper, and Chinese 5-spice powder.

1.
Combine all ingredients except beef in a bowl, mixing thoroughly.

2.
Make sure every bit of fat has been removed from meat. Rub with beer mixture, coating thoroughly.

3.
Layer strips of meat in deep bowl or crock. Place a plate and heavy weight on top. Allow to stand in cool place or refrigerate 8 to 18 hours.

4.
Drain and lay strips in smoker or hang over a smoky fire. Smoke over low heat 3 to 4 hours. Lay on racks or hang in a well-ventilated place to complete drying.

1/2 cup light soy sauce
1/4 cup porter
1/4 cup brown sugar
2 teaspoons whole black peppercorns, freshly ground
1/2 to 1 teaspoon red chili flakes, coarsely ground
1 1/2 teaspoons onion powder
1 teaspoon Chinese 5-spice powder (star anise, fennel, cinnamon, cloves and pepper or ginger)
3 cloves garlic, minced and mashed
4 pounds beef, fat removed, cut in long strips with the grain

NOTE
Lean brisket or flank steak is traditional but bottom round makes a good substitute. For tender, easy-chewing jerky, try top sirloin.

BEERISH MEATBALLS

These full-flavored morsels are not the usual meatballs. They are robed in luscious beer sauce to form a triumphant alliance that lingers in the memory.

Serves 6 for main course, 12 for appetizers

1.
Mix the first eleven ingredients in a large bowl. Steep 15 minutes.

2.
Combine next four ingredients with steeped spices, mixing thoroughly. Refrigerate 1 hour before forming into balls.

3.
While meat is chilling, heat large skillet or wok on medium-high. Swirl with 2 tablespoons oil and stir-fry onions until golden brown but still crisp.

4.
Heat large, heavy skillet on medium, add olive oil to coat, and brown meatballs on all sides.

5.
Layer browned meatballs and onions in a large Dutch oven. Pour prepared sauce over top. Cover and simmer slowly 45 minutes. Serve hot with sauce.

1.
Heat skillet used to brown meatballs on medium, add 1/4 cup oil and sauté onions until wilted and light golden. ▼

MEATBALLS
1/2 cup grated onion
2 tablespoons Oktoberfest beer
1/2 tablespoon salt
1 teaspoon thyme
2 teaspoons dried parsley
1 teaspoon freshly ground red chili flakes
1 teaspoon cayenne
1/2 teaspoon ground allspice
1/2 teaspoon freshly ground black pepper
1/2 teaspoon sugar
4 cloves garlic, finely minced and mashed

2/3 cup dried bread crumbs
2 eggs
1/3 cup finely chopped parsley
2 pounds lean boneless beef or pork, freshly ground

2 tablespoons vegetable oil
4 cups onions, coarsely chopped

4 tablespoons olive oil for browning

SAUCE
1/4 cup vegetable oil
2 medium onions, coarsely chopped
1/4 cup flour
1 1/3 cups hot beef broth
2/3 cup Oktoberfest beer
1 cup sour cream
1 tablespoon paprika
1/2 teaspoon cayenne
2 cups sliced mushrooms
salt and pepper to taste
1/2 cup finely minced Italian (flat-leafed) parsley for garnish

2.

Sprinkle flour over onions, cook, stirring constantly, until golden brown.

3.

Slowly whisk in hot broth. When smooth, stir in beer, sour cream, spices, and mushrooms (do not boil). Season to taste.

SOUTH-OF-THE-BORDER ROAST RUB

T he longer the roast stands with the rub on it, the more flavorful the final outcome!

1.

Combine ingredients and rub generously on roast. Wrap tightly in plastic wrap and place in refrigerator 6 to 48 hours.

2.

Let stand at room temperature 1 hour before roasting.

2 teaspoons toasted coriander seed
1/2 teaspoon toasted cumin seed
2 teaspoons mild red chili powder, toasted
1/2 to 1 teaspoon hot red chili powder, toasted
4 to 5 large cloves garlic, crushed
2 tablespoons lime juice or wine vinegar
2 tablespoons smoked beer
2 tablespoons olive oil

STUFFED LEG OF LAMB

Serves 8

When nothing less than a stupendous entrée will suffice, this fits the bill. The boneless, butterflied leg is marinated, spread with savory filling, rolled, and roasted. When cut, the swirls of stuffing make a striking presentation. The two sauces are equally noteworthy; choose your favorite.

1.

Combine marinade ingredients. Rub lamb inside and out with marinade. Cover and marinate in refrigerator 6 to 12 hours.

2.

Combine stuffing ingredients and spread evenly over lamb. Roll loosely to enclose stuffing, pushing it back in at edges.

3.

Secure with lacing pins, small skewers, or trussing thread. Place on greased rack in large pan. Pour 3 cups water into pan.

4.

Roast in preheated 400° oven. Turn after 30 minutes (protect your hands and turn very carefully). If lamb is browning too quickly, cover loosely with foil (shiny-side up).

5.

After 1 hour, remove pan juices. Lower heat to 325° and roast 25 to 30 minutes more or until internal temperature reaches 145°. Remove and place on hot platter. Cover with foil and let stand 15 minutes. ▼

1 leg of lamb, boned and butterflied

MARINADE
1/2 cup balsamic vinegar
1/2 cup Belgian ale
1 1/2 teaspoons each dried rosemary and thyme
4 cloves garlic, lightly crushed
1/2 cup olive oil
2 tablespoons light soy sauce

STUFFING
3 shallots, coarsely chopped
1/2 pound fresh mushrooms, stemmed and sliced
1/2 cup pine nuts (pignoli) toasted 10 minutes in 350° oven
1 bunch fresh spinach, washed, stemmed, and chopped
2 cloves garlic, finely chopped
1/4 cup Italian (flat-leafed) parsley, finely chopped (no stems)
1 teaspoon dried tarragon
1 cup ricotta
1/4 cup grated hard cheese (fontinella, asiago, or Muenster)
2 beaten eggs
4 cups fresh bread crumbs
1/2 teaspoon each salt and pepper
lacing pins, small skewers, or trussing thread
3 cups water
meat thermometer

1.

On medium heat combine sugar and pears in large skillet (not cast iron), stirring until sugar is dissolved. Turn heat to medium-high and add pear nectar.

2.

Cook until mixture caramelizes (turns dark brown and syrupy) 20 to 25 minutes, stirring frequently and scraping the bottom well. Remove from heat and stir in 1/2 cup Belgian ale and set aside.

3.

Heat butter in large sauté pan. Add shallots, salt, and cinnamon, sautéing until tender. Add caramelized pears, chopped mint, and pan juices, and cook about 12 minutes, stirring occasionally. Remove from heat and serve.

PEAR & MINT SAUCE

1/2 cup brown sugar, firmly packed
5 large Bosc pears, peeled, cored, and
   coarsely chopped
1 cup pear nectar or apple cider
1/2 cup Belgian ale
2 tablespoons unsalted butter
2 shallots, finely chopped
1/2 teaspoon salt
scant teaspoon ground cinnamon
2 tablespoons finely chopped mint, to taste
1 cup pan juices, fat removed

1.

Sauté onion on high in olive oil until brown and caramelized.

2.

Lower heat and add pan juices, ale, and vinegar. Simmer 4 minutes, add pomegranate seeds, adjust tartness with sugar, and remove from heat.

BEER & BALSAMIC SAUCE WITH POMEGRANATE SEEDS

2 tablespoons olive oil
1 small onion, finely chopped
1 1/2 cups pan juices, fat removed
1/2 cup Belgian ale
1/2 cup balsamic vinegar
1/2 cup fresh pomegranate seeds or coarsely
   chopped Italian (flat-leafed) parsley
sugar to taste

Trappist beer is any beer brewed by one of six brewing abbeys in Belgium and the Netherlands. The ales are top-fermented, amber to brown, and range from 5.7 to 12 percent alcohol by volume. They are fruity in taste and sometimes bittersweet; they are bottle-conditioned by priming and re-yeasting.

CANDY'S TACOS

This is the genuine article – strips of meat lightly sautéed with seasonings and cradled in soft corn tortillas. You will be forever spoiled once you taste these out-of-this-world tacos. Be sure to try the smoked meat variation, it is absolutely dynamite!

Serves 4

MEAT

4 cloves garlic, peeled, minced, and mashed

3 tablespoons Pipian paste (purée of pumpkin seeds and chili)

1/2 cup Bavarian light lager or German Pilsener

2 pounds lean beef or pork, sliced thinly

3 tablespoons olive oil

TORTILLAS

16 to 20 light-colored corn tortillas, fresh and flexible

5 tablespoons vegetable oil for brushing oven-proof dish lined with large dish towel

1.

Combine garlic, Pipian paste, and beer in a bowl, mixing to form a smooth, soft paste.

2.

Coat meat thoroughly with mixture. Allow to stand at room temperature 30 to 45 minutes.

3.

Prepare tortillas by lightly brushing one side with vegetable oil. Tortillas can be prepared up to 12 hours before using if stacked in a sealed plastic bag in the refrigerator.

4.

Toast tortillas over medium heat in cast-iron skillet until they begin to bubble, turn, and cook other side. Stack on oven-proof dish and cover with towel. Place dish in 125° to 150° oven until ready to serve.

5.

When tortillas are ready, heat large, heavy skillet on medium-high and brown meat quickly in olive oil just until all signs of pink are gone. Remove and place in heated dish. Repeat with remaining meat. Serve immediately wrapped in warm tortillas.

SERVING SUGGESTIONS

Set out shredded lettuce, sour cream, grated white Mexican cheese, Pico de Gallo (see page 221), and invite everyone to help themselves. Oh yes, chill down lots of cerveza!

VARIATION

For an incredible taste sensation, slowly smoke beef, pork, or poultry 20 to 30 minutes until smoky in flavor but not fully cooked. Allow to rest 20 minutes, slice thinly, and toss with Pipian mixture. Continue with step 5.

CHIMICHANGAS

8 cups cooked seasoned meat (recipes
  follow) or refried beans
8 extra-large flour tortillas
vegetable oil

1.

Place about 1 cup meat mixture on tortilla and roll up, burrito style, folding in ends to encase meat, and seal. Place on a cookie sheet, cover with towel, and repeat until all are filled.

2.

TO PAN-FRY: Heat 2 inches of vegetable oil in a deep skillet. Carefully lower two chimichangas into fat, cover with spatter screen, and fry until golden brown on one side. Turn using two spatulas (not tongs, they puncture the tortilla) and brown on other side. Remove and drain on paper towels. Keep warm in oven until all are cooked.

3.

TO BAKE: Lightly oil broiler pan and preheat oven to 450°. Brush chimichangas with oil and bake until top is golden, turn, and continue baking until lightly browned and crisp. Serve immediately.

Serves 8

Few who enter the hallowed halls of a good Mexican restaurant can pass up chimichangas. Try this version, a large flour tortilla filled with Basic Chimichanga Meat (page 137), or Red Chili Meat (page 138), Green Chili Meat (page 139), or Frijoles Borrachos (beans cooked in beer, page 55). Fry or bake the "chimi" until brown and crisp.

SERVING SUGGESTIONS

Serve on bed of shredded lettuce with homemade sour cream (Crème Fraîche, page 35) and guacamole sprinkled with cilantro and chopped green onions, or homemade Pico de Gallo (see page 221). Serve fresh radishes and lime wedges on the side.

BASIC CHIMICHANGA MEAT

Serves 6 to 8

The mainstay of many Southwestern dishes including tacos, enchiladas, and chimichangas. All take on a fascinating new dimension when made with this flavorsome beer-laced meat.

4 pounds chuck roast, bone-in (arm, chuck, or 7-bone) or pork roast
3 cups German Pilsener or Bavarian lager
6 cups water
5 large cloves garlic, peeled and mashed
2 onions, chopped
1/2 to 1 teaspoon red chili flakes (optional)
1 teaspoon coarse salt
1 teaspoon freshly ground black pepper

1.

Cut roast into large chunks. In Dutch oven or stock pot, add beer and about 6 cups water. Bring to a rapid boil.

2.

Slide meat into boiling liquid one piece at a time, allowing liquid to return to a full boil before adding more.

3.

Lower heat to medium-low and remove foam. When residue no longer rises, add garlic, onions, chili flakes, salt, and pepper. Partly cover pan and simmer slowly 1 1/2 to 2 hours or until meat is very tender.

4.

Remove meat and cool, reserving broth. When cool enough to handle, remove gristle and fat, pull into long shreds, and refrigerate if not using immediately.

HELPFUL HINT

Refrigerate broth until fat is hard, discard, and freeze broth for soup, enchilada sauce, or any dish requiring rich broth.

RED CHILI MEAT

Serves 6 to 8

This rich blend of red chili, garlic, herbs, and spices spiked with just a bit of beer is a wonderful way to add an exciting dimension to meat.

1.

Soak mulato and pasilla chili pods in hot water until soft. Drain, place in blender and purée with garlic, coriander, cumin, peppercorns, vinegar, and beer.

2.

Heat oil in large skillet on low. Add chili mixture and slowly sautè stirring frequently to prevent scorching, 3 to 4 minutes.

3.

Stir in 1 1/2 cups broth and shredded meat. Continue cooking on low 15 minutes. Cover, remove from heat, and let stand 15 minutes for flavors to mingle.

3 dried mulato chilies, seeds and veins removed (see Note)
3 dried pasilla chilies, seeds and veins removed (see Note)
4 cloves garlic, peeled
1 teaspoon freshly ground coriander seeds
1/2 teaspoon cumin seeds
12 black peppercorns, freshly crushed
1/4 cup mild red wine vinegar
1/2 cup Pilsener-style beer
1/4 cup oil, margarine, or lard
1 1/2 cups broth from cooked meat (page 137)
1 batch Basic Chimichanga Meat (page 137).

NOTE

If these chili varieties are not available, substitute 1/2 cup mild red chili powder, toasted briefly in cast-iron skillet. To make Red Chili with chicken, substitute 1 1/2 cups chicken broth and 6 to 7 cups roasted, shredded chicken for the broth and beef.

GREEN CHILI MEAT

Serves 6 to 8

This recipe is adapted from my Aunt Dot's recipe. She is my foremost authority on green chili. The Basic Chimichanga Meat is covered with green chili sauce made from broth, freshly roasted green chilies, and cornstarch. Uncomplicated to make, yet bursting with green chili flavor.

1.

Place 1 1/4 cups broth and green chilies in large pan. Heat on medium until hot.

2.

Mix cornstarch with 1/4 cup cold broth. Pour slowly into simmering broth, stirring constantly until thick and clear.

3.

Add shredded meat to thickened sauce. Simmer 5 minutes, cover, and remove from heat. Allow meat to absorb green chili flavor 15 to 20 minutes before using.

1 1/2 cups broth from Basic Chimichanga Meat (1/4 cup of it cold)
9 to 12 freshly roasted, peeled, sliced green chilies (or canned green chilies, sliced)
2 tablespoons cornstarch
1 batch Basic Chimichanga Meat (page 137)

HELPFUL HINTS

If you prefer a juicier chili, simply double the amount of broth.

FAJITAS

The sizzling meat and vegetable dish served with warm tortillas and salsa typifies the easygoing Southwestern cuisine that has been taking our nation by storm. The two fundamentals for memorable fajitas are a flavorful marinade and the proper cooking method, which is to cook the meat whole, let it stand for a short time, slice, and cook briefly in a very hot pan. To eliminate the extra step of tenderizing, use top sirloin instead of the more traditional skirt steak. Be sure to chill down lots of brew to go with this feast.

MARINADE

2/3 cup of Homebrewed Steak Sauce (page 214)

juice of 1 lime

3 to 4 serrano chilies, finely chopped (or 1 to 2 chopped jalapeños)

1/2 cup extra-virgin olive oil

1 teaspoon each freshly ground cumin, coriander seed, and black pepper

2 1/2 to 3 pounds top sirloin (2/3 to 3/4 inch thick)

FAJITAS

4 bell peppers (for color use red, yellow, and green)

3 large onions

6 roasted, peeled Anaheim chilies (or canned green chilies)

1/3 cup olive or peanut oil (more may be needed)

2 tablespoons melted butter mixed with 1 tablespoon oil

1.

Combine marinade ingredients and marinate meat 4 to 6 hours in refrigerator, turning once.

2.

While marinating, seed and slice bell peppers 1/3 inch thick and cut onions 1/2 inch thick, separate into rings. Roast, peel, and pull chilies into strips (see pages 281 and 282). Place chilies and onions in separate bowls.

3.

Drain meat, pat dry, and grill, broil, or pan-fry on very high heat 3 to 4 minutes per side. The outside should be seared and brown, leaving the inside rare. Cover with foil and let rest 20 to 30 minutes, allowing juices to settle before slicing.

4.

Heat large, heavy skillet (cast iron works best) on medium-high. When very hot carefully add oil, heat briefly, and toss in half the onion rings, turning with tongs until browned but still crisp. Set aside in large bowl.

5.

Repeat with peppers, cooking in two batches, and add to onions. ▼

6.

Slice meat across the grain in long strips 1/4 to 1/3 inch thick. Reheat skillet on high, heat 3 tablespoons peanut oil, and add meat, stir-frying just until hot.

7.

Add the sautéed vegetable mixture and chili strips to meat and toss quickly to heat through. Place on a large hot platter and immediately pour the butter-oil mixture over the top. If platter is hot enough it will sizzle and sputter. Serve immediately with lime wedges, lots of hot flour or corn tortillas, and your favorite salsa.

BEER-BECUED PORK RIBS

1.

In a small skillet melt butter and sauté onion on medium-low until limp and translucent. Add garlic and continue to cook, stirring occasionally until onion is limp, set aside.

2.

In a blender or food processor, purée plums and tomato sauce until smooth.

3.

In a 3-quart pan heat beer to medium simmer and add bouillon cubes, stirring until dissolved. Add vinegar, liquid smoke, brown sugar, spices, sautéed onion, and plum-tomato mixture.   ▼

1/4 cup butter, olive, or other vegetable oil
1 large onion, finely chopped
6 cloves garlic, minced and mashed with 1
   teaspoon salt
1 cup pitted plums, fresh or canned, or
   whole cranberry sauce
12 ounces tomato sauce or crushed
   tomatoes in purée
12 ounces brown ale
2 large or 4 small beef or chicken bouillon
   cubes
1/2 cup red wine vinegar
1 teaspoon bottled liquid smoke
1/2 cup dark brown sugar
1 teaspoon each ginger, cayenne (or hot
   red chili powder), crushed coriander
   seed, black pepper, cumin seed, and
   mustard seed
5 to 8 pounds pork ribs, country-style,
   back, or baby back
freshly ground black pepper and allspice

Serves 4 to 8

Not for the faint of heart, this thick, fruity sauce based on plums, tomatoes, beer, and spices has genuine sinus-clearing properties. The well-balanced full flavor complements pork so perfectly it is hard to imagine eating ribs without it.

4.

Bring to a slow simmer and cook, stirring frequently, until very thick, 45 minutes to 1 hour.

5.

Wipe ribs to remove fat and bone particles and keep whole to retain moisture. Sprinkle liberally with pepper and allspice. Let stand at room temperature 30 minutes.

6.

Heat coals very hot and set grill close to them. Quickly sear ribs, making sure they don't scorch. Remove, raise grill to highest position, and place lightly oiled heavy-duty foil on grill. Puncture for ventilation.

7.

Place meat on greased foil, brush liberally with sauce, close lid, and cook 5 to 7 minutes. Turn and sauce again. Continue saucing and turning every 5 to 7 minutes until cooked through and tender, from 45 to 75 minutes, depending on the cut of rib and grill heat.

HELPFUL HINTS

❧ The faster meat cooks, the more it shrinks and the less time it has to absorb those marvelous basting sauces you so carefully prepared.

❧ Be wary of market specials when purchasing meat for barbecue. Although tempting, they often are from older, tougher animals. The extra money spent on top-quality meat is well worth the peace of mind that your barbecue is going to be juicy and tender.

Trappist monasteries are justly famous for their beers. The Trappists do not eat meat, and at one time also ruled out fish and cheese. The abbot of one monastery noted, "Without the nutrients in our beer, we would have died."

IMPECCABLE PORK ROAST

Serves 6 to 12

Succulent and flavorful, this culinary triumph is ever so simple to prepare.

1 1/2 cups pale ale, English bitter, or light porter
1/2 cup extra-virgin olive oil
1 teaspoon ground red chili flakes
6 to 8 large cloves garlic, split in half
1 tablespoon kosher salt
2 1/2 tablespoons dried thyme, rosemary, or basil
1 tablespoon freshly ground black pepper
4- to 8-pound pork roast (shoulder, loin, or fresh ham)
meat thermometer

1.

Combine beer, olive oil, and red chili flakes in small bowl, set aside. Stir garlic, salt, herbs, and black pepper together until well blended, set aside.

2.

Place roast fat-side up on work surface, trim fat, and cut 1/2-inch slits, about 3 slits per rib, or one every 2 inches.

3.

Stuff slits with a piece of herb-laden garlic. Rub remaining herb mixture on roast and let stand at room temperature 20 minutes.

4.

Pour beer and oil mixture over roast and let stand 45 more minutes. Place on greased rack in greased roasting pan and put in preheated 325° oven.

5.

Baste frequently with beer and oil mixture along with pan juices. Roast until meat thermometer registers 165°.

6.

Remove roast, cover with foil, let rest 15 minutes to allow juices to set before carving.

NOTE

The internal temperature of pork should be 170° to 175° to be juicy and succulent when served. The internal temperature will rise 5° to 10° after taken from oven, so it should be removed when the internal temperature is 165° to 170°.

SOUTHWEST STUFFED PORK IN CLAY

1.

Combine the first seven of ingredients, whisking thoroughly. Pour over split pork loin and marinate overnight in refrigerator.

2.

Combine next six of ingredients, tossing lightly to make stuffing.

3.

Heat olive oil over medium, sauté onion and garlic just until wilted and translucent. Add to stuffing mixture.

4.

Place a piece of baking parchment on work surface. Place six 12-inch lengths of cooking twine across center of parchment. Completely cover parchment and twine with a layer of wet cornhusks.

5.

Place half the loin in the center of the cornhusks and twine, cut side-up. Arrange a layer of green chilies on the meat. ▼

MARINADE

1/2 cup Oktoberfest, altbier, brown ale, or porter
1/4 cup extra-virgin olive oil
1 canned chipotle chili, finely chopped
1 teaspoon chipotle chili juice from can
4 cloves garlic, finely minced and crushed
1 teaspoon kosher salt
1 tablespoon dried oregano
1 6 to 8-pound boneless pork loin, split in half lengthwise

STUFFING

4 ounces Queso Anejo, crumbled, or Muenster
4 ounces Queso Oaxaca, sliced thinly, or provolone
1/3 cup toasted pine nuts or walnuts
2 teaspoons each coriander and cumin seeds, toasted
2 lightly toasted corn tortillas, finely crumbled
1 serrano, yellow banana, or red Fresno chili, finely minced

2 tablespoons olive oil
1 small onion, finely minced
2 cloves garlic, finely minced
1 package cornhusks, soaked
sheet baking parchment
cooking twine
4 large whole green chilies (canned Anaheim chilies may be used), split open
2 large roasted red bell peppers, split open
12 to 15 pounds organic Hawaiian red or white clay
meat thermometer

Serves 10 to 14

Meltingly tender, this dramatic pork roast is perfect for a formal fall dinner. Marinated and stuffed, the entrée consists of beer-marinated pork loin split and stuffed with layers of mild green chilies, Mexican cheese, and roasted red chilies. The roast is wrapped in cornhusks, enveloped in organic Hawaiian clay, and baked slowly. The flavor of pit barbecue comes to the oven!

6.

Cover with stuffing. Completely blanket stuffing with roasted red bell peppers.

7.

Place remaining pork on top, cover top and sides of roast with wet cornhusks, and secure with twine, completely encasing the roast.

8.

Roll or pat clay into a rectangle large enough to encase the pork about 3/4 to 1 inch thick. Center pork on clay and cover it completely, smoothing cracks and seams. If desired, mold a fanciful figure of a pig or score the clay.

9.

Place on baking sheet in a 275° oven. The clay will develop one or two steam cracks. Insert meat thermometer into the cracks and bake 6 to 7 hours. Be sure internal temperature is at least 170°.

10.

To serve, present in clay on a sturdy tray. Use a small hammer to break casing, transfer roast to a separate platter, and open parchment and cornhusks.

NOTES

❧ Use a large, plastic trash bag underneath the clay during preparation. This way you can "lift" the clay around the roast easily and keep the clay from sticking to the counter.

❧ Although less dramatic, this can also be baked in a clay cooker or covered roasting pan.

CARNITAS

These "little meats" are glazed and crispy outside, tender and bursting with flavor inside. Serve as part of a Southwestern buffet with lots of fresh tortillas, 2 or 3 different salsas (see pages 220 and 221), guacamole, or a bowl of Crème Fraîche (page 35).

4 pounds boneless pork (butt or shoulder)
3 cups altbier
2 1/2 cups water
1/2 teaspoon freshly cracked pepper
7 cloves garlic, peeled and mashed
1 teaspoon toasted coriander, lightly crushed
1/2 teaspoon toasted cumin, lightly crushed
1 teaspoon crushed red pepper flakes
2 teaspoons coarse salt
1 to 2 tablespoons olive oil

1.

Cut pork into large cubes or thick strips.

2.

In a heavy Dutch oven or deep skillet, heat beer and water to a rolling boil. Add meat one handful at a time, allowing the liquid to return to a full boil before adding more.

3.

When all the meat has been added, lower to medium simmer, and skim foam. Once foam has subsided, add remaining ingredients except olive oil.

4.

Cover and simmer slowly 45 minutes or until meat is tender. Remove lid, raise heat to a slow boil.

5.

Continue cooking until liquid has completely evaporated. As the liquid is cooked off you will need to lower the heat to avoid scorching. Add 1 to 2 tablespoons olive oil, if necessary.

6.

Cook until browned and crisp on the outside. Remove from heat and serve hot.

NOTE

Cooking meat in this fashion will give an intensity of flavor that is rarely encountered.

MEXICAN PULLED PORK

This is the traditional shredded pork used for tacos and flautas.

Serves 10 to 12

1/4 cup olive oil

5 pounds boneless pork roast cut into large pieces (4 x 4 inches)

1 onion, coarsely chopped

8 cloves garlic, mashed

2 tablespoons oregano

1 1/2 tablespoons kosher salt

2 teaspoons crushed black pepper

1 tablespoon hot red chili flakes

1 cup pale ale

3 cups water

3 tablespoons olive or vegetable oil

1 large onion, halved and sliced

2 bell peppers, cut into strips

6 Anaheim chilies, roasted, peeled, and cut in strips (or canned)

1.
Heat oil in a heavy skillet, add pork a few pieces at a time, and quickly sear on both sides.

2.
When all the pieces have been browned, place meat in a heavy Dutch oven. Add onion, garlic, oregano, salt, black pepper, and red chili flakes.

3.
Pour beer and water over meat, cover and simmer 2 hours or until pork pulls apart easily with a fork.

4.
Remove meat from liquid, pull into shreds, and return to liquid.

5.
Sauté onions and bell peppers in olive oil until golden around edges. Add Anaheim chilies and cook 2 minutes.

6.
Stir sautéed vegetables into pork, cook briskly until liquid evaporates, stirring frequently.

SWEET-&-SOUR PORK

Serves 6

Tender chunks of pork are crispy outside, juicy inside, and served with crisp vegetables. The unique sweet-and-sour sauce makes a memorable dish and will spoil you forever.

1.

Combine light soy sauce, ale, sesame oil, and garlic. Add pork and refrigerate 45 minutes.

2.

Preheat oven to 200°. Line baking pan with paper towels. Drain pork and lightly coat one-fourth with cornstarch, shaking off excess (see Note).

3.

In a wok heat 2 cups peanut oil just below the smoking stage (between 355° and 370°.) Fry one-fourth of the pork until golden brown and crispy. While cooking, coat another fourth of the meat. Remove each batch with a slotted spoon and place on paper-lined baking pan in the oven.

4.

Remove oil from wok and add 2 to 3 tablespoons fresh oil. Stir-fry carrots, onions, and bell peppers individually until bright in color and lightly cooked. Add oil as necessary. Transfer as finished to a large bowl. ▼

MEAT

2 1/2 tablespoons light soy sauce
2 tablespoons Belgian ale
2 teaspoons dark sesame oil
1 large clove garlic, peeled and lightly mashed
2 pounds boneless lean pork, cut into 1-inch cubes
paper towels
1 cup cornstarch for coating
2 2/3 cups peanut or canola oil

VEGETABLES

2 medium carrots, sliced diagonally, 1/4-inch thick
2 medium onions, quartered, each quarter cut into thirds
2 large red bell peppers, seeded and cut into 1-inch chunks
2 large green bell peppers, seeded and cut into 1-inch chunks
5 green onions, cut diagonally into 1-inch pieces
1/3 cup raw or brown sugar
1 large fresh pineapple, peeled, cored, and cut into 1-inch chunks or 2 cans pineapple chunks, drained
1-inch chunk fresh ginger, peeled and sliced 1/4 inch thick
1/3 cup Bavarian dark

5.

Add 3 tablespoons oil, bring wok to medium, and add raw sugar, stirring 2 minutes. Raise to medium-high, add pineapple, ginger, and beer. Cook until liquid is absorbed and pineapple is glazed, set aside.

6.

To make sauce mix 1/2 cup beer with cornstarch, soy sauce, and wine vinegar, stir until smooth.

7.

Pour cranberries into hot wok and heat. Add beer mixture and crushed peppercorns. Simmer until thickened.

8.

Toss stir-fried vegetables and glazed pineapple chunks into sauce. Heat through and add pork just before serving to retain crispness.

SAUCE

1/2 cup brown ale
1 tablespoon cornstarch
2 tablespoons light soy sauce
1/4 to 1/3 cup red wine vinegar (use more
  for a tarter flavor)
1 can whole cranberries
4 crushed Szechwan peppercorns
  (optional)

NOTES

❧ Coat small amounts of pork at a time. If allowed to stand, coating will absorb oil and become soggy.

❧ To prepare ahead follow this order: cut meat into chunks, combine marinade ingredients, cut and refrigerate vegetables, glaze pineapple, and simmer sauce ingredients. To serve, marinate meat and cook, sauté vegetables, reheat sauce, and combine.

APPLE & HAM PIE WITH CURRY SAUCE

Serves 8

A savory pie of ham, apples, and onions simmered in a rousing sauce seasoned with spices and curry. This makes a stunning breakfast, brunch, or supper dish.

3 tablespoons butter
2 large onions, coarsely chopped
4 shallots, finely minced
1/2 cup flour
1/2 cup frozen apple juice concentrate, thawed and undiluted, heated until hot
1 cup India pale ale, hot
1/3 cup firmly packed brown sugar
2 to 3 tablespoons curry powder (to taste)
1 teaspoon ground ginger
pinch freshly grated nutmeg
1/4 teaspoon cloves
2 pounds ham, Canadian bacon, or smoked pork chops, coarsely chopped
4 large tart apples, peeled, cored, sliced, and halved
1 batch of Easy-Roll Savory Pie Crust (recipe follows)
1 large egg yolk, beaten (optional)

1.
In a heavy skillet heat butter until foam subsides. Add onions and shallots and sauté just until limp. Set aside in large bowl.

2.
To hot skillet add flour and cook, stirring constantly 4 minutes. Remove from heat and stir in apple juice and beer, scraping bottom well. When mixture is smooth, pour over onions.

3.
Stir brown sugar, curry powder, ginger, nutmeg, and cloves into onion mixture. Toss in ham and apples, coating thoroughly.

4.
Pour filling into prepared 10-inch crust, cover with top crust, and seal edges.

5.
Cut vent holes and brush with beaten egg yolk. Heat oven to 425° and place pie on the lower rack. After 15 minutes turn heat to 350° and cover top loosely with foil. Bake 60 minutes.

6.
Cool 30 minutes before serving. ▼

1.

In a food processor fitted with steel blade, process flour, salt, butter, margarine, and herbs just until crumbly. With motor running, slowly add enough beer to form ball.

2.

Remove and knead gently 10 to 12 strokes. Cover with plastic wrap and refrigerate 20 minutes.

3.

Divide dough and roll half into a thin circle to fit pie pan. Gently roll crust up onto rolling pin and unroll over pie plate.

4.

Ease crust into pan, leaving a half-inch overhang. Roll out top crust, fill pie and cover. Pinch edges to seal. Cut vents before baking.

EASY-ROLL SAVORY PIE CRUST

2 1/2 cups unbleached flour
1 teaspoon salt (optional)
5 tablespoons butter (cold)
5 tablespoons margarine (cold)
1 teaspoon dried savory or thyme
2 to 4 tablespoons cold India pale ale or
    light lager

HELPFUL HINT

Use this flavorful crust for quiche, steak and mushroom pie, homemade pot pies, vegetable and cheese pie, and Cornish pasties.

BRATWURST

Serves 8 to 10

Fresh lean, juicy bratwurst with the proper balance of seasonings is not easy to come by, especially here in Arizona. Have no fear, with some basic equipment you can make your own, even if you are a novice cook. Serve these at your next Oktoberfest along with Sweet-N-Hot Beer Mustard (page 218) and Curried Sauce (page 213).

1 1/2 pounds lean veal
4 pounds of lean pork
1/2 pound pork trimmings (fat)
1 1/2 tablespoons salt
1 1/2 teaspoons mace
1 1/2 teaspoons nutmeg
1 1/2 teaspoons white pepper
2 teaspoon ground ginger
2 cups whole milk, chilled
1 cup fine white bread crumbs
1/2 cup Märzen or Vienna-style beer
1 egg
15 feet of sausage casings

1.
Grind veal and pork with trimmings very finely.

2.
Combine remaining ingredients (except casings) in a separate bowl, blending thoroughly.

3.
In a bowl combine meat with other ingredients using a mixer or large spoon until thoroughly blended.

4.
To stuff sausages, prepare casings purchased from butcher. Rinse inside and out under cool water.

5.
Following directions on sausage stuffer, gently slide about four feet of casing onto end without tearing. Tie knot to close casing.

6.
If you do not own a stuffer, push casing onto a funnel with a 1-inch opening. Fill funnel with sausage mixture and use a piece of clean wooden dowel to push into sausage casing. Fill as evenly as possible.

7.
Tie off each sausage by twisting casing every 4 to 5 inches.

8.
Sausages taste best if aged 24 hours in refrigerator. To cook, simply grill, boil, or steam until cooked through. Using beer to boil or steam bratwurst gives a super taste sensation.

COUNTRY-STYLE PÂTÉ

Serves 6 to 8 as an appetizer

Imagine yourself in a meadow with an array of tasty delights spread before you. Start with a stein of beer, loaf of black Russian rye, chunk of fresh cheese, seasonal fruit, pungent radishes, thinly sliced onions, and a crock of incredible country-style pâté. What more could one desire for the perfect European picnic?

6 tablespoons butter
2 shallots, sliced
6 ounces chicken livers
8 ounces homemade bulk sausage (recipe follows)
1/2 cup Märzen or Vienna-style beer
1/2 cup heavy whipping cream

1.
In a sauté pan melt butter over medium until foam subsides. Add shallots and sauté until limp. Add chicken livers and sauté until just cooked through, set aside.

2.
Sauté sausage until browned, drain fat.

3.
Combine cooked chicken livers and sausage in food processor and add beer. With motor running slowly add cream and mix until silky smooth.

4.
Place in crock, cover, and refrigerate 6 hours to develop flavor.

NOTE
Even if you are not fond of pâté, this is one you may take a liking to. The liver flavor is so subdued by spices and beer that it becomes a meat spread rather than a more traditional-tasting liver pâté.

Vienna beer was originally brewed in the city from which it takes its name. The style is often considered synonymous with Märzen. It is a bottom-fermented amber beer, lightly hopped, malty, and fairly strong.

HOMEMADE BULK SAUSAGE

Makes 1 pound

Although this recipe is provided for making pâté, it is one of the tastiest bulk breakfast sausages you will find. Prepared without the white pepper found in many commercial sausages, it lets the full flavor of meat and spices shine through.

1 pound lean pork or 1 pound medium lean beef
1/2 teaspoon each dried thyme, basil, oregano, and parsley
1/2 teaspoon crumbed sage or 1/4 teaspoon rubbed sage
2 tablespoons balsamic or other flavored vinegar
1 teaspoon each salt and black pepper
1/2 teaspoon coriander seeds, finely crushed
1/8 to 1/4 teaspoon cayenne
2 large cloves garlic, mashed

1.
Combine ingredients in large bowl and mix well.

2.
Let stand in refrigerator 2 to 24 hours before using.

PORK SPEEDIES

Serves 8 to 12

Although Speedies are a culinary phenomenon of Upstate New York, they are absolutely delicious and deserve to be shared with the rest of the beer-loving world. Made with lean pork, lamb, or fresh game, Speedies are marinated in a spicy herb mixture before grilling and nestled in a fresh roll. Eater beware, they are addictive!

1.

Combine first twelve ingredients and pour over pork cubes. Marinate at least 24 hours.

2.

Skewer pork, alternating with onions, peppers, potatoes, and apples before grilling or broiling. Serve hot in a crusty roll.

1 cup Bavarian dark beer

1/2 cup red wine vinegar

1/2 cup olive oil

1 1/2 teaspoons dried basil

1 1/2 teaspoons dried parsley flakes

2 1/2 teaspoons dried oregano

1/2 teaspoon dried thyme

1/2 to 1 teaspoon red pepper flakes

juice of 1/2 lemon

1/2 small onion, finely grated or puréed

4 to 8 cloves garlic (to taste) mashed with 2 teaspoons kosher salt

1 teaspoon freshly ground black pepper

4 pounds lean pork, cut into 1-inch cubes

2 large onions, cut in chunks

2 red or green bell peppers, cut in chunks

1 pound each small boiled potatoes and apples, cut in chunks

*B*abe Ruth *was known to order midnight snacks of half a dozen sandwiches, a platter of pigs knuckles and a pitcher of beer. It didn't seem to affect his ability to hit home runs the next day.*

NOTES

NOTES

CHAPTER 7
POULTRY

M ost Americans do not view food in the same way their parents did. There are Middle Eastern restaurants in Iowa and Mexican restaurants in Maine.

Because of the shrinking culinary world, many people find they are turning to food that can be transformed into more exciting fare. As you will find in this chapter, there is no better combination for innovative cooking then beer and poultry.

The subtle flavor of poultry lends itself beautifully to enhancement with beer-based marinades, sauces, and stuffings. Where a supper of plain baked chicken breast is usually considered boring, the same is positively mouth-watering when first marinated in a zippy alliance of beer, spices, garlic, and herbs. Please see pages 18 and 19 for basic instructions on cooking poultry.

The following is such a small sample of the endless potential for combining beer and poultry that I am overwhelmed by the multitude of recipes that were not included due to lack of space!

CREATING YOUR OWN RECIPES

When making a tomato-based barbecue sauce, substitute a rich beer (smoked, bock, Bavarian dark, or brown ale) for half the tomato purée. You will maintain the tomato flavor and acquire the full-bodied flavor of beer.

To marinate and baste chicken for grilling or roasting, try this simple marinade: 1 cup beer (American light lager or pale ale) mixed with 1/4 cup olive or other vegetable oil, 1 tablespoon lemon or lime juice, and your favorite herbs and spices. ▼

Southwestern chili beer is sold in Europe and Belgian framboise (raspberry lambic) is available in Arizona. Food is no longer viewed within the narrow parameters that once dictated we eat pot roast on Sunday and fish on Friday.

Malaysian Chicken, ►
page 179.

To marinate and baste dark-meat poultry such as duck or goose, use 1 cup full-bodied beer (porter, strong ale, Bavarian dark, altbier, or herb beer) mixed with 1/4 cup frozen fruit juice concentrate, thawed and undiluted (mandarin orange is delicious), herbs, and garlic for an exquisite flavor.

To add beer to poultry stuffing, moisten with a medium- to light-bodied beer (German or American light lager, weissbier, mead, or cider) instead of broth or water.

When making wild rice or brown rice stuffing, use equal amounts of water or broth and medium-bodied beer (India pale ale, light bock, Oktoberfest, or dunkelweizen). The malt and hops transform the rice and permeate the bird as it roasts.

SOUTHWEST CHICKEN KEBABS

Serves 6 to 8

All preparation except skewering and grilling can be done the night before for these appetizing chunks of spicy grilled chicken.

MARINADE

1 1/2 cups brown or Belgian ale
1/4 cup frozen pineapple juice concentrate, undiluted
1/4 cup frozen orange juice concentrate, undiluted
juice of 2 limes
1/2 cup extra-virgin olive oil
1/2 teaspoon each whole cloves and whole allspice
1 stick cinnamon
3 serrano chilies, sliced thinly or 1 jalapeno or chipotle chili
1/2 teaspoon each coriander and cumin seeds, toasted lightly
1/4 cup A-1 Steak Sauce

KEBABS

12 large chicken breast halves, skin and fat removed

24 small white boiling onions
2 red bell peppers
2 yellow or green bell peppers
1/4 cup olive oil
2 cloves garlic, peeled and lightly mashed with 1 teaspoon kosher salt
24 long bamboo skewers, soaked overnight in water

1.

Combine marinade ingredients, whisking well. Let stand at room temperature 30 minutes.

2.

Pour marinade over chicken, turning to coat evenly. Cover and marinate overnight in refrigerator.

3.

Boil a pot of salted water, drop in unpeeled onions, and time for 1 minute. Plunge momentarily in a bowl of ice water and place in colander to drain.

4.

Cut the root off each onion and slide skin off.

5.

Split and seed bell peppers. Cut each half into sixths.

6.

Toss peppers and onions with olive oil and garlic. Cover and let stand overnight.

7.

Cut each breast half into about 6 pieces. Alternate red pepper, chicken, onion, and yellow or green peppers on skewers. Cover and refrigerate until ready to grill.

8.

Grill on each side just until golden and cooked through.

SAFFRON CHICKEN

An unusual recipe for grilled or skewered chicken breast combining beer, lemon juice, yogurt, and saffron. Serve with grilled tomatoes and basmati rice for an unparalleled supper delight.

1.

Cut chicken breasts into 1 1/2-inch cubes.

2.

Combine onion, lemon juice, beer, yogurt, salt, and pepper. Add chicken pieces, coating well, cover, and refrigerate 4 to 8 hours.

3.

Remove chicken from marinade and reserve. Pat chicken dry with paper towels and slide pieces onto skewers.

4.

Heat 3 tablespoons beer until hot and dissolve saffron in it. Melt butter and add to saffron liquid, mixing well.

5.

Brush chicken generously with mixture and barbecue or grill.

2 1/2 pounds boneless, skinless chicken or turkey breast
2/3 cup puréed or finely grated onion
1/3 cup fresh lemon juice
1/3 cup wheat or Kölsch-style beer
1/2 cup plain yogurt
2 teaspoons salt
1/2 teaspoon freshly ground black pepper
3 tablespoons weissbier
1/4 teaspoon saffron threads, finely ground
6 tablespoons butter

SERVING SUGGESTION

Serve with vegetable kebabs of zucchini, onion, bell pepper, mushroom, and cherry tomato brushed with olive oil. Grill until edges of vegetables are lightly charred.

PERFECTLY ROASTED CHICKEN

Serves 4

*S*imple ingredients give this flawless chicken an intense malty essence that is divine.

1 3 to 4 pound chicken, cleaned of fat, rinsed, and patted dry
juice of 1 lemon
1 1/2 teaspoons kosher salt (to taste)
1 teaspoon freshly crushed black pepper
1 large clove garlic
1 tablespoon dried sage or thyme (for fresh sage use 1 teaspoon)
4 tablespoons butter or margarine, softened
cooking twine
1 1/2 cups Vienna or Märzen-style beer
meat thermometer

1.
Rub chicken inside and out with lemon juice. Sprinkle inside with half the salt and pepper.

2.
With side of a cleaver, mash garlic and remaining salt to form a paste and mix with sage and butter.

3.
Carefully lift skin on each side of the chicken breast and push some of the mixture under. Rub the remaining mixture over the outside.

4.
Truss (see Note) and place chicken breast-side down on well-greased rack in a shallow pan.

5.
Pour beer into pan and place in 425° oven for 40 minutes, basting every 10 minutes with beer and pan drippings.

6.
Turn breast-side up and roast 25 minutes, basting every 8 minutes. Continue roasting and basting until meat thermometer inserted into the thickest part of the thigh registers 160°. The juices should run clear when you puncture the skin at the thigh joint.

7.
Remove from pan and place on heated platter. Cover with foil and allow to rest 10 minutes before carving. Serve with pan juices or make into gravy. Or save pan juices to simmer with the carcass for a delicious soup.

NOTE
Using cooking twine, tie the legs together, turn and tie wings together.

VARIATION
You can use the same recipe and cooking method for a small fresh turkey.

BETTER CORDON BLEU

1.

Combine beer, olive oil, lime juice, garlic, and tarragon.

2.

Form a pocket in the breast by inserting a sharp knife into thickest side and cutting horizontally. Place between two pieces of wax paper and gently pound until evenly flattened (do not pound until thin, simply create a uniform thickness).

3.

Marinate chicken in beer mixture 4 to 8 hours in refrigerator. Drain and pat chicken dry when ready to stuff.

4.

Spread 3/4 teaspoon mustard on each piece of ham, place cheese on top and fold ham around cheese. Place in pocket with fold-side out to deter cheese from leaking.

Serves 4

Besides getting a terrific uplift from beer, these chicken breasts are lightly breaded and sautéed instead of being baked for tender, juicy, simply scrumptious results.

1 cup Bavarian light lager or German Pilsener
1/4 cup olive oil
juice of 1 lime
1 clove garlic, minced and mashed
2 teaspoons tarragon
4 large skinless, boneless chicken breast halves
wax paper
1 tablespoon Sweet-N-Hot Beer Mustard (page 218)
4 3 x 2-inch slices of Black Forest ham (or prosciutto)
4 3 x 1-inch thick slices Finnish lappi cheese (or Gruyère)
1/2 cup flour
1/2 teaspoon salt
1/4 teaspoon each paprika and freshly ground black pepper
1/8 teaspoon cayenne
1/3 cup buttermilk
1 stick unsalted butter

5.

Combine flour, salt, paprika, pepper, and cayenne. Just before cooking dip chicken in buttermilk and dredge lightly in seasoned flour.

6.

Heat butter in heavy sauté pan on medium until foam subsides. Brown breasts lightly on each side. Lower heat to medium-low and cook about 6 minutes. Turn and continue cooking until done. Remove to heated platter. Serve with Pilsener Sauce, recipe follows. ▼

PILSENER SAUCE

A light and lovely sauce, this is exceptional on pasta tossed with bits of leftover chicken, ham, and fresh peas.

Makes 4 half-cup servings

1 1/2 cups chicken broth
1/2 cup German Pilsener or Bavarian light lager
1/2 teaspoon tarragon or thyme
4 tablespoons pan drippings (add butter if needed)
4 tablespoons flour

1.

Combine broth, beer, and tarragon and heat until hot.

2.

Heat drippings in pan on medium, add flour, and cook, stirring constantly, 4 minutes.

3.

Whisking continuously, slowly add hot broth mixture and continue stirring until thickened. Serve over Better Cordon Bleu.

EXOTIC WINGS OF ASIA

Serves 2 to 4

Gingery, flaming Buffalo wings in a captivating garlicky sauce.

MARINADE

2/3 cup American light lager or Pilsener

3 tablespoons frozen orange juice concentrate

1 tablespoon dark soy sauce

1 teaspoon finely grated fresh ginger

1/2 teaspoon Chinese 5-spice powder (star anise, fennel, cinnamon, cloves and pepper or ginger)

1 clove garlic, finely minced and mashed

3 tablespoons cornstarch

36 chicken wings

oil for frying

paper towels

ASIAN WING SAUCE

1 1/2 cups American light lager or Pilsener

1/2 cup soy sauce

2 tablespoons Red Curry Paste (see page 285)

1 teaspoon sesame oil

1 tablespoon oil

1 teaspoon Szechwan peppercorns (see page 286)

1 large clove garlic, thinly sliced

1 small onion, finely minced

1 1/2 tablespoons cornstarch

1.

Blend first 7 ingredients and marinate wings in refrigerator 4 to 6 hours.

2.

Drain and pat dry. Heat oil to 375° in a deep skillet. Fry wings a few at a time until crisp and cooked through, drain on paper towels.

1.

Combine first 4 ingredients and set aside.

2.

Heat oil over medium and sauté peppercorns and garlic briefly. Remove from pan and set aside. Sauté onion in remaining oil until limp and translucent.

3.

Lightly crush peppercorns and stir with garlic, onions, and cornstarch into beer mixture. Whisk until cornstarch is dissolved. Cook on medium, stirring constantly, until thickened.

4.

Pour hot sauce over fried wings and serve immediately.

VARIATION

Bake at 300° or grill over very low heat until tender before saucing.

WINGS OF THE COMANCHERO

Smoky chipotle chilies give an extra lift to these fiery sauced wings.

2/3 cup Homebrewed Steak Sauce (page 214)
2 cloves garlic, minced and mashed
3 tablespoons cornstarch

36 chicken wings
oil for frying
paper towels

1.
Blend first 3 ingredients and marinate wings in refrigerator 4 to 6 hours.

2.
Drain and pat dry. Heat oil to 375° in a deep skillet. Fry wings a few at a time until crisp and cooked through, drain on paper towels.

COMANCHERO WING SAUCE
1 1/2 cups tomato juice
1/2 cup altbier or Scottish ale
1/2 to 1 teaspoon hot red chili powder
1 canned or dried reconstituted chipotle chili
2 cloves garlic, minced and mashed
1 teaspoon paprika
1/2 teaspoon liquid smoke
1/4 to 1/2 teaspoon salt (optional)

1.
Simmer all ingredients uncovered for 40 minutes, stirring frequently.

2.
Pour hot sauce over fried wings and serve immediately. If a dipping sauce is desired blue cheese is a great accompaniment for these wings.

VARIATION
Bake at 300° or grill over very low heat until tender before saucing.

BLAZING GOLDEN MUSTARD WINGS

Buffalo wings with a fabulous twist are ensconced in a pungent, potent mustard sauce.

Serves 2 to 4

2/3 cup pale ale or India pale ale
1/3 cup honey, warmed
1 clove garlic, finely minced and mashed
1/8 to 1/4 teaspoon cayenne
3 tablespoons cornstarch

36 chicken wings
oil for frying
paper towels

1.
Blend first 5 ingredients and marinate wings in refrigerator 4 to 6 hours.

2.
Drain and pat dry. Heat oil to 375° in a deep skillet. Fry wings a few at a time until crisp and cooked through, drain on paper towels.

GOLDEN MUSTARD WING SAUCE

2 cups pale ale or India pale ale
1/3 cup dried yellow mustard
1/4 cup brown sugar
2 teaspoons hot mustard powder or hot red chili powder
1 1/2 tablespoons cornstarch

4 tablespoons butter
1 small onion, finely minced

1.
Combine first 5 ingredients and let stand one-half hour.

2.
Heat butter over medium and sauté onion until limp and translucent.

3.
Stir beer mixture into onions. Cook over medium, stirring constantly until thickened.

4.
Pour hot sauce over fried wings and serve.

Fiery Buffalo wings were invented by a Buffalo, New York, bar owner as an incentive for bar patrons to consume lots of brew.

ALMOND TURKEY SCALOPPINE

Rounds of turkey breast, marinated in beer, soy sauce, and ginger are cloaked in chopped almonds, sautéed, and served with a hot-n-spicy dipping sauce. Great party fare, these are not to be missed!

1.
Combine beer, ginger, soy sauce, sesame oil, chili, and garlic. Pour over turkey medallions and coat thoroughly. Cover and refrigerate 2 hours.

2.
Combine egg whites and cornstarch. Dip each marinated round in cornstarch-egg mixture and coat completely with almonds. Place on parchment.

3.
Heat 4 tablespoons oil in heavy 10-inch skillet on medium. Arrange about 8 turkey rounds in hot oil and sauté until almonds turn light gold.

1 1/2 cups Oktoberfest beer
1/2-inch piece fresh ginger, thinly sliced and mashed
3 tablespoons dark soy sauce
1 teaspoon dark sesame oil
1/8 to 1/4 teaspoon ground hot Thai chili
1 clove garlic, finely minced
2 pounds turkey breast, cut into 2-inch medallions 1/2-inch thick

4 egg whites
1/3 cup cornstarch
3 cups blanched almonds, finely chopped
4 tablespoons peanut oil for sautéing
baking parchment
paper towels

4.
Turn and continue sautéing until golden and cooked through. Remove and place on a pan lined with paper towels. Keep in a warm oven until all are cooked.

NOTE

Chicken breast fillets, also known as "tenders," are a perfect substitute for turkey.

HOT-N-SPICY DIPPING SAUCE

Although my favorite dipping sauce for these crunchy almond-coated delicacies is Thai Sweet Hot Sauce for Chicken found in Asian grocery stores, this version makes an excellent substitute.

1.
Thoroughly whisk all ingredients in heavy saucepan.

2.
Cook on medium, stirring constantly, until thick and clear. Serve warm.

3/4 cup Oktoberfest beer
3/4 cup chicken broth
2 tablespoons frozen orange juice concentrate
1/4 cup light soy sauce
1 teaspoon finely grated fresh ginger
1/4 to 1/2 teaspoon ground hot Thai or other red chili (to taste)
2 teaspoons oyster sauce
1 large clove garlic, thinly sliced
3 tablespoons cornstarch

SIZZLING CHICKEN OR TURKEY FAJITAS

1.

Combine first six ingredients. Reduce by 2/3 on medium-high, cool.

2.

Remove whole spices and add remaining marinade ingredients.

1.

If grilling meat, leave whole to marinate. If stir-frying, cut breasts into 1/3-inch thick slices to marinate.

2.

In a glass or stainless-steel bowl, marinate meat in refrigerator 2 to 8 hours. While meat is marinating, prepare vegetables.

3.

When meat is ready, heat a heavy skillet, add 3 tablespoons oil, and toss in sliced onions, browning quickly but removing before they soften. Place in large oven-proof bowl while repeating with the meat. Keep warm in a 200° oven.

4.

Add 1 tablespoon oil and toss in bell pepper, again cooking briefly to brown but removing before soft. Remove and add to onions. ▼

MARINADE

12 ounces canned fruit nectar (see Notes)
1/2 cup brown ale
1/2 teaspoon each whole cloves and whole allspice
1 stick cinnamon
1/2 teaspoon ground red chilies or 2 serrano chilies, sliced thinly
1/2 teaspoon each toasted crushed coriander and cumin seed

1/2 cup Homebrewed Steak Sauce (see page 214)
juice of 1/2 orange
juice of 2 limes
1/2 cup extra-virgin olive oil

FAJITAS

2 pounds skinless boneless chicken or turkey breasts
1/4 to 1/2 cup olive or peanut oil
6 freshly roasted green chilies, peeled and sliced (or canned)
2 large onions, sliced 1/3 inch thick
2 bell peppers, sliced thin (red or yellow for color)
4 green onions, cut 1-inch long
1 cup drained, sliced nopalitos (pickled canned cactus pads, optional)
1 tablespoon each melted butter and olive or peanut oil mixed

Serves 2 to 4

Tender pieces of savory marinated chicken or turkey and colorful, crunchy vegetables make a spectacular entrée for an informal evening of good eating. Be sure to serve in a piping hot cast-iron skillet so they will sizzle dramatically as you carry them to the table. I have provided two methods for cooking fajitas. The first is to slice the meat before cooking and stir-fry. The second is to grill for a smoky flavor, slice, and quickly cook a second time just before serving.

5.

Repeat with nopalitos and add to onions and peppers. Remove skillet from heat and toss in sliced chilies just to warm. Add to cooked vegetables.

6.

METHOD I

STIR-FRYING THE MEAT

This is a fast and easy way to prepare fajitas. Be sure to drain thoroughly before cooking.

A.

Reheat skillet on medium-high with 2 tablespoons oil. When very hot, add one-third of the chicken, stirring constantly, and cook until meat turns opaque and is lightly browned. Remove and repeat with remaining chicken.

B.

Combine vegetables, meat, green chilies, and green onions, toss and quickly pour on the melted butter and oil. Serve while sizzling.

6.

METHOD II

GRILLING THE MEAT

This method is a little more time-consuming, but will give an exquisite, smoky essence to fajitas that is well worth the effort.

A.

Place handful of soaked wood chips on hot charcoal in grill. Add meat and cook just enough to sear and lightly brown the outside; the inside will be raw. Cool completely before slicing into 1/3-inch thick strips.

B.

Reheat skillet on medium-high with 3 tablespoons oil. When very hot, add partially cooked chicken, stirring constantly, and cook until meat is opaque and lightly browned.

C.

Combine vegetables, meat, green chilies, and green onions, toss quickly, and pour on the melted butter and oil. Serve while sizzling.

NOTES

❧ Orange, apricot, or peach nectar is a good base. Papaya, mango, or guava are fascinating when used alone or with the basic flavors.

❧ Serve fajitas with lots of hot flour and corn tortillas and lime wedges to squeeze over.

STUFFED GAME HENS

Elegant and sophisticated, stuffed game hens are perfect for special-occasion suppers. The stuffing is made of wild rice simmered in hard cider or mead and combined with sautéed vegetables. The hens are roasted with herbed butter under the skin and basted with beer for tender and juicy results.

WILD RICE STUFFING
1 tablespoon butter
1/3 cup wild rice
1 cup of hard cider or mead
4 tablespoons butter or margarine
1 small carrot, julienned
1 small leek, split, washed, and chopped
6 shallots, finely chopped
1/2 cup chopped Italian (flat-leafed) parsley, loosely packed
1 small can water chestnuts, thinly sliced
2 cups finely shredded Italian or French bread
1/2 teaspoon each dried thyme and tarragon

GAME HENS
6 game hens
1 fresh lemon or 2 limes, quartered
kosher salt and freshly ground black pepper
1/2 pound butter, room temperature
1/3 cup fresh thyme, finely chopped
2 large shallots, crushed in garlic press
twine
2 cups wheat beer or hard cider

1.
In a small saucepan melt 1 table-spoon butter over medium heat. Add rice and sauté, stirring constantly, 10 minutes. Add cider, cover, and simmer on medium-low for 40 minutes. Uncover and continue simmering 10 minutes or until all liquid is absorbed. Cool.

2.
In a sauté pan, melt 4 tablespoons butter and sauté carrot until it begins to soften. Add chopped leek and sauté just until limp. Stir in shallots, cook 1 minute and remove from heat.

3.
Combine sautéed vegetables with cooked rice, parsley, water chestnuts, bread crumbs, thyme, and tarragon, mixing well.

1.
Rinse game hens and pat dry. Rub inside and out with quartered lemon. Sprinkle cavity lightly with salt and pepper.

2.
In a small bowl combine butter, thyme, and crushed shallots, mashing well to incorporate thoroughly, set aside. ▼

3.

Slip a finger beneath skin on one side of the breast. Press two teaspoons herbed butter into opening. Repeat with the other side.

4.

Lightly stuff each hen 3/4 full. Place a small piece of aluminum foil over cavity to hold in stuffing and retain juices. Truss birds lightly with twine to hold legs and wings against the body.

5.

Rub hens with some of the remaining herb butter. Salt and pepper lightly and place breast down on a greased roasting rack in a shallow pan (see Note). Melt remaining herb butter and combine with beer for basting.

6.

Roast at 400° for 30 minutes, basting every 10 minutes with butter-beer baste. Turn hens and roast 30 more minutes, basting every 10 minutes. Hens are done when leg moves freely, or pierce the thickest part of thigh to make sure juices run almost clear. Do not overcook or they will become tough and tasteless.

7.

Place hens on warmed platter and cover with foil to keep hot. Pour off drippings and remove fat.

ROASTED GAME HEN SAUCE

1 1/2 to 2 cups pan juices, fat removed (add chicken stock, if necessary)
1/3 cup wheat beer or hard cider
3 tablespoons balsamic or fruit vinegar (blueberry, raspberry)
1/4 cup honey
2 shallots, finely minced
1/2 cup Italian (flat-leafed) parsley, chopped

1.

Pour beer and vinegar into hot roasting pan and deglaze (see page 282).

2.

In a small saucepan, combine pan juices, honey, and shallots. Simmer on medium-high until reduced to 2 cups. Add parsley and serve over hot game hens.

NOTE

A roasting rack is essential to keep hens from literally "stewing in their own juices."

THE QUINTESSENTIAL GAME HEN

The fine flavors of aged blue cheese, grapes, and toasted walnuts transform game hens into an exquisite and memorable dining experience.

STUFFING

1/2 cup basmati rice, washed thoroughly and soaked 8 to 12 hours
1/3 cup weissbier or water
1 to 2 tablespoons olive oil
pinch salt
2 large shallots, thinly sliced
1/4 cup Italian (flat-leafed) parsley, finely chopped
1/3 cup mild blue cheese or 1/2 cup Gorgonzola, crumbled
1 cup small seedless green grapes
1/2 cup toasted walnuts, coarsely crushed
pinch of freshly ground black pepper

1.

Combine drained rice with beer in small saucepan. Add 1 teaspoon olive oil and pinch of salt. Cover and simmer 10 minutes. Remove from heat and let stand, covered, 10 minutes to cool.

2.

In a small skillet, sauté shallots in olive oil until soft and translucent, cool.

3.

Combine parsley, cheese, grapes, and shallots. Toss in the cooled rice, toasted walnuts, and pepper.

4.

Stuff, roast, and sauce game hens according to recipe on page 171.

SOUTH-OF-THE-BORDER CORDON BLEU

Serves 4

These stuffed chicken breasts unite a variety of flavors found in the Southwest – chicken, spices, chilies, cheese and, of course, cerveza.

2 large, split chicken breasts, halved, skinned, and boned

MARINADE

1 cup Vienna-style beer
1/3 cup olive oil
1 teaspoon each toasted coriander and cumin seeds, ground
1 large serrano chili, finely sliced
2 teaspoons sugar

4 tablespoons Cilantro Pesto (page 216)
4 small whole canned green chilies (or fresh roasted)
4 pieces cheese cut to fit pocket (Mexican cheese or Muenster)
1/2 cup flour (approximately)
1/2 teaspoon salt
1/2 teaspoon paprika
1/4 teaspoon freshly ground black pepper
3/4 cup buttermilk
1/2 cup butter
1/4 cup each beer, water, and lime juice

1.

Form a pocket in the breast by inserting a sharp knife into the thickest side and cutting horizontally (see page 162). Place between two pieces of wax paper and gently pound until evenly flattened (do not pound until thin, simply create a uniform thickness).

2.

Pour marinade over chicken and marinate in refrigerator 4 to 8 hours. Drain and pat chicken dry when ready to stuff.

3.

Spread inside of each breast with 1 tablespoon of cilantro pesto. Stuff chili with cheese and place stuffed chili into pocket.

4.

Combine flour, salt, paprika, and pepper. Dip each breast in buttermilk and dredge lightly in seasoned flour. Refrigerate 5 minutes.

5.

In a heavy skillet melt butter over medium until foam subsides. Add chicken and sauté until golden brown on each side. ▼

6.

Drain on paper towels and place in 250° oven until ready to serve. If not serving within 10 minutes, lay a piece of foil lightly over chicken to keep from drying out.

7.

Pour beer mixture into hot pan and scrape the bottom well. Reduce by one-fourth. Pour into a gravy server. These breasts can be served up to 30 minutes after cooking if kept hot.

1.

Spread 1 tablespoon sour cream (or Crème Fraîche) and 1 tablespoon almonds on each slice of ham.

2.

Place cheese slice on ham, roll and stuff inside a chili. Place stuffed chili in pocket of chicken breast. Continue with step number 4.

NOTE

Since variety is the spice of life, try stuffing the breasts with the following ingredients for a change of pace.

FILLING

4 tablespoons sour cream or Crème Fraîche (see page 35)

4 tablespoons sliced almonds, lightly toasted

4 slices of Black Forest ham or prosciutto

4 slices Muenster, Swiss or Gruyère cheese

4 small whole canned green chilies (or fresh roasted)

WOK COOKING

Wok cooking is a wholesome, rapid method that preserves the color, flavor, and texture of food. There are certain basics to wok cooking that will help you turn out flawless dishes every time.

BASIC STIR-FRYING ORDER

Most stir-fried dishes follow a basic cooking order.

1.
Stir-fry meat first then remove from wok and set aside.

2.
Stir-fry firm vegetables next (carrots, broccoli, celery) until partially cooked.

3.
Push vegetables up sides of wok, add sauce and thicken slightly.

4.
Stir in the more delicate ingredients (scallions, fresh ginger, spinach).

5.
Return meat last, toss to coat with sauce, and reheat briefly.

HELPFUL HINTS

❧ Cutting food into small, uniform pieces provides more cooking surface, allowing for quick, efficient cooking.

❧ To slice meat thinly, partially freeze before cutting.

❧ Stir-frying means just that — constantly stirring food while it cooks. Moisture released by the food is constantly in contact with a hot surface, causing it to evaporate immediately. If not constantly stirred, the food will simmer in the moisture rather than stir-frying.

❧ Never try to cook more than 1 pound of meat or vegetables at a time. This allows space in the wok to move the food and helps the wok retain heat.

❧ Stir-frying requires very high heat, so use oil with a high flame point, such as peanut or canola. Add oil to hot wok.

❧ Traditionally, whole nuts are fried briefly in very hot oil then added at the end of stir-frying. Oven-roasting nuts at 350° until golden will give similar results without adding oil.

❧ Always serve stir-fried foods immediately.

ALMOND CHICKEN

Serves 2 to 4

Tantalizing and scrumptious, this is a favorite of many. The beer-marinated chicken, lightly cooked vegetables, and toasted almonds combine for a delectable supper.

1.

Combine dark soy sauce, beer, dried pepper flakes, and cornstarch in a small bowl. Cut chicken into 3/4-inch cubes or strips, add to the marinade, and set aside.

2.

Chop and prepare vegetables, placing each in a separate bowl. Combine chicken stock, beer, light soy sauce, sugar, and cornstarch.

3.

Heat wok on medium-high. Swirl in about 1/2 cup oil. Add garlic and ginger, stir-frying until fragrant (1 to 3 minutes). Strain and set aside.

4.

Add chicken to the hot flavored oil, stir-frying until opaque (about 1 minute). Remove and set aside.

5.

Swirl another 1/4 cup oil in wok and add cabbage and celery. Stir-fry 30 seconds. Push vegetables up sides of wok.

6.

Stir sauce and pour into wok, stirring constantly until it thickens. Push vegetables down into the sauce and add scallions and chicken. Cook just long enough to reheat chicken and thicken sauce.

1 1/2 tablespoons dark soy sauce
3 tablespoons Pilsener-style beer
1/4 teaspoon dried red pepper flakes
1 tablespoon cornstarch
2 whole chicken breasts, skinned and boned
1/3 cup strong chicken stock
1/4 cup pale ale or German light lager or Pilsener
2 tablespoons light soy sauce
1 tablespoon sugar
1/4 cup cornstarch
3/4 cup oil for stir-frying (peanut or canola)
2 cloves garlic, sliced thinly (optional)
1/2 inch fresh ginger, peeled and sliced thinly (optional)
4 cups shredded napa or bok choy cabbage
1 cup celery, thinly sliced
6 scallions, cut diagonally 3/4 inch long
1 cup blanched almonds, toasted lightly
garnish with sliced scallion and sesame seeds (optional)

7.

Stir in almonds and immediately transfer to a serving platter or individual dishes. Garnish with sliced scallion and sesame seeds, if desired.

KUNG PAO CHICKEN

Serves 2 to 4

An incendiary dish that will warm you on a wintry day or cool you on a blistering one (it can make 115° seem chilly!). Of course, adjust the amount of chilies to produce the desired intensity.

1.
Combine dark soy sauce, beer, and cornstarch in a small bowl. Add chicken to marinate. Set aside.

2.
Combine stock, beer, wine vinegar, soy sauce, sugar, and cornstarch in a separate bowl. Set aside.

3.
Heat wok on high and swirl with about 1/2 cup oil. Add chicken, stir-frying just until glazed and cooked through. Remove and set aside.

4.
Swirl another 1/4 cup oil in wok and add chilies, peppercorns, garlic, shallots, ginger, and green onions, cooking about 1 minute.

5.
Push vegetables up sides of wok, stir sauce mixture and pour into bottom of wok, stirring constantly until it thickens.

6.
Push down the vegetables, add chicken, and cook just until chicken is heated through and glazed. Stir in peanuts and transfer to a serving platter or individual plates. Serve immediately.

1 tablespoon dark soy sauce

2 tablespoons brown ale or Bavarian dark

1 tablespoon cornstarch

2 whole chicken breasts, skinned, boned, and cut into chunks

1/3 cup chicken stock

1/2 cup German Pilsener or light lager

3 tablespoons red wine vinegar

3 1/2 tablespoons light soy sauce

1 tablespoon sugar

2 tablespoons cornstarch

3/4 cup peanut or canola oil for frying

4 to 6 large red Chinese chilies, soaked in water 1 hour and chopped coarsely

1 teaspoon Szechwan peppercorns

5 cloves garlic, sliced thinly

4 large shallots, sliced thinly

1-inch piece fresh ginger, peeled and sliced thinly

8 large green onions, chopped in inch-long pieces

1 cup dry-roasted peanuts

CARIBBEAN CHICKEN

The combination of cooling coconut milk, beer, toasty almonds, and fiery spices makes this chicken dish one of contrast and fascinating flavors.

1/2 cup blanched almonds
2 cups coconut milk
1/4 cup peanut or canola oil
1 large onion, finely chopped
4 large cloves garlic, finely minced and mashed
3/4-inch piece fresh ginger, peeled and lightly mashed
4 chicken breasts, skinned, split and boned
1 1/2 cups India pale ale
1/2 cup flour mixed with 1/2 teaspoon each salt, pepper, and paprika
1 teaspoon freshly ground cumin
1 teaspoon salt (optional)
15 small dried hot red Asian chilies
juice of 1 lime
1/2 cup freshly chopped cilantro (or Italian flat-leafed parsley)
4 large scallions, finely chopped

1.

In heavy skillet, toast almonds lightly to a pale gold color. Place in blender with coconut milk and blend until smooth. Set aside.

2.

Heat 2 tablespoons oil over medium and sauté onion, garlic, and ginger until onion is wilted. Remove and set aside.

3.

Moisten chicken breasts with 1/2 cup ale. Coat lightly with seasoned flour.

4.

Turn heat up to medium-high, add about 1/4 cup oil, and brown breasts lightly on both sides.

5.

Add coconut-almond mixture, 1 cup ale, sautéed onion mixture, cumin, salt, and chilies to chicken and bring to a slow simmer. Keep heat low or coconut milk will curdle.

6.

Simmer, uncovered, 35 minutes. Remove chicken and add lime juice, chopped cilantro, and scallions, stirring gently. Remove ginger and discard. Serve chicken and sauce over steamed rice.

MALAYSIAN CHICKEN

Serves 4 to 6

This is another exotic dish that uses coconut milk with hot and spicy ingredients. The beer-glazed pineapple adds an indescribable flavor to this intriguing combination.

2/3 cup coconut milk
1/3 cup Pilsener-style beer
1 1/2 tablespoons cornstarch
1 to 2 teaspoons Chinese hot red curry paste (to taste)
1/4 cup peanut oil
3 chicken breasts, boneless, skinless, and cut into half-inch strips
2 whole cans pineapple chunks, drained
6 chunks raw sugar, finely ground in blender or food processor
1/4 cup weissbier or fruit lambic
1 tablespoon light soy sauce
1 3-inch chunk fresh ginger, peeled, split, and crushed
2 carrots, julienned
4 large scallions, sliced diagonally
2 cloves garlic, finely chopped and mashed
1 small bunch fresh cilantro, trimmed and coarsely chopped
2 to 3 hot Thai chilies, sliced 1/4 inch thick (optional)

1.

Mix coconut milk, beer, cornstarch, and curry paste in a small bowl and set aside.

2.

Heat wok to medium-high and add 1/4 cup peanut oil. Add chicken and cook quickly until barely opaque. Remove and set aside.

3.

Turn heat to high, add another tablespoon of oil and swirl to coat. Add pineapple, ground sugar, beer, soy sauce, and crushed ginger. Cook until liquid evaporates and pineapple takes on a glaze. Set pineapple aside and discard ginger.

4.

Swirl in 1 tablespoon oil, add carrots, and cook until slightly limp. Add scallions and garlic and cook briefly.

5.

Push vegetables up sides of wok, add coconut milk mixture to the bottom, and stir until thickened. Keep heat low or coconut milk will curdle.

6.

Push vegetables back down and stir to coat. Add chicken, pineapple, cilantro, and chopped Thai chili, then simmer 8 to 10 minutes. Serve immediately with cooked rice.

NOTES

NOTES

CHAPTER 8
BREADS

Certain food and beverage combinations are so harmonious their alliance is never questioned. Cold milk and warm chocolate chip cookies, rich burgundy wine and rare prime rib, sparkling Champagne and fine caviar, and last but not least, a cooling tankard of beer and warm slabs of fresh bread. Beer and bread are an intriguing and complex union that captures our hearts.

When eaten together, the lavish essence of malted grain, hops, and brewers yeast in beer intensifies the rich grain and yeast flavors so prized in bread. To combine the exceptional qualities of each by using beer in the preparation of bread is a creative and rewarding process.

Before beginning this pleasurable task, make sure your baking will have the proper groundwork for success. Countless people believe the mysteries of yeast baking are far beyond them. For them I have broken the process into five distinct steps and explained each fully. Please see page 19 and pages 23 and 24 for basics that will help make each venture into the kitchen a culinary triumph.

CREATING YOUR OWN BEER BREAD RECIPES

Using any standard bread recipe, you can devise your own original beer bread simply by substituting one liquid for another.

If a recipe calls for 2 cups of water, replace a portion or all with beer.

If a recipe calls for 2 cups of whole milk or buttermilk, substitute 1 3/4 cups of beer (or beer-water combination) plus 1 cup of reconstituted powdered milk or powdered buttermilk.

If a recipe calls for 2 cups of potato water, simmer a large unpeeled diced potato in 2 1/2 cups of beer or beer-water combination. Measure the liquid before adding to the bread.

Italian Pepperoni Bread, page 193. ▶

GENERAL YEAST BREAD DIRECTIONS

1.

In a large bowl sprinkle yeast over 1 cup of bread flour. Pour in warm liquid and whisk thoroughly. Allow to rest in a warm spot for 10 to 20 minutes.

2.

Whisk in sugar, powdered milk, oil, eggs, salt, spices, special flours, and other flavorings.

3.

Stir in remaining flour one cup at a time, using your hands once the dough becomes too heavy for a spatula. Continue adding flour until dough begins to pull away from sides of the bowl and kneading can begin.

4.

Knead vigorously by pushing, folding, and turning, adding only enough flour to prevent the dough from sticking to your hands or kneading surface.

5.

When dough is smooth and elastic, coat the inside of a large bowl with 1 tablespoon vegetable oil. Press the ball of dough into the bowl and turn it over, coating the entire surface with oil.

6.

Cover and allow to rise in a warm spot until doubled. When doubled in bulk, punch down, divide in half, and allow to rest 5 minutes, covered.

7.

To shape the dough into loaves, coat an area of the counter with a few drops of oil. Pat the dough into an 8 x 10-inch rectangle.

8.

Starting at the narrow end, roll firmly but gently into a cylinder. Do not stretch the dough. Pinch ends and turn them under toward the seam side. Forcefully slam the dough onto the counter, seam-side down, two or three times to seal and remove large air bubbles.

9.

Place the loaves seam-side down in generously greased loaf pans. Cover and allow to rise until doubled.   ▼

HELPFUL HINTS

❧ When covering dough to rise, plastic wrap works especially well, particularly in dry climates. If you live in a humid climate, a towel works fine (no terry cloth — it sticks to the dough and leaves lint). In cold climates a smooth woolen cloth is preferred to retain warmth.

❧ If the dough looks like it is tearing while you are kneading, stop folding and instead press and push on it to continue the kneading process. Continuing to fold the dough will tear the fragile structure formed by gluten.

❧ To glaze or flavor the tops of your bread, many combinations can be used. Water makes a crusty loaf, milk or cream makes a tender crust, whole egg or egg white gives a glossy finish, and egg yolk gives a rich golden color.

❧ My favorite glaze is one I created for finicky kids and husbands. Whisk 1 to 2 tablespoons warm honey with 1 egg white and brush it on liberally. (For homebrewers, substitute malt extract for the honey). It makes an irresistible glossy, sweet crust favored by all.

WONDERFUL TANGY FRENCH BREAD

1.

In a large bowl, sprinkle 1 cup flour, sugar, and yeast. Pour in warm beer and water, and whisk thoroughly. Cover and allow to rest in a warm spot 10 to 20 minutes.

2.

Add oil, salt, and 2 more cups flour. Continue with steps 3 to 6 of the general bread-making directions on page 182.

3.

If you are making the traditional thin baguettes, divide dough into fourths. If you are making large, long loaves, divide in half.

4.

Carefully coax the soft dough into long, even loaves by rolling and slapping lightly onto the counter. Place each loaf into French bread pans that have been greased and sprinkled with cornmeal or onto a similarly prepared baking sheet.

5.

Cover and allow loaves to rise at room temperature until double. Brush tops with beaten egg white or spray with water (see Note). Using a sharp knife, lightly score top of each loaf with 4 or 5 diagonal

Makes two long loaves

Adding beer may not be conventional, but the tangy flavor is sensational and the texture outstanding.

7 to 8 cups bread flour
1 tablespoon sugar
2 tablespoons yeast
1 cup warm pale ale or India pale ale (110°)
1 1/3 cups water (110°)
1 tablespoon oil or melted shortening
1 1/2 tablespoons coarse or kosher salt
1 egg white (optional) for brushing loaves
cornmeal for sprinkling on baking pans

cuts. This will prevent the loaf from cracking or bursting from internal moisture released while baking.

6.

Preheat oven to 350° with a pan of hot water to add humidity. Remove the pan and place bread in the hot, humid oven. Bake for 20 to 25 minutes or until loaves are golden brown and crusty.

POTPOURRI

2 teaspoons freshly chopped basil
1 teaspoon freshly chopped thyme
1 teaspoon freshly chopped tarragon
1 teaspoon freshly chopped marjoram
1 teaspoon finely grated lemon zest

NOTE

If you prefer your bread really crusty, use a spray bottle to spritz with water after the first 5 minutes of baking and again after 10 more minutes.

VARIATIONS

❧ Create a glorious herbed loaf when summer bestows a bounty of fresh herbs. Simply stir the potpourri into the warm liquid used in the recipe.

❧ Try adding grated carrot to the herbed dough for bread with attractive flecks of green and orange.

SCHERMERHORN HONEY-BRAN BREAD

Makes 2 loaves

Full-flavored and tender, this multigrain bread is a family favorite and a winner with the sandwich crowd.

7 cups bread flour (approximately)
2 tablespoons dry yeast
2 cups warm Oktoberfest or brown ale (110°)
1/2 cup cornmeal
3 cups bran cereal or 1 1/2 cups bran flakes
2/3 cup dry powdered milk
3 eggs, room temperature, separated
1/2 cup vegetable oil
3/4 cup honey
1 teaspoon salt

1 tablespoon vegetable oil
1 egg white
1 tablespoon warm honey

1.

Place 1 cup flour in a large bowl. Stir in dry yeast and pour warm beer over, and whisk thoroughly. Cover and allow to rest in a warm, draft-free spot 10 to 20 minutes to form a sponge.

2.

Add the next 7 ingredients to the yeast mixture (reserving 1 egg white) and whisk until combined.

3.

Continue with steps 3 through 9 of the general bread-making directions on page 182.

4.

Brush tops with 1 egg white beaten with 1 tablespoon honey to combine thoroughly.

5.

Bake at 350° in lightly greased loaf pans for 25 to 30 minutes, until the tops are browned and, when tipped out of the pan, the bottoms are golden.

VARIATION

Add toasted sunflower seeds and/or crushed granola in place of bran.

SWEDISH RYE BREAD

This dense bread is fragrant with orange zest, honey, rye, beer, and spices. It's a light-colored loaf, well-suited for sandwiches or hors d'oeuvres.

Makes 2 loaves

3 cups medium rye flour
2 tablespoons dry yeast
1 1/2 cups porter (110°)
1/2 cup honey, warmed
3 tablespoons finely minced orange zest
3 eggs
1/4 cup vegetable oil
1/2 teaspoon cinnamon
1/2 teaspoon ground ginger
1/4 teaspoon ground cardamom
1/4 cup cornmeal
4 cups bread flour
1 egg white, beaten
2 tablespoons honey

1.

Place 1 cup of rye flour in a large bowl. Stir in dry yeast, pour warm beer over, and whisk thoroughly. Cover and allow to rest in a warm spot 15 to 20 minutes.

2.

Stir in honey, zest, eggs, oil, spices, cornmeal, and remaining rye flour, beating until smooth.

3.

Continue with steps 3 through 9 of the general bread-making directions on page 182.

4.

Prepare glaze by beating the remaining egg white with 2 table-spoons warmed honey. Brush tops of loaves gently with glaze.

5.

Bake at 350° for 25 to 30 minutes until tops are golden and, when tipped out of the pan, the bottoms are light golden brown.

NOTE

Rye bread often takes 2 to 3 hours to rise until doubled — be patient!

VARIATIONS

❧ Stir in 2 tablespoons caraway seeds with the orange zest.

❧ Shape into round peasant loaves. Smooth dough into a circle with seams on the bottom. On an ungreased counter, place the dough seam-side down and put your hands on either side of the loaf. Begin gently turning the loaf in one direction. The dough will stick slightly to the counter causing the seam to twist and seal itself. The loaf will literally pull itself into a uniform shape. Lightly score top with a sharp knife just before baking.

𝒯he Little Mermaid, the statue that greets travelers to Copenhagen, was donated to the city by a director of the Carlsberg Brewery and the Carlsberg Foundation, which owns Carlsberg Beer. The beer's earnings are distributed through the Foundation to support Danish arts and science.

CURRIED BREAD

1.
Place 1 cup flour in large bowl. Stir in dry yeast, pour warm beer and water over, and whisk thoroughly. Cover and allow to rest in a warm spot for 15 to 20 minutes.

2.
Continue with steps 2 through 9 of the general bread-making directions on page 182.

3.
Prepare glaze by beating the remaining egg white with 1 tablespoon warmed honey. Brush tops gently with glaze.

4.
Bake at 350° for 25 to 30 minutes until the tops are golden and, if tipped out of the pan, the bottoms are light golden brown.

7 to 8 cups bread flour
2 tablespoons dry yeast
1 1/2 cups India pale ale (110°)
1/2 cup water (110°)
2/3 cup sugar
1/3 cup vegetable oil
3 extra-large eggs, room temperature
1/3 cup quality curry powder (see Note)
1 tablespoon salt
1 tablespoon vegetable oil
1 egg white
1 tablespoon warm honey

Makes 2 loaves

Unrivaled in zesty flavor, this easy-slicing bread is sensational for sandwiches. Standard ham-and-Swiss sandwiches taste amazingly innovative when served on this golden loaf. And toasted, well, plain bread never tasted this good! This is another multipurpose dough that bakes up beautifully in all shapes and sizes.

NOTE
Whenever possible, purchase curry powder from East Indian or Middle Eastern markets for fresh, distinctive, and pungent blends.

HONEY WHEAT WALNUT BREAD

Makes 2 loaves

A substantial loaf, this has a crunchy texture and heavenly flavor. The addition of roasted, beer-simmered wheat kernels permeates the loaf with the essence of wheat. Further accented by toasted walnuts, this hearty bread will keep you going all day.

1 1/2 cups cracked wheat kernels
2 1/2 cups dunkelweizen
1/2 cup honey or brown sugar
6 to 7 cups bread flour
2 tablespoons dry yeast
1 1/2 cups warm water (110°)
1/3 cup vegetable oil (110°)
2/3 cup honey
1 teaspoon salt
1 cup toasted walnuts, coarsely chopped
1 egg white whisked with 1 or 2
  tablespoons warmed honey for glaze

1.

Roast the wheat kernels in a 400° oven, stirring frequently until golden brown. Combine in pan with beer and 1/2 cup honey. Simmer on low 1 hour, covered. Uncover, raise heat slightly, and simmer an additional hour or until most of the liquid has been absorbed. Remove from heat and allow to cool completely.

2.

Grind the cooked wheat in a food processor or blender until fine but not puréed. Set aside.

3.

Place 1 cup flour in large bowl. Stir in dry yeast, pour in warm water, and whisk thoroughly. Cover and allow to rest 15 to 20 minutes.

4.

Whisk oil, 2/3 cup honey, salt, walnuts, and cooked wheat into yeast mixture.

5.

Continue with steps 3 through 9 of the general bread-making directions on page 182.

6.

Brush with glaze and bake at 350° for 25 to 30 minutes or until tops are golden and bottoms are browned.

VARIATIONS

❀ Precooking grains and adding them to bread is a marvelous way to add nutrition, flavor, and variety in your baking. The next time you have leftover cooked grains such as brown rice or barley, use them for making bread!

❀ For homebrewers who always have extra malted barley on hand, crack and cook it in place of wheat. Use a complementing malty beer for liquid.

ALE & EGG BREAD

This is a great all-round bread, moist, finely textured, and replete with the essence of beer. The dough is easily formed into braids or dinner rolls, hamburger or hot dog buns.

7 to 8 cups bread flour
2 tablespoons dry yeast
1 cup warmed brown, pale, or India pale ale (110°)
1 cup water (110°)
2 tablespoons sugar
1 cup dry powdered milk
1/4 cup vegetable oil
3 large eggs, room temperature
1 tablespoon salt
1 egg white beaten with 1 tablespoon warmed honey for glaze

1.

In a large bowl mix 1 cup flour and dry yeast. Pour the warm beer and water over, and whisk thoroughly. Allow to rest in a warm, draft-free spot for 15 to 20 minutes.

2.

Proceed with steps 2 through 9 of the general bread-making directions on page 182.

3.

Gently and generously brush tops with glaze.

4.

Bake at 350° for 30 to 35 minutes or until tops are golden and bottoms are browned.

VARIATIONS

❧ Add various herbs (tarragon, basil, thyme) to the batter for a rich egg-and-herb bread.

❧ Sprinkle top of loaves with poppy or sesame seeds after brushing with glaze.

❧ For a stupendous three-color holiday loaf, form the entire batch of dough into one grand braid and place on a very large baking sheet lined with parchment. After brushing with glaze, sprinkle sesame seeds on one strand of the braid, poppy seeds on the other, and cinnamon sugar on the third.

BLACK RUSSIAN RYE BREAD

1.

Place 1 cup rye flour in a large bowl and stir in dry yeast. Pour warm beer over, and whisk thoroughly. Cover and allow to rest in a warm spot for 15 to 20 minutes.

2.

Stir butter, eggs, honey, caraway, cocoa, and salt into the yeast mixture, whisking until well-combined. Add remaining rye flour 1 cup at a time.

3.

Continue with steps 3 through 6 of the general bread-making directions on page 182.

4.

Form dough into oblong or round peasant loaves (see variation page 186). Place on well-greased parchment, cover, and allow to rise until doubled.

5.

Brush tops with glaze. Lightly score with a sharp serrated knife. Bake at 350° for 30 to 35 minutes, until the tops are dark and the bottoms well-browned.

4 cups medium or dark rye flour
2 tablespoons dry yeast
2 cups stout (110°)
4 tablespoons butter, melted
2 eggs
1/2 cup honey
3 tablespoons caraway seed
1/4 cup cocoa powder
1 tablespoon salt
3 to 4 cups bread flour
baking parchment
1 egg white mixed with 2 tablespoons
   warm honey for glaze

Makes 2 round peasant loaves

Lush with the essence of rye, stout, and chocolate, this peasant bread is an Old World indulgence when served alongside a bowl of hearty stew. It is a memorable appetizer when sliced thin, spread with dilled cream cheese, and crowned with Dilled Smoky Salmon (page 101).

SERVING SUGGESTIONS

This robust Black Russian Rye is heavenly with slabs of cured ham, country-style cheese, sliced onions, and fresh radishes dipped in salt.

POTATO BREAD

Makes 2 loaves

Beer and potatoes seem to have a special affinity for one another. Here they are combined in a delectable loaf enhanced with dill. This is the consummate loaf of potato bread.

2 large baking potatoes, peeled and cubed
1 1/2 cups American light lager
2/3 cup water
2 tablespoons dry yeast
6 to 6 1/2 cups bread flour
1/2 cup dry powdered milk
3 tablespoons sugar
3 tablespoons oil
1 tablespoon dried dill or 3 tablespoons
  fresh dill, chopped
2 to 3 tablespoons milk

1.

In a covered saucepan simmer cubed potatoes in beer and water until very tender. With a slotted spoon, remove potatoes and set aside. Measure and save 2 cups of potato liquid. Cool to 110°.

2.

In a separate bowl, combine yeast with 1 cup bread flour. Whisk in 2 cups potato liquid and powdered milk. Allow to stand 15 to 20 minutes.

3.

Mash potato and add, along with sugar, oil, and dill, to yeast mixture.

4.

Proceed with steps 3 to 9 of the general bread-making directions on page 182.

5.

Just before placing loaves in oven, brush with milk. Bake until pale golden on top and bottom. Cool thoroughly before slicing.

N O T E

This bread slices well, has a long shelf life, and is excellent toasted. It can be formed into dinner rolls and braids. For a change of pace, form into hamburger buns for your next cookout.

HEARTY BEER-N-OAT BREAD

Makes 2 loaves

This solid loaf is brimming with the flavor and texture of oats, a portion of which is processed until flourlike and the remainder toasted whole. Embellished with nuts and ale, this praiseworthy loaf will quickly become a family favorite.

4 cups old-fashioned oats
4 to 5 cups bread flour
2 tablespoons dry yeast
1 1/2 cups water (110°)
1 1/2 cups India pale ale
1/2 cup dry milk powder
1/2 to 2/3 cup firmly packed brown sugar
1 cup toasted walnuts or pecans, crushed (optional)
1 tablespoon salt

1 egg, beaten
4 tablespoons oats (optional)

1.

Process 2 cups of oats in a blender or food processor until the texture of coarse flour. Toast the remaining 2 cups in a 350° oven, stirring frequently until golden brown. Set aside.

2.

In a bowl combine 1 cup bread flour, yeast, and warm water, whisking until well-combined. Set aside for 15 to 20 minutes.

3.

In a large bowl combine ale, dry milk powder, brown sugar, toasted nuts, salt, and both types of oats. Pour yeast mixture over the top and stir.

4.

Continue with steps 3 through 9 of the general bread-making directions on page 182.

5.

Just before placing bread in the oven, brush with egg and sprinkle oats on top. Bake until golden on top and bottom.

America's oldest existing brewery is high in the mountains of Ecuador. The brewery is part of a monastery begun in Quito in 1534.

ITALIAN PEPPERONI BREAD

Makes 2 loaves

This distinctive bread makes a savory gift for that exceptional someone on your gift list.

6 to 6 1/2 cups bread flour
2 tablespoons dry yeast
1 cup water (110°)
1 cup pale ale or German Pilsener (110°)
2 tablespoons vegetable oil
1 tablespoon sugar
1 tablespoon kosher salt
1/4 cup Parmesan, Romano or other hard cheese, grated
2 tablespoons dried minced onion
2 tablespoons oregano
2 teaspoons crushed rosemary
1 1/2 teaspoons finely crushed black pepper
1 1/3 cups finely chopped hard pepperoni
cornmeal for sprinkling the baking pans
1 egg white (optional) for brushing the loaves

1.

Whisk 1 cup flour and dry yeast in a large bowl. Add warm water and beer and whisk thoroughly. Cover and allow to rest in a warm place 10 to 20 minutes.

2.

Continue with steps 2 through 4 of the general bread-making directions on page 182, adding all ingredients up to the pepperoni.

3.

Pat dough into a flat circle and sprinkle with pepperoni. Fold over and seal. Continue kneading for an additional 4 to 5 minutes.

4.

When dough becomes smooth and elastic and pepperoni pieces are evenly distributed, place in a lightly oiled bowl and turn over, coating the entire surface with oil. Cover and allow to rise again until doubled.

5.

Punch down and let rest 5 minutes, covered.

6.

Form dough into the desired shape and place in lightly greased pans sprinkled with cornmeal. Allow to rise again until doubled.

7.

Brush tops with beaten egg white. Score with 4 to 5 diagonal cuts.

8.

Place bread in 350° oven and bake 20 to 25 minutes or until loaves are golden and crusty.

STUFFED BREAD

BREAD DOUGH

8 to 9 cups bread flour
1 tablespoon dry yeast
2 cups water (110°)
1 1/2 cups American light lager (110°)

HERB SPREAD

1 tablespoon sugar
2 teaspoons herb combination (rosemary, basil, thyme)
1 teaspoon freshly ground black pepper
1 teaspoon paprika
1/2 cup grated hard cheese (Parmesan or Romano)
1/2 cup vegetable oil
1 tablespoon salt

Makes 2 stuffed loaves

Every culture seems to have some delicious version of bread stuffed with meats and vegetables. This recipe combines beer-enhanced bread stuffed with sausage, cheese, and vegetables to form two large turnovers.

1.

In a large bowl sprinkle 1 cup flour with dry yeast. Whisk in warm water and beer. Cover and allow to rest in a warm place for 10 to 20 minutes.

2.

Continue with steps 2 through 6 of the general bread-making directions on page 182.

ASSEMBLING

1.

During the first rising, combine filling ingredients.

2.

Divide dough in half and roll each half into an 18-inch circle, keeping dough thinner around edges.

3.

Spread a 12-inch circle in the center with 1 tablespoon herb spread and place about 3 cups of filling (recipes follow) on half of the dough.

4.

Fold top over filling until it is fully encased and seal, making a large turnover. Place on greased baking sheet. Repeat with other loaf.

5.

Brush tops with oil, cover, and allow to rise in a warm place 15 to 20 minutes only. Bake at 350° for 25 to 30 minutes or until the top is golden and the bottom is lightly browned.

SUGGESTED FILLINGS

MEAT

Sliced sausage, thinly sliced roasted meat, poultry, or barbe-cued meats. Use leftover meats such as hamburger or thinly sliced steak.

VEGGIES

Lightly roasted peppers, raw broccoli florets (they steam to perfection in the dough), sautéed mushrooms, sautéed onions, boiled or baked potatoes. ▼

CHEESE

Ricotta cheese and any compatible melting cheese such as cheddar, Muenster, Mozzarella, provolone or Swiss.

MISCELLANEOUS

Toasted nuts, sesame seeds, cooked beans.

SAUCES

My favorite is pesto but any of the following are tasty and easy to prepare. Pesto (see page 216), barbecue sauce, Sweet-N-Hot Beer Mustard (see page 218), salad dressing or chunky spaghetti sauce.

ZUCCHINI SPICE BREAD

Makes 2 loaves

This supermoist bread makes a perfect gift any time of the year.

1.

Beat eggs, sugar, and half the oil until very light and fluffy. Stir in remaining oil, zucchini, malt extract or honey, and vanilla.

2.

Combine the dry ingredients and stir well.

3.

Add wet ingredients to the dry ingredients, stirring just until combined.

4.

Divide batter between two well-greased loaf pans and bake at 350° for 45 minutes or until a toothpick inserted in the middle comes out clean. Cool 10 minutes before turning out onto a cooling rack.

3 extra-large eggs
1 1/2 cups sugar
3/4 cup vegetable oil
2 cups grated zucchini
1/3 cup unhopped amber malt extract or honey
1 teaspoon vanilla
2 cups flour
2 teaspoons baking soda
1 teaspoon baking powder
1 1/2 to 2 teaspoons Chinese 5-spice powder (star anise, fennel, cinnamon, cloves and pepper or ginger)
1 to 1 1/2 teaspoons cinnamon
1/2 teaspoon allspice
1/2 teaspoon nutmeg
1 teaspoon salt
1 cup toasted walnuts, finely chopped (optional)
2 teaspoons orange zest, finely minced (optional)

CINNAMON- SWIRL RAISIN BREAD

Ah, one of life's special indulgences is cinnamon-raisin bread. Try this fragrant and beautiful bread to restore hope.

3 tablespoons dry yeast

7 to 8 cups bread flour (approximately)

1 1/2 cups light-bodied fruit beer or
   weissbier (110°)

1/2 cup water (110°)

1 cup dry milk powder

3 large eggs (room temperature)

1 teaspoons salt

1/2 to 2/3 cup sugar

1 cup raisins plumped in 1/2 cup water,
   beer, brandy, or wine

1/2 cup vegetable oil or melted margarine

2/3 cup granulated sugar mixed with 1 1/2
   tablespoons cinnamon

3 tablespoons milk or cream

1.

In a large stainless-steel or ceramic bowl whisk the dry yeast with 1 cup of the bread flour. Whisk in the warmed beer and water, cover, and allow to stand in a warm place 15 to 20 minutes.

2.

Beat powdered milk, eggs, salt, sugar, raisins, and oil into the yeast mixture. Add 2 cups bread flour and beat until dough is smooth.

3.

Continue with steps 3 through 7 of the general bread-making directions on page 182.

4.

Sprinkle each rectangle of dough with half the sugar and cinnamon mixture. Continue with steps 8 and 9 on page 182.

5.

Brush the raised loaves with milk or cream and bake at 350° until golden on top and bottom. Allow to cool 5 minutes before taking out of the pan. Cool completely before slicing.

HOMEMADE BAGELS

Makes 2 dozen

Chewy and full-flavored, these bagels freeze well and lend themselves to numerous breakfast or sandwich fillings.

1.

Stir dry yeast with powdered milk and 1 cup bread flour. Whisk in warm beer and water and allow to rest for 15 minutes.

2.

Continue with steps 2 through 6 on page 182.

3.

Form a piece the size of an egg into a smooth ball. Poke your thumb through the middle and pull dough into a bagel. Place on a baking sheet and cover with a cloth towel. Repeat with remaining dough.

4.

Boil water and add sugar and salt. Place bagels in the boiling water 3 or 4 at a time and poach 3 minutes, turn, and poach other side 3 minutes.

5.

Remove and place on a lightly oiled parchment-covered baking sheet.

6.

When the pan is filled but bagels don't touch, brush with beaten egg. Bake at 375° for 25 minutes or until golden.

2 tablespoons dry yeast
1/2 cup dry powdered milk
5 to 6 cups bread flour
1 cup American light lager (110°)
1 cup water (110°)
1/4 cup oil
3 tablespoons sugar
1 1/2 tablespoons salt
3 eggs
4 to 5 quarts boiling water
2 tablespoons sugar
1 tablespoon salt
1 beaten egg
baking parchment

VARIATIONS

The addition of flavorings such as herbs or spices, nuts, raisins, chopped pimento, rye or whole-wheat flour offer a profusion of variations limited only by your pantry.

TOSTADA SHELLS

Serves 6

These shells are included here because they make such wonderful bases for all types of meals. Spread with a little of the Frijoles Borrachos (page 55) and topped with lots of shredded lettuce and Pico de Gallo (page 221) they are great for suppers or picnics. Add cooked meats, vegetables, and avocados for endless variety.

6 corn tortillas (soft and pliable)

1.
To prepare tortillas, lightly brush one side with vegetable oil or rub with a stick of margarine so each has a light coating. Stack tortillas butter-side up.

2.
On a large cookie sheet, lay a few tortillas (they can overlap slightly) and toast at 400°.

3.
The shells are done when they are a light golden brown. Remove and repeat with remainder of the tortillas. Allow to cool completely before storing.

NOTE
These tostada shells are not greasy and retain their crispness. They travel well for picnics or camping if packed in a cardboard box lined with a large plastic bag.

FEATHERY BISCUITS

An all-in-one mixture that makes light, fluffy biscuits. We love to take this camping, so I've given camp stove directions, too.

2 1/2 cups unbleached flour
1 tablespoon baking powder, sifted
1/2 teaspoon salt (optional)
1/2 cup dry powdered milk
1 1/2 teaspoons mixed herbs or parsley and herbs (optional)
6 tablespoons butter or margarine
1/2 cup weissbier or German Pilsener
1/4 cup water

1.

Mix dry ingredients and cut margarine into the mixture, working until crumbly. Store in sealed plastic bag if not using immediately.

2.

To make biscuits, stir beer and water into flour mixture until barely moistened and it begins to pull into a ball. If making drop biscuits, drop dough by large spoonfuls onto a greased baking sheet.

3.

If rolling and cutting the biscuits, knead 8 to 9 strokes, roll or pat 3/4-inch thick, cut and place on a greased baking sheet.

4.

Bake at 350° for 15 to 18 minutes or until the tops are a light gold.

CAMPING DIRECTIONS

1.

Rub oil on the inside of a heavy cast-iron skillet and cast-iron lid. Place the lid directly on the heat (camp stove or campfire) to get very hot.

2.

Pat the biscuit mixture into oiled skillet or drop the batter in by spoonfuls.

3.

Cover with the hot lid. Place over a medium-low flame or in the hot coals for about 20 minutes. Check after 15 minutes.

If the lid is flat and you are using a campfire, place a shovelful of hot ashes on top of the pot for even baking.

VARIATIONS

Try adding grated cheese or finely chopped ham to the biscuits.

HELPFUL HINT

If you have ever eaten banana bread or biscuits with mouth-puckering specks of baking soda throughout, you know first-hand why baking soda and baking powder should be sifted before using.

SAVORY SCONES

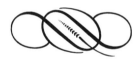

Makes 10 to 12

S cones are rich biscuits that can be sweet or savory. This recipe incorporates bits of cheese and beer-soaked ham for a hearty breakfast or dinner biscuit.

1/2 cup ham, diced finely
3 tablespoons Belgian ale
2 cups all-purpose flour
1 tablespoon sugar
2 teaspoons baking powder
1 teaspoon dried herbs (thyme, savory, dill)
1/4 teaspoon salt
8 tablespoons butter
2/3 cup grated Grùyere or Swiss cheese
1 extra-large egg, beaten
3 tablespoons Belgian ale
3 tablespoons light cream or milk

1.
Combine ham and 3 tablespoons ale in a saucepan and heat until hot. Cover and let stand 15 to 30 minutes.

2.
In a medium bowl stir flour, sugar, baking powder, herbs and salt. Cut in butter until crumbly and stir in cheese.

3.
Beat egg, ale, and cream, make a well in the flour mixture and add the egg mixture and ham. Stir gently to distribute moisture until dough forms a ball.

4.
Knead gently 5 to 8 strokes. Roll or pat 3/4 inch thick. Cut with a 2-inch biscuit cutter dipped in flour between biscuits.

5.
Place on ungreased baking sheet and bake on center shelf at 400° for 12 to 15 minutes or until pale gold on top. Serve immediately with fresh butter.

NOTE
The uncooked cut scones can be frozen. Separate with wax paper or plastic wrap to freeze in an airtight container. Bake frozen scones on a baking sheet at 400° for 15 to 17 minutes.

The word "bridal" is derived from an English custom dating to the Middle Ages in which a bride would brew a special batch of "bride's ale" for the wedding feast. Drinkers of the ale would then contribute money.

MARVELOUS CORN MUFFINS

These are simply the best-tasting corn muffins – moist, tender, and full of wholesome corn flavor.

greased muffin pan
1 cup yellow cornmeal
1 1/4 cups unbleached flour
1/2 cup sugar (more or less to taste)
2 teaspoons baking powder, sifted
1/2 teaspoon baking soda, sifted
1/2 teaspoon salt
1 egg
1/4 cup oil
1 cup creamed corn or fresh corn puréed in
  a blender
1/2 cup Pilsener or pale ale (see Note)
1/4 cup dry powdered milk

1.

Preheat oven to 375°. Generously grease 12 standard muffin cups.

2.

Combine cornmeal, flour, sugar, baking powder, soda, and salt in a large bowl and whisk until combined.

3.

Mix egg, oil, corn, beer, and powdered milk in another bowl and beat until thoroughly combined.

4.

Add wet ingredients to the dry ingredients, stirring just until moistened.

5.

Spoon into prepared muffin pan, filling 3/4 full. Bake until muffins are springy to the touch and golden brown.

NOTE

The liquid content of corn will affect the amount of beer needed. Use the amount called for and if the batter seems dry, add an additional 2 tablespoons beer, or if too moist add flour.

HELPFUL HINTS

❧ The essential technique for making tender, high-rising muffins is to handle the batter as little as possible.

❧ Always combine dry ingredients in one bowl and wet ingredients in another to keep stirring to a minimum.

❧ Using a large spatula, gently mix until ingredients are moistened and combined. Small lumps will disappear during baking.

❧ Always have your oven fully preheated for consistent baking and peaked muffins. Standard muffins usually bake at 400°, small muffins at 350°, and oversized Texas muffins at 375°.

❧ Muffins are done when the tops feel springy.

❧ When converting a standard 12-muffin recipe to make 6 Texas muffins you will need to make 1 1/2 batches (3 standard muffins = 1 Texas muffin).

TEXAS-SIZED SPICE MUFFINS

1.

Preheat oven to 400°. Generously grease Texas-sized muffin pan.

2.

Mix flour, powdered milk, sugars, baking powder, soda, salt, and spices in a large bowl and whisk until blended.

3.

Combine marmalade, vanilla, eggs, beer, and oil in another bowl and beat until thoroughly mixed.

4.

Stir the wet ingredients into the dry ingredients quickly, just until moistened. The varying liquid content of the marmalade will cause the amount of buttermilk needed to vary.

5.

Spoon into prepared tins, filling 3/4 full. Bake until springy to the touch and golden brown.

3 cups unbleached flour
2/3 cup dry powdered milk
1/4 cup granulated sugar (optional)
1/2 cup firmly packed brown sugar
2 1/2 teaspoons baking powder
1/2 teaspoon baking soda
1 teaspoon salt
2 teaspoons cinnamon
1 teaspoon ground ginger
1/2 teaspoon each ground allspice,
  nutmeg, coriander, and cloves
3/4 cup marmalade or preserves (see Note)
1 teaspoon vanilla extract
2 eggs
1 cup Oktoberfest or altbier
1/2 cup vegetable oil (corn or safflower)
2 to 4 tablespoons buttermilk, if moisture
  is needed

Makes 6 Texas or 18 regular muffins

Oversized muffins make a great lunch when paired with fruit or salad. These are absolutely delicious and the recipe is versatile, allowing you to use up bits and pieces of leftover fruits or preserves. Next time someone special needs a pick-me-up, offer one of these scrumptious, oversized muffins wrapped in colored plastic wrap.

NOTE

Use 3/4 cup finely chopped fresh apricots or other fruit in place of marmalade. An additional 1/4 cup of liquid may be needed if using fresh fruit in place of preserves.

VARIATIONS

❦ Toast oats, coconut, or nuts and add to dry ingredients.

❦ Use 1 cup whole-wheat flour in place 1 cup unbleached flour.

SAVORY BREAKFAST MUFFINS

Makes 12

Curry-flavored and golden brown, these rich, savory muffins are enhanced with bits of Canadian bacon and cheese. They make great breakfast or picnic fare.

2 cups unbleached flour
1 cup chopped Canadian bacon
1 cup grated Gruyère or Swiss cheese, chilled
1 teaspoon dried mixed herbs (thyme, tarragon)
1/4 cup sugar
2 teaspoons baking powder
1/2 teaspoon baking soda
1/2 teaspoon salt
1/2 teaspoon crushed black pepper
1 teaspoon finely minced lemon zest
2 tablespoons quality curry powder
2/3 cup buttermilk
1/3 cup pale ale
1 large egg
1/3 cup vegetable oil

1.
Preheat oven to 400°. Generously grease muffin tins using a pastry brush.

2.
Combine the first 11 ingredients, tossing well to distribute the ham and cheese.

3.
Combine buttermilk, ale, egg, and oil, stir well.

4.
Stir the buttermilk mixture into the dry ingredients quickly, stirring gently just until moistened (about 25 strokes).

5.
Spoon the batter equally among the muffin tins, filling them about 3/4 full.

6.
Bake for 25 minutes. The muffins should be springy to the touch and golden brown.

WHEAT, NUT & DATE MUFFINS

Makes 12

*S*tudded with nuts and moist dates combined with the full flavor of bock beer, these muffins are perfect for using up leftover oatmeal, hot cereal, or brown rice.

2 cups unbleached flour
1 cup chopped dates
1/2 cup toasted nuts (almonds, pecans, walnuts)
1/2 cup sugar
1 teaspoon baking powder
1 teaspoon baking soda
1/2 teaspoon salt
2 teaspoons Chinese 5-spice powder (or cinnamon)
1 cup cooked oatmeal, cracked wheat, four-grain cereal, or brown rice
2 teaspoons grated orange zest
1/2 cup buttermilk mixed with 1/4 cup dry powdered milk
1/2 cup bock beer
1 large egg
1/4 cup vegetable oil
1/3 cup raw sugar (or brown sugar)

1.
Preheat oven to 400°. Generously grease muffin tins.

2.
Mix the dry ingredients in a large bowl.

3.
Mix the wet ingredients in a bowl, whisking well to incorporate.

4.
Stir the wet ingredients into the dry just until moistened.

5.
Spoon the batter equally among the muffin tins, filling them about 3/4 full. Sprinkle the tops with sugar.

6.
Bake until springy to the touch and a nice golden brown. Allow to cool 5 minutes.

CINNAMON ROLLS

Some of the most memorable cinnamon rolls you will ever sample. The dough is easy to work with and tastes incredible. They can be refrigerated overnight and baked in the morning. Go ahead, treat yourself!

DOUGH

1 cup weissbier (110°)
1 cup water (110°)
1 cup dry powdered milk
3 tablespoons dry yeast
8 cups bread flour (approximately)
4 eggs, room temperature
2 teaspoons salt
1/2 cup sugar
1/2 cup melted margarine
baking parchment

FILLING

2 cups firmly packed brown sugar
3 tablespoons ground cinnamon
3 tablespoons unbleached flour
1 stick butter or margarine, very soft
1/2 cup cream or milk

GLAZE

3 cups powdered sugar
1/3 to 1/2 cup frozen orange or fruit juice
   concentrate, undiluted
2 teaspoons ground cinnamon

1.

Warm beer, water, and powdered milk in a saucepan or microwave to lukewarm (105° to 110°). In a large stainless-steel or ceramic bowl, dissolve yeast in warm beer along with 1 cup bread flour. Whisk thoroughly. Allow to stand in a warm place 15 to 20 minutes.

2.

Continue with steps 2 to 6 of the general bread-making directions on page 182.

3.

While dough is rising, mix brown sugar, cinnamon, flour, and butter in a bowl until crumbly.

4.

Roll half the dough into a 12 x 16-inch rectangle. Sprinkle surface (except for a 1-inch border around the edges) evenly with half the cinnamon sugar.

5.

Starting with the wide edge, firmly roll the dough, taking care not to stretch or roll it too loosely. Pinch seams together tightly.

6.

Using a sharp serrated knife cut dough into 1 1/2- to 2-inch slices.

7.

Place rolls in a pan lined with lightly buttered parchment. Place rolls snugly in the pan or the filling will seep out. The number of rolls will vary depending on how thick they are cut.

8.

Allow to rise just until halfway doubled. Brush the tops with cream. ▼

9.

Bake at 350° on lower oven shelf about 25 to 35 minutes. Time will vary depending on the size of the rolls and the size of the pan. When done, the center rolls should be golden on top and firm in the middle.

10.

Remove pan from oven. Stir powdered sugar, cinnamon, and juice concentrate until smooth and generously glaze the warm rolls in the pan.

VARIATION

These rolls rise well overnight in the refrigerator. Reduce yeast to 2 tablespoons. Cover the baking pan loosely with plastic wrap so the rolls have room to rise but don't dry out. Refrigerate until ready to bake. Remove from refrigerator, bring to room temperature and bake at 350° for 25 to 35 minutes. Glaze as in step 10.

PECAN STICKY BUNS

1.

Mix yeast and powdered milk with 1 cup bread flour. Whisk in the warmed beer and water. Allow to stand in a warm place 15 to 20 minutes.

2.

Continue with steps 2 through 6 of the general bread-making directions on page 182.

3.

While dough is rising prepare the syrup.   ▼

2 tablespoons dry yeast
1/2 cup dry powdered milk
4 cups bread flour (approximately)
2/3 cup German Pilsener or pale ale (110°)
1/3 cup water (110°)
2 large eggs, room temperature
1 teaspoons salt
1/3 cup sugar
1/4 cup melted margarine

SYRUP

1/2 cup amber beer
1 1/2 cups firmly packed brown sugar
4 tablespoons butter
1 teaspoon vanilla or 2 teaspoons rum vanilla (see Note)
2 cups coarsely chopped toasted pecans
1/3 cup granulated sugar mixed with 2 teaspoons cinnamon

Makes 1 1/2 to 2 dozen

By using beer in the syrup of these pecan sticky buns the flavor is enhanced and the cloying sweetness is tempered.

1.

In a heavy saucepan heat the beer, brown sugar, and butter on medium-low, stirring until sugar dissolves.

2.

Turn heat to medium and stop stirring. When the mixture comes to a boil, lower heat to medium-low and simmer 8 minutes without stirring.

3.

Remove, stir in vanilla, and allow to cool 5 minutes.

4.

Pour 2/3 of the warm syrup into the generously buttered 12 x 12-inch baking pan and sprinkle with toasted pecans. Set the remaining syrup aside in a warm spot.

5.

When the dough has doubled in bulk, punch it down and allow to rest covered for 5 minutes. Roll the dough into a 12 x 20-inch rectangle. Sprinkle cinnamon sugar over the top.

6.

Starting with the wide end, carefully and evenly roll the dough, taking care not to stretch or roll it too loosely.

7.

Pinch ends tightly. With a sharp serrated knife cut dough into 1/2-inch slices.

8.

Place rolls on the syrup in the pan. Drizzle remaining syrup over the top, cover, and allow to almost double in bulk.

9.

Bake at 350° about 25 minutes. Time will vary depending on the size of the pan and rolls. They should be golden on top and cooked through the middle.

10.

Remove pan from oven and allow to cool 5 minutes before inverting over a serving platter. Be sure to scrape any remaining syrup out of the pan and spread over the top of the buns.

NOTE

Rum vanilla is delicious and easy to make. Simply buy a bottle of dark rum, split a vanilla bean, and place it in the bottle. Age for at least 2 weeks; 2 months is better.

YEASTY BELGIAN WAFFLES

Makes 10 to 12

3 cups unbleached flour
1 tablespoon dry yeast
1 1/2 cups warm water (110°)
1 1/2 cups warm Oktoberfest (110°)
1/2 cup sugar
2 large eggs
1/2 teaspoon salt
6 tablespoons melted butter
1/4 cup vegetable oil
1 teaspoon vanilla extract

Light and ethereal, these yeasty waffles are much more than breakfast fare. Try them as a base for fresh fruit topped with whipped cream or for ice cream sundaes.

1.

Stir 1 cup flour with yeast. Whisk in warmed water and beer. Cover and let stand in a warm place for 15 minutes.

2.

Beat sugar, eggs, and salt until lemon colored and fluffy. In a separate bowl stir butter, oil, and vanilla.

3.

Combine the ingredients and beat 2 minutes. Cover and refrigerate from 4 hours to overnight.

4.

Stir the batter and cook in a generously greased Belgian waffle maker until crisp and brown. Serve immediately or cool on a rack before storing in airtight container.

SERVING SUGGESTION

Try these with the sweet Beer Syrup on page 231 for an eye-opening beer-enhanced breakfast.

CHAPTER 9
SAUCES, SIDES & GARNISHES

W hen it comes to sauces and sides, beer becomes an instrument of flavor that can be wielded just about everywhere. Whether making a dynamite beer-n-honey mustard that can be used to make a mustard-honey salad dressing, or a home-brewed steak sauce that can be the base for fabulous fajitas, or a luscious raspberry salad dressing, your creative genius will have a heyday. Please see pages 19 and 20 for basic tips on making classic sauces and gravies.

CREATING YOUR OWN WITH BEER

The key is to examine the basic ingredients and see if some form of beer can be added, or substituted in place of an ingredient, to enliven the flavor.

Beer can be substituted whenever sherry, vinegar, wine, broth, or fruit juice are called for. The key is in the amount and type of beer being substituted.

For example, if a delicate sauce for chicken calls for 2 cups of broth, try using 2/3 cup of weissbier and 1 1/3 cups of broth. Taste and decide if the flavor is balanced or if the amount of beer needs to be adjusted.

There is a fine-tuning that comes from cooking with beer. It is fine to use weissbier for a citrusy flavor, but remember some weissbiers are wheatier or fruitier in flavor and the citrus non-existent.

Unfortunately, beer does not come labeled with a description of its subtle character. So, horrifying as it sounds, you will be forced to taste and judge the beer's flavor before deciding which and how much to use. It's a tough job, but someone has to do it!

See Chapter 4 for additional salad dressing recipes.

Spicy Fruit Salsa, page 221. ►

PLUM BEER-BECUE SAUCE

This thick, fruit sauce is rich and aggressive, leaving a fiery aftertaste. A great way to add zing to a gift basket!

1 large onion, finely chopped
1/4 cup olive oil
6 cloves garlic, minced and smashed
2 cups plums, fresh or canned (no pits)
1 1/2 cups crushed tomatoes
12 ounces Bavaria dark beer
2 large or 4 small bouillon cubes, beef, chicken, or vegetarian
1 teaspoon bottled liquid smoke
1/2 cup red wine vinegar
1/2 cup dark brown sugar
1 teaspoon each ginger and cayenne (or hot red chili powder)
1 teaspoon each freshly crushed coriander seed, black pepper, cumin seed, and mustard seed

1.

In a small skillet, sauté onion in olive oil over medium-low until limp and translucent. Add garlic and continue to cook, stirring occasionally until limp. Set aside.

2.

In a blender or food processor, purée the plums and crushed tomatoes.

3.

In a 3-quart saucepan, heat beer and bouillon cubes until dissolved. Add remaining ingredients, including sautéed onion, garlic, and plum-tomato purée.

4.

Bring to a slow simmer and cook, stirring frequently, until very thick, 45 minutes to 1 hour. Cool and refrigerate or preserve with proper canning method for future use.

CURRIED SAUCE

Makes about 2 cups

A flavorful sauce, the perfect complement to homemade bratwurst (page 152).

3 tablespoons oil
1 onion, finely minced
1 cup water minus 2 tablespoons
1 cup Munich pale lager
3 tablespoons malt vinegar
2 tablespoons sugar
2 to 4 tablespoons curry powder
1 tablespoon cornstarch

1.

Heat oil in a large saucepan on medium. Add onions and cook slowly until very soft and translucent.

2.

Add water, beer, vinegar, and sugar, cover, and continue to cook on medium-low 30 minutes.

3.

Add curry powder and stir thoroughly. Cover and cook an additional 15 minutes.

4.

Mix cornstarch with 2 tablespoons water and whisk into the hot mixture. Cook until thickened and clear. Taste and adjust seasonings if necessary.

Bitter is a golden-brown to copper-colored top-fermented beer with a pronounced flavor of hops. It is dry and lightly carbonated and is sometimes referred to as the draft equivalent of pale ale in Britain.

HOMEBREWED STEAK SAUCE

Makes about 3 cups

A pungent, tart sauce not overly sweet, lending itself nicely to barbecue as a basting sauce or marinade.

1 1/2 cups Bavarian dark
1/3 cup dry sherry
1/4 cup honey
1/3 cup malt vinegar
1/3 cup dark soy sauce
1/2 teaspoon liquid smoke (hickory or mesquite)
1/2 medium yellow or white onion, coarsely chopped
4 large cloves garlic, peeled
1/2 cup raisins
1/4 teaspoon hot red chili flakes (to taste)
1 tablespoon freshly zested orange rind
1/2 teaspoon each freshly ground black pepper and coriander seed

1.
Combine ingredients in a blender and purée until smooth.

2.
Pour into a medium saucepan and bring to a slow simmer. Simmer for 20 minutes.

FETA CHEESE SAUCE

Makes about 4 cups

This ever-so-simple sauce is prepared in the food processor and served at room temperature over cooked pasta salad or vegetables.

1 cup feta cheese, drained
1 cup yogurt
1/2 cup sour cream (or additional yogurt for a tangy taste)
1 cup mayonnaise
2 tablespoons olive oil
1/4 cup balsamic vinegar
1/4 cup Belgian ale or English bitter
2 or 3 large cloves garlic, finely minced
1 tablespoon Italian (flat-leafed) parsley, finely chopped
1 teaspoon each of oregano, basil, orange zest
freshly cracked black pepper to taste

1.
Combine all ingredients in a food processor and process until smooth. Allow to stand for 30 minutes before serving.

CHEESE SAUCE WITH A TWIST

A perfect sauce when you want something unique to dress up the standard pasta, steamed veggies (cauliflower is wonderful), or chicken. The twist comes from the addition of Southwestern spices and strips of green chilies.

Makes about 4 cups

3 tablespoons butter or margarine
1 onion, finely chopped
1/2 cup green chilies (fresh roasted or canned), pulled into strips
1 teaspoon freshly ground black pepper
1/2 teaspoon cayenne
1/2 teaspoon crushed oregano
1/4 teaspoon crushed coriander seed
1/2 teaspoon minced garlic
1/2 cup German Pilsener
1 cup heavy cream
1 1/2 cups grated Muenster or cheddar cheese
1 cup sour cream
freshly chopped cilantro or Italian (flat-leafed) parsley for garnish

1.
Melt butter in a heavy sauté pan until the foam subsides. Add onions and cook just until wilted.

2.
Add the green chili strips, black pepper, cayenne, oregano, coriander, and garlic. Sauté 4 minutes over medium-low, stirring frequently.

3.
Stir in beer and simmer an additional 4 minutes. Pour in heavy cream and continue to simmer 10 minutes, stirring often.

4.
Remove from heat and add grated cheese and sour cream. Stir gently in one direction just until the cheese is melted and sour cream is blended. Serve immediately, garnished with cilantro or parsley.

PESTO

Pesto is a concentrated combination of herbs, garlic, oil, and cheese in spreadable form. It may not have beer in it but it complements pasta, pizza, spaghetti squash, and sautéed vegetables of all sorts. Or try pesto in Stuffed Bread (page 194).

2 to 2 1/2 cups fresh basil leaves
5 cloves garlic
2 peeled shallots
1 cup toasted pignoli (or) walnuts
1 cup extra-virgin olive oil
1 cup grated hard cheese (Parmesan, Romano, fontinella)
1/2 teaspoon freshly ground black pepper
salt to taste

1.

Using a food processor or blender, purée basil leaves, garlic, shallots, and nuts.

2.

With the motor running, add olive oil in a slow stream. Add grated cheese, pepper, and salt, processing just long enough to mix thoroughly. Refrigerate, covered, until ready to use, or freeze in small batches.

CILANTRO PESTO

Delightfully piquant, this pesto can transform many ho-hum dishes into southwest delights (try it over pasta!).

1 1/2 cups cilantro leaves
1 cup fresh basil leaves, firmly packed
6 to 7 large cloves of garlic
2 peeled shallots (optional)
2/3 cup green pumpkin seeds
1/2 cup salty Mexican cheese
1 teaspoon toasted coriander seed, crushed
1 teaspoon finely minced yellow (banana) or serrano chili
1/2 teaspoon freshly ground black pepper
2/3 to 3/4 cup fruity olive oil

1.

Using a food processor or blender, process the cilantro, basil leaves, garlic, shallots, and pumpkin seeds, until chopped.

2.

With the processor running, add the cheese, coriander seed, chili, and black pepper. Process until smooth. ▼

3.

In a slow, steady stream add the olive oil while the processor is running.

4.

Cover and refrigerate until ready to use. This can also be frozen in small batches for later use.

MUSTARD SAUCE

Makes 2/3 cup

Tastes wonderful paired with potatoes and other gently cooked vegetables such as green beans or asparagus. And it makes a dynamite salad dressing.

1.

Whisk all ingredients and allow to stand 1 hour before serving.

1/4 cup extra-virgin olive oil
2 tablespoons freshly squeezed lime juice
2 tablespoons homemade Sweet-N-Hot Beer Mustard (page 218)
2 tablespoons mayonnaise
1 large clove garlic, finely mashed with pinch coarse salt
1 tablespoon freshly chopped parsley
1/4 teaspoon each thyme, savory, and tarragon

MUSTARD SALAD DRESSING

Makes 1 cup

Use the Mustard Sauce to make a delightful salad dressing.

1.

Combine Mustard Sauce with oil, lime juice, garlic, and spices.

2/3 cup Mustard Sauce
1/4 cup olive oil
2 tablespoons lime juice
1 clove minced garlic
1 teaspoon each dried parsley, thyme, oregano, basil, savory, and tarragon

SWEET-N-HOT BEER MUSTARD

Makes about 1 cup

By far the most addictive mustard you will ever encounter. The balance of sweet and hot makes this perfect for salad dressings, sauces, and grilled meats.

1/4 cup dry yellow mustard powder

1/3 cup India pale ale, brown ale, or Bavarian dark

2 tablespoons rice vinegar

scant 1/4 cup sugar

1 tablespoon prepared horseradish

2 beaten egg yolks (or 1 tablespoon cornstarch)

1.
Whisk together all ingredients except egg yolks. Cover and let stand 30 minutes.

2.
Whisk in yolks and place on top of double boiler. Cook on medium-low until thickened, whisking constantly. Cool and keep up to three weeks in the refrigerator.

VARIATIONS

❧ Curry Mustard: In place of 1 tablespoon horseradish, use 1/2 tablespoon horseradish plus 1 tablespoon curry powder (to taste).

❧ Honey Mustard: Use 1/3 to 1/2 cup honey in place of sugar and use 3 egg yolks instead of 2.

❧ Herbed Mustard: Add 1 tablespoon fresh herb (finely chopped) or 1 teaspoon dried herbs, such as basil, thyme, or tarragon.

SPICED BEER & FRUIT GRAVY

Makes about 5 cups

This fabulous combination of fruit, pan juices, and spices is exceptional served with roast pork, duck, ham, or goose.

1 cup brown sugar, firmly packed
5 cups apples, peeled, cored, and coarsely chopped
1/2 cup raisins
2 cups cider or nut brown ale
1/4 cup pan drippings from roast (or 4 tablespoons unsalted butter)
2/3 cup finely chopped onions
2/3 cup finely chopped celery
1/2 teaspoon salt
1/2 to 3/4 teaspoon hot chili powder or cayenne
scant teaspoon ground cinnamon
1 3/4 cup pan juices (fat removed) or stock

1.

Combine sugar and apples in a large skillet (not cast iron) and cook over medium, stirring until sugar is dissolved. Raise heat to high and cook 1 minute, stirring once or twice.

2.

Stir in raisins and 1 cup cider. Continue cooking until the mixture caramelizes (turns dark brown and syrupy), 20 to 25 minutes, stirring frequently and scraping the pan well. Remove from heat and stir in remaining cider; set aside.

3.

Heat the pan drippings in a large sauté pan. Add onions, celery, and seasonings, sautéing over medium-high until tender (3 minutes). Stir continuously.

4.

Add caramelized apples and pan drippings and simmer 15 minutes, stirring constantly. Serve hot over slices of roast pork, duck, goose, or ham.

SALSA RANCHERO

Makes about
2 1/2 cups

This zesty salsa complements the flavor of just about any dish.

4 large plum tomatoes or 6 medium
   tomatoes
2 large cloves garlic
3 to 4 serrano chilies, toasted
2 tablespoons olive oil
1 large onion, coarsely chopped
1/2 cup German Pilsener or chili beer
1/2 teaspoon salt (approximately)
1/2 teaspoon sugar
freshly ground black pepper
2 tablespoons chopped cilantro or 2
   teaspoons dried oregano

1.
Peel and seed the tomatoes. Place in a blender or food processor. Add garlic and toasted chilies and purée.

2.
Heat olive oil in a skillet on medium, toss in onion, and cook until pale gold.

3.
Add puréed tomatoes to onion in skillet. If you are using dried oregano, add it now. Simmer over medium until sauce thickens, about 8 minutes. Taste and adjust salt, sugar, and pepper. If using cilantro, stir in just before serving.

PICO DE GALLO

1.

Combine ingredients and allow to stand 30 minutes.

3 medium, ripe tomatoes, seeded and chopped
2 large cloves garlic, minced
1 each small white, red, and yellow onion, finely chopped
8 scallions, coarsely chopped
2 fresh serrano chilies, finely minced
1 yellow banana chili, finely minced
1 small can sliced black olives, drained
1/3 cup American lager or rice vinegar or juice from 1 large lime
1 small bunch cilantro, rinsed and coarsely chopped or use 1 tablespoon dried oregano

Makes about 5 cups

The ultimate vegetable salsa – spicy, chunky, and delicious on just about everything. Try stuffing this along with slices of avocado in your next omelet for an eye-opening treat.

NOTE
Wear rubber gloves when working with fresh chilies and be careful to protect your eyes.

SPICY FRUIT SALSA

1.

Combine all ingredients in a stainless-steal or ceramic bowl and allow to stand at room temperature for 1 hour.

2.

Refrigerate and use within 2 to 3 days.

2/3 cup green onion, very finely chopped
1 1/2 cups mango or pineapple, finely chopped
1 1/2 cups papaya, nectarine, or firm peaches, finely chopped
2 large cloves garlic, finely minced
2 fresh serrano chilies, finely minced
2 yellow banana chilies, finely minced
1 teaspoon cumin seeds, toasted and finely crushed
2 teaspoons freshly grated ginger
1/3 cup fruity lambic-style beer
1 small bunch cilantro, rinsed and coarsely chopped

Makes about 3 cups

This zesty combination of fruit, spices, lambic, and chilies is sure to become a hit. For an incredibly fast, unusual supper, serve this alongside grilled chicken or pork.

BREWHOUSE STEAK RUB

Makes about
3 1/2 cups

A steak rub is a combination of herbs, spices, and other flavorful ingredients that is rubbed into the surface of meat 30 to 60 minutes before grilling or broiling. Equally delicious on beef, pork, or poultry, this zesty amalgam of fruit, beer, herbs, and spices will spoil you forever. Packed in small jars, this makes a great holiday gift.

1 1/2 cups canned plums, no pits
1 cup beer (your choice, each variety lends its own subtlety)
1/2 cup extra-virgin olive oil
1/3 cup firmly packed brown sugar
1 tablespoon liquid smoke
2 teaspoons salt
6 large cloves garlic, mashed
2 teaspoons crushed hot red peppers
scant teaspoon crushed coriander seed
scant teaspoon freshly ground black pepper

1.
Combine all ingredients in a food processor and process until very smooth.

2.
Allow to stand 2 hours at room temperature before using. Refrigerate remainder.

BAKED STUFFED ONIONS

Serves 6

These lovely onions are stuffed with a combination of gorgonzola, provolone, and pesto, then laced with a bit of porter, whiskey, and buttered bread crumbs before baking to perfection.

6 large yellow onions, unpeeled
2 tablespoons pesto (scant)
1/2 cup toasted crushed walnuts or pecans
6 ounces gorgonzola, crumbled
8 ounces provolone, grated
3 tablespoons porter
1 tablespoon sipping whiskey
1/4 cup butter, melted
1/2 cup fresh bread crumbs
2 tablespoons butter, melted

1.

Bake onions in a pan in a pre-heated 375° oven for 35 to 45 minutes or until they feel like a properly baked potato when squeezed slightly. Cool briefly.

2.

Remove skins and cut off both ends. Remove inner onion layers leaving the thick shell intact.

3.

Chop the inner layers from 3 of the onions and toss lightly with pesto and nuts. Add gorgonzola and provolone.

4.

Stuff onions with the cheese mixture. Place each onion upright in a buttered large muffin tin or individual baking dishes. Raise the oven heat to 475°.

5.

Combine porter and whiskey with 1/4 cup melted butter. Spoon over onions.

6.

Combine bread crumbs and 2 tablespoons melted butter, divide equally over top.

7.

Bake at 475° for 8 to 10 minutes or until the tops are golden.

ONIONS STUFFED WITH APPLES & SAUSAGE

Serves 6

The phenomenal flavors of glazed apples, onions, and sausage combine for a stunning side dish or elegant entrée.

6 large yellow onions, unpeeled
2 tablespoons butter
2 medium apples, peeled, cored, and chopped
1/2 cup pale ale
2 tablespoons brown sugar
1/2 teaspoon Chinese 5-spice powder (star anise, fennel, cinnamon, cloves, and pepper or ginger)
1/3 pound lean spicy sausage, cooked and drained thoroughly (see page 154 to make your own)
1 cup fresh soft bread crumbs
1/4 cup pale ale
1/2 cup fresh bread crumbs
1/4 cup grated fontinella or Parmesan cheese
3 tablespoons butter, melted and cooled slightly

1.

Place onions in a pan and bake in a preheated 375° oven for 35 to 45 minutes or until they feel like a properly baked potato when squeezed lightly. Cool briefly.

2.

Meanwhile, heat a heavy skillet on medium, add butter and sauté the apples for 5 minutes.

3.

Add the pale ale, sugar, and Chinese 5-spice powder, raise heat to medium-high, and cook until all liquid has evaporated and the apples are glazed. Remove and cool.

4.

Remove the onion skins and cut both ends off. Remove the inner onion leaving the thick shell intact.

5.

Chop 2 of the inner onions and toss with the sausage, glazed apples, and bread crumbs. Stuff onion shells with this mixture.

6.

Place each onion upright in a buttered Texas muffin tin or individual baking dishes. Raise oven heat to 400°.

7.

Spoon ale over the top of the onions. Toss together the bread crumbs, cheese, and melted butter. Sprinkle over the onions.

8.

Bake 15 to 20 minutes or until the tops are golden.

SCALLOPED APPLES, POTATOES, & ONIONS

Serves 6 to 8

Few combinations are as compatible as this. Glorified with butter, beer, cream, and herbs, it is heavenly eating.

4 tablespoons unbleached flour

2 teaspoons kosher salt

1/2 teaspoon freshly ground black pepper

1 teaspoon crushed thyme

1/4 to 1/2 teaspoon cayenne or finely crushed hot red chili flakes

1 1/2 pounds White Rose or Russet potatoes, peeled and sliced thinly

6 tablespoons butter, melted and cooled slightly

1 pound Granny Smith apples, peeled, cored, and sliced thinly

1 cup heavy cream

1 cup brown ale or cider

2 large cloves garlic, finely minced

1/2 to 2/3 cup grated Swiss cheese

1.

Generously butter a 3-quart casserole. Combine the flour, salt, pepper, thyme, and cayenne.

2.

Toss the potato slices with half the butter, repeat with the apple slices.

3.

Overlap half the potatoes in the casserole. Sprinkle with one-fourth of the flour mixture. Place half the apple and onion slices over the potatoes and sprinkle with one-fourth of the flour. Repeat with remaining potatoes, apples, and onions.

4.

Combine the cream, ale, and garlic and pour over the casserole. Cover with foil and bake 50 minutes at 375°.

5.

Remove the foil, reduce temperature to 350° and bake 35 minutes. Sprinkle the top with cheese and bake 15 minutes or until golden.

SPANISH RICE

A lovely, light-textured and flavorful rice. Add a bit of leftover meat (chicken is great), sautéed ground beef, or lots of fresh vegetables for an economical, fabulous meal.

1 cup chicken, beef, or vegetable stock
1 cup brown ale or Bavarian dark
2 cups tomato juice
1 teaspoon salt
1 teaspoon freshly ground pepper
1/2 teaspoon freshly ground coriander (optional)
1 teaspoon dried, crushed hot red chilies
1/2 cup olive oil
1 small yellow onion, finely chopped
2 cloves finely chopped garlic
2 cups long-grain white rice
5 finely chopped green onions
2/3 cup coarsely chopped fresh cilantro, or 2 teaspoons dried oregano added to rice with stock

1.
Combine stock, beer, tomato juice, salt, pepper, coriander, and chilies in a bowl and set aside.

2.
In a heavy sauté pan, heat oil on medium and add chopped yellow onion. Cook just until limp, then add garlic and sauté another 2 minutes.

3.
Using a slotted spoon remove onion mixture to a Dutch oven. Add rice to remaining oil and sauté, stirring constantly, until rice takes on a light-brown toasted color.

4.
Transfer rice to the Dutch oven and add the stock mixture, stirring well. Bring to a rapid boil then lower to a slow simmer. Cover and cook 20 minutes.

5.
Remove from heat and allow to rest 5 minutes. Stir in green onions and cilantro and serve.

VARIATIONS

Add sliced black olives, peas, or corn; use all broth or all tomato juice; add toasted sliced almonds; add slices of freshly roasted green chilies.

MÄRZEN-GLAZED NEW POTATOES

These tasty, braised potatoes have a more intense flavor than their boiled cousins.

Serves 4 to 6

3 tablespoons butter
2 tablespoons olive oil
1 1/2 pounds new red potatoes
(or quartered medium red potatoes)
1/2 cup Märzen beer
1 1/2 teaspoons thyme, crushed rosemary
or mixed herbs
1 teaspoon kosher salt
1/2 teaspoon freshly ground black pepper
1/4 cup finely chopped Italian (flat-leafed)
parsley

1.
Heat the butter and olive oil in a heavy pan over medium until hot. Add the potatoes and sauté, stirring occasionally for 10 minutes.

2.
Add the beer and herbs, simmering briskly until the beer is reduced to 1 to 2 tablespoons on the bottom of the pan.

3.
Season with salt and pepper. Cover, lower heat to low, and cook 10 minutes, stirring every 3 minutes.

4.
Remove the lid, turn the heat up to medium. Brown the potatoes, shaking the pan frequently to prevent scorching. Garnish with chopped parsley.

Märzenbier, *sometimes called Vienna, is a blond bottom-fermented German beer with medium to strong alcohol content. Historically it was brewed especially strong in March to survive the many months of maturation and was not served until Oktoberfest.*

HERBED BUTTER

The base for some wonderful dishes, everything from herbed vegetables to a luscious hot steak. Adjust herbs to your preferences and ingredients on hand.

1.

Cream butter with salt and beer.

2.

Blend in remaining ingredients and let stand at room temperature at least 1 hour.

1 cup butter, room temperature
1/4 teaspoon salt
2 tablespoons light lager or pale ale
1 teaspoon chervil
2 tablespoons minced chives
1 shallot, finely minced
1 scant teaspoon dried thyme, basil, marjoram, or mixed herbs
1 tablespoon fresh Italian (flat-leafed) parsley, minced (optional)
1 small clove garlic, finely minced (optional)
1/4 teaspoon finely ground black pepper

APPLE CIDER BUTTER

This is not the usual puréed apple butter. Flavored with cider or mead and plenty of spices, it is a chunky, intensely flavored spread. If you live near apple country, take advantage of the fall harvest and preserve sizable amounts for holiday gifts.

1.

Peel, core, and thinly slice apples. Place with cider and apple juice in a heavy 6-quart Dutch oven. Cover and simmer slowly until apples are tender.

2.

Using a potato masher or back of a large spoon, lightly mash until you have a 60-to-40 ratio of mashed-to-chunky pieces. ▼

6 pounds flavorful cooking apples (Granny Smith, Winesap, Pippin)
1 cup cider or sweet mead
1/2 cup frozen apple juice concentrate (undiluted), or strong fresh cider
cheesecloth bag
1 teaspoon whole cloves
1 teaspoon whole allspice
pinch of salt
1 1/2 cups granulated sugar
1 1/2 cups firmly packed brown sugar
juice and finely minced zest of 1 lemon
4 thick cinnamon sticks
1/2 teaspoon ground nutmeg

3.

Tie cloves and allspice into cheesecloth and add to apples along with salt, sugars, lemon juice, cinnamon sticks, and nutmeg. Stir and slowly bring to a rapid boil. Lower to medium.

4.

Cook, stirring constantly, until apple butter falls in a sheet from a metal spoon. Remove and discard cinnamon sticks and spice bag.

5.

Ladle into hot sterilized jars and seal by proper canning method or cool and place in a crock for immediate use.

VARIATIONS

❧ Robust cooking pears such as Bosc can be used to replace half the apples for an apple-pear cider butter.

❧ Add 1/2 cup apple brandy after cooling for a delightful morning eye-opener.

EUREKA DRESSING

1.

Warm butter and syrup on medium-low, add sugar and stir until dissolved.

2.

Add beer and cream. Bring to a slow boil and cook without stirring for 6 minutes. Cool.

3.

When cool, combine the caramel sauce with vinegar and allow to stand 10 minutes before using. Refrigerate remaining dressing, warm gently on stove or in microwave oven, stirring well before using.

1/2 cup unsalted butter

1/3 cup Lyles Golden Syrup (see Note) or corn syrup

1 cup raw sugar, ground finely in a blender

1/2 cup Vienna lager

1/2 cup heavy cream

1/3 to 1/2 cup balsamic vinegar (to taste)

Makes about 2 1/2 cup

During a cooking class I demonstrated a lovely caramel dressing for fresh fruit salad. In a moment of inspiration I stirred in some balsamic vinegar and eureka, a to-die-for dressing, the likes of which you have never encountered!

NOTE

Lyles Golden Syrup is a buttery caramel-flavored cane syrup made in England.

VARIATION

Add poppy seeds when stirring in the vinegar for an incredible poppy-seed dressing.

RASPBERRY DRESSING

A delightfully light salad dressing suffused with the intensity of raspberries.

Makes about 2 cups

1 shallot, peeled and quartered
1 1/4 cups vegetable oil
1/2 cup framboise
1 to 2 tablespoons seedless raspberry
preserves warmed (to taste)
1/3 cup fresh or frozen raspberries, lightly
crushed
salt and pepper to taste

1.

Press the shallot through a garlic press, discarding dry pulp. Whisk together shallot, oil, framboise, and preserves.

2.

When ready to serve, stir in crushed raspberries. Season to taste.

CREAMY WEISSBIER DRESSING

Makes 1 1/2 cups

8 ounces cream cheese
1/3 cup honey (to taste)
3 tablespoons weissbier or pale ale
1/4 teaspoon almond extract
1 teaspoon cinnamon

1.

Process cream cheese and honey in a mixer or food processor until smooth and fluffy.

2.

Add beer, almond extract, and cinnamon. Allow to stand 10 minutes before using.

BEER SYRUP

Try Belgian waffles with a spoonful of this beer-flavored syrup on top!

Makes about
2 cups

1/2 stick butter
2 eggs
2 cups sugar
3/4 cup doppelbock, old ale, Scotch ale, or
  other full-bodied beer
1 teaspoon vanilla

1.

Melt butter in a large saucepan. In a medium bowl, beat eggs into sugar until fluffy. Slowly add beer, whisking thoroughly.

2.

Add beer mixture to the butter and stir. Slowly bring to a full rolling boil. Boil on medium 6 to 8 minutes without stirring.

3.

Remove and stir in vanilla. Cool and store in refrigerator.

Doppelbock, or *"double"* bock, is a stronger version of bock beer. It ranges from 7.5 percent up to 13 percent alcohol by volume. It was first brewed in Bavaria by Italian monks who named the brew Salvator, or Saviour.

Early Americans were proud of their beer. In 1788, Boston minister Jeremy Belknap sent his recipe for spruce beer to Dr. Benjamin Rush. He called it "the most superlatively excellent beer in the world (made) by boiling the spruce in maple sap; I know of no other liquor in the universe that can match it."

CHAPTER 10
DESSERTS

The very thought of combining beer and sugar is considered shocking to the uninitiated. After all, beer doesn't go with anything sweet, or does

it? The answer is not just yes, but absolutely! Desserts prepared with beer have a delectable quality all their own. Few ingredients impart such uniqueness to dessert as the flavor of quality beer.

Those very characteristics we appreciate in an outstanding beer — the exquisite interplay of grain with the bitter qualities of hops — will magically balance the overwhelming sweetness of sugar, which so often dominates the world of desserts.

This weaving of qualities makes the addition of beer to desserts not only exciting, but downright indispensable.

A classic example of this unlikely marriage is Jessie Mahoney's Chocolate, Stout and Bourbon Pie (see page 255). A modest blend of sugar, eggs, chocolate, stout, and whiskey is transformed into an incredibly sumptuous dessert, extraordinarily rich yet not overly sweet.

Before you get started, let me remind you that desserts often demand specific times and ingredients. It is crucial that you read the recipe through before beginning and that you have all ingredients measured and assembled beforehand. To review some of the basic techniques in making great desserts see pages 13 through 15.

CREATING YOUR OWN DESSERT RECIPES

When adding beer to a dessert recipe, remember that texture will play a big role in the amount of beer you can use. ▼

Enchanted Apricot Tart, page 271. ►

When the recipe calls for water you can substitute all or part with beer.

Using beer in place of dairy products in a dessert recipe is a little more complex but can be accomplished with a few guidelines. Milk-based dairy products add tenderness, flavor, and are often used for leavening. Study the function of each dairy product before substituting with beer.

Milk, cream, or sour cream are added to leavened desserts (cake, biscuits) for tenderness, leavening, and flavor. They can be replaced by combining beer with other dairy products.

When a recipe calls for 1 cup milk, substitute 3/4 cup beer combined with 1/2 cup dry milk powder.

If a recipe calls for 1 cup light cream or half-and-half, substitute 1/2 cup beer combined with 1/2 cup heavy cream.

When heavy cream is used in a recipe that will be cooked, for each cup of heavy cream substitute 1/4 cup of beer combined with 3/4 cup of whipping cream.

When sour cream is used in a recipe that will be cooked, for each cup of sour cream substitute 1/3 cup beer combined with 1/3 cup dry milk powder and 2/3 cup sour cream.

Beer cannot be used to replace cream if the cream must be whipped.

When you desire an abundance of beer essence but are limited in the amount you can add, use a robust, hearty-flavored beer.

BUTTER-N-BEER CAKE

Makes an 8-inch 2-layer cake

Surprisingly easy to prepare, this scrumptious butter cake is moist and delectable. Most yellow butter cakes are typically mild, but the beer provides substantial flavoring. No need to fret that the frosting will overwhelm the flavor of this cake!

2 8-inch round buttered cake pans
2 cups unbleached flour
1 1/2 cups sugar
1 teaspoon salt
3 teaspoons baking powder (sifted)
1/2 teaspoon baking soda (sifted)
1 cup weissbier
1/2 cup dry powdered milk
2 teaspoons vanilla
3 large eggs
1/2 cup butter, room temperature

1.
Heat oven to 350°. Butter and flour 2 8-inch round cake pans.

2.
Combine flour, sugar, salt, baking powder, and soda in a large bowl. In a separate bowl combine beer, powered milk, vanilla, and eggs, whisking well.

3.
Add butter to the dry ingredients and mix until crumbly. Add 1/3 of the liquid to the flour and beat 4 minutes. Add remaining liquid and beat 2 minutes.

4.
Divide batter evenly between pans. Bake at 350° for 25 minutes or until a pick inserted into the middle comes out clean. Cool 5 minutes before inverting onto a cooling rack.

5.
Frost with fruit frostings (see page 236) or as desired.

VARIATION
Add 2 tablespoons finely chopped lemon or orange zest to the batter for a citrus cake.

VERSATILE FRUIT FROSTINGS

1.

Beat butter until very soft, add powdered sugar and beat until crumbly. Scrape the sides of the bowl often.

2.

Add the vanilla and juice concentrate and beat until light and fluffy.

3.

If more moisture is needed add milk, cream, or beer 1 teaspoon at a time.

1/2 cup butter, room temperature
3 1/2 cups powdered sugar, sifted
1 teaspoon vanilla
3 to 4 tablespoons frozen juice
   concentrate, thawed and undiluted

Makes 1 cup

The variety of interesting frozen juice concentrates on the market makes this a quick and refreshing frosting. In a flash you can create tropical passion fruit-banana frosting, mandarin-tangerine frosting, or quick orange- or apple-cinnamon frosting.

Beer and pastry have a long tradition together. In private homes in eighteenth and nineteenth century America, ale and cakes were commonly served as refreshments for guests. Many late nineteenth and early twentieth century saloons sold large wedges of homemade pie to customers to accompany their beer.

APPLE & BRIE TURNOVERS

These exceptional turnovers are a combination of beer-glazed apples crowned with blue-veined Brie and wrapped in puff pastry. Because of the convenience of store-bought puff pastry, this sophisticated turnover is wonderfully simple to prepare.

Makes 2 large turnovers or 4 to 8 small turnovers

1.
Defrost puff pastry 20 minutes and place in the refrigerator until ready to fill.

2.
Peel, core, and thinly slice apples, sprinkle with mead, tossing well to coat. Stir together sugar and cornstarch, set aside.

3.
Heat butter in a heavy-bottomed skillet on medium heat until the foam subsides. Add apples and coat with butter. Turn up heat to medium-high and sauté just until limp. Remove apples with a slotted spoon. Reduce the juices on high until only 2 tablespoons remain. Reserve for glaze.

4.
Sprinkle the sugar and cornstarch mixture over apples and toss well. Stir in cinnamon, vanilla, brandy, and preserves. Cool. ▼

1 box frozen puff pastry dough, thawed (2 sheets)
6 large Granny Smith apples
1/3 cup mead or still cider
1/2 to 2/3 cup sugar
2 tablespoons cornstarch
3 tablespoons butter
1 teaspoon each vanilla extract and ground cinnamon
1 tablespoon apple, apricot, or plain brandy (optional)
1/3 cup orange marmalade or apricot preserves
8 to 10 ounces blue-veined Brie (or classic Brie, if not available) with rind, chilled and sliced
2/3 cup toasted walnuts, coarsely chopped (optional)
1 beaten egg
1/3 cup superfine sugar (run through a blender or food processor)

5.

For 2 large turnovers, place half the apples in the middle of one puff pastry square. Top with half the Brie slices, sprinkle with half the nuts, and fold the top over into a triangle. Pinch edges together, crimping to seal.

For smaller turnovers, cut each square of dough into halves or fourths and continue, using smaller amounts of filling and making 4 to 8 individual turnovers.

6.

Slit top decoratively and brush with beaten egg and reduced juices (glaze). Place in refrigerator until 30 minutes before serving.

7.

Quickly brush with glaze again, reopen slits if necessary and sprinkle with superfine sugar. Place in a 375° oven for 35 to 40 minutes while you are enjoying supper.

8.

When finished baking, allow to cool briefly on the baking sheet.

SERVING SUGGESTION

Serve warm with a sprinkling of powdered sugar and a dollop of cream or scoop of French vanilla ice cream.

APPLE CRISP

**Makes 1
12 x 12-inch dish**

1.

In a large bowl, combine sugars, oats, flour, cinnamon, ginger, nutmeg, and salt. Cut in butter until crumbly and evenly distributed.

2.

Peel, core, and slice apples and toss in bowl with cider. Sprinkle one-quarter of the flour mixture over the apples and stir lightly.

3.

Generously butter a 12 x 12-inch baking dish, add apples, and sprinkle the remaining flour mixture over top.

4.

Place on lower oven rack and bake at 350° for about 45 to 50 minutes, or until apples are tender and the top brown and bubbly. Cool slightly before serving.

1 1/2 cups brown sugar
1/2 cup granulated sugar (optional)
2 cups rolled oats
1 1/3 cups unbleached flour
1 1/2 tablespoons cinnamon
2 teaspoons ground ginger
1/2 teaspoon freshly grated nutmeg
1 teaspoon salt (optional)
2 sticks cold butter or margarine
8 large Granny Smith or 12 cups sliced cooking apples
3/4 cup still or sparkling cider
12 x 12-inch baking dish

Ah, the aroma of apple crisp bubbling in the oven is one that few can resist. This version uses cider to intensify the apple essence. Serve hot with a scoop of French vanilla ice cream or a drizzling of heavy cream for sheer decadence.

VARIATIONS

❧ Soak raisins in cider or brandy and add before baking.

❧ Use a combination of fresh fruits in season — apples and pears, plums and nectarines, apricots and peaches — for a wide variety of crisps.

PEACH COBBLER

Another traditional fruit dessert, cobblers are a kissin' cousin to crisps but crowned with biscuits in place of crumb topping. A charming finish to any meal, and the beer adds a downright scrumptious distinction.

1.

Combine flour, sugar, baking powder, and salt. Cut in butter until crumbly. Add egg, vanilla, and beer. Stir just until the dough clings together.

2.

Knead gently 8 strokes. Cover and allow to rest while you pre-pare fruit. Roll or pat dough 3/4 inch thick and cut into rounds or fanciful shapes.

BISCUIT TOPPING
1 1/2 cups unbleached flour
1/3 cup sugar
1 1/2 teaspoons baking powder
pinch of salt
6 tablespoons butter
1 egg yolk, lightly beaten
1 teaspoon vanilla
1/2 cup pale ale mixed with 1/3 cup dry
   powdered milk

1.

Generously butter a 8 x 8-inch baking dish. Mix sugar, corn-starch, cinnamon, and zest, set aside. Heat oven to 350°.

2.

Slice peaches thickly and arrange in dish, cover with berries. Scatter the sugar mixture evenly over the fruit and sprinkle with beer.

3.

Top with biscuits and dust lightly with sugar. Bake on shelf in lower half of oven until fruit is thick and bubbly and biscuits are golden. Cool 10 minutes before serving.

FRUIT FILLING
1/2 to 3/4 cup sugar (to taste)
1/4 cup cornstarch
1 teaspoon cinnamon
2 teaspoons finely chopped lemon zest
4 cups peaches (or plums or cherries)
1 pint blueberries
1/2 cup peach beer or other light-bodied
   fruit beer
sugar for sprinkling top

HELPFUL HINTS

❧ Use a baking pan or dish with high sides to prevent boilover.

❧ If the biscuits are browning faster than the fruit is cooking, lay a piece of foil shiny-side down over the top.

SWEET POTATO PIE

A unique combination, beer and sweet potatoes unite in a charming pie of fascinating character. Don't forget to spoon warm Lagered Caramel Sauce (page 253) over the top!

Makes 1
10-inch pie

1.

In a food processor fitted with a steel blade, process the flour, sugar, salt, butter, and margarine just until crumbly. Add almond extract to the water and slowly, while the motor is running, add to the flour mixture.

2.

Process until dough begins to cling and form a ball. Knead gently by hand exactly 12 times. Wrap in plastic wrap and refrigerate 30 minutes.

3.

Roll crust on a lightly floured surface from the center using light strokes. When about half the size you will need, roll crust onto the rolling pin and lightly flour the work surface again. Lay out the crust and roll until large enough to fit 10-inch pie pan.

4.

Gently roll crust onto the rolling pin and unroll over the pan, making sure the dough does not stretch. Form a tall fluted edge. Refrigerate 30 minutes. ▼

SWEET PIE CRUST
1 1/4 cups unbleached flour
1/4 cup granulated sugar
1/2 teaspoon salt (optional)
3 tablespoons butter (cold)
3 tablespoons margarine (cold)
1/2 teaspoon almond or vanilla extract
1 to 2 tablespoons cold water or American light lager
plastic wrap

SWEET POTATO FILLING
3 large sweet potatoes
4 tablespoons butter
1 1/2 cups light brown sugar
1/2 teaspoon salt
1/2 teaspoon ground allspice
1 teaspoon ground ginger
4 extra-large eggs
1 cup brown ale
1/2 cup dry powdered milk
1 cup buttermilk

HELPFUL HINT

❧ To support a tall fluted edge, wrap a 2-inch-wide strip of foil around outside edge of the pan before baking.

❧ If you do not have a food processor, a sturdy hand-held pastry blender will provide the same results.

1.

Prick sweet potatoes well with a fork and bake in the oven or microwave until tender. Cool briefly, split, and scoop out pulp. Mash and measure the cooked pulp (there should be about 3 1/2 cups). Stir butter into the hot pulp.

2.

In a separate bowl combine sugar, salt, allspice, ginger, and eggs. Beat until light and fluffy. Add beer, powdered milk, butter-milk, and potato pulp, whisking thoroughly.

3.

Pour into prepared crust and bake at 450° for 10 minutes. Reduce to 325° and bake 45 to 50 minutes (or until the filling is set). Cool and serve with Lagered Caramel Sauce or lightly whipped cream.

NUT BRITTLE

1.

In a heavy pan combine sugar, syrup, beer, and salt. Thoroughly dissolve sugar over medium-low, stirring constantly.

2.

Raise heat to medium-high and cook, without stirring, until syrup measures 300° on a candy ther-mometer. In the meantime, com-bine melted butter, nuts, soda, and vanilla. Set aside in a warm place.

▼

Makes 1 1/2 pounds

2 cups sugar
1 cup Lyles Golden Syrup (see Note) or corn syrup
1/2 cup Vienna beer
pinch of salt
candy thermometer
3 tablespoons butter, melted
2 cups roasted unsalted peanuts
1 1/2 teaspoons baking soda
1 teaspoon vanilla

Ordinary brittle will never do once you have tasted this luscious beer-enhanced version. Try the hazelnut-cashew variety for the ultimate brittle experience!

3.

Remove syrup from heat and immediately stir in the butter-nut mixture. Work fast, this hardens quickly.

4.

Pour into buttered 9 x 12-inch baking pan and cool. Break into pieces and store in an airtight container.

NOTE

Lyles Golden Syrup is a buttery caramel-flavored cane syrup made in England.

VARIATIONS

❧ Use 1 cup roasted cashews and 1 cup roasted hazelnuts (with skins removed) for an indulgent confection.

❧ For homebrewers, try using pale malt in place of the nuts for beer brittle that is beer enhanced from top to bottom.

AMBER RICE PUDDING

Serves 12 to 14

A rich caramel-flavored rice pudding bursting with the essence of cinnamon and brown ale. For extra flavor, try soaking raisins in mead, wine, or brandy before baking.

6 cups whole milk
4 tablespoons butter
1 cinnamon stick
4 cups short-grain white rice
3 cups brown ale
1 cup milk
6 large eggs
3 cups white or dark raisins
2 large tart apples, peeled, cored, and grated (optional)
1 tablespoon ground cinnamon
1 1/2 tablespoons vanilla
1 cup honey
2 cups brown sugar

1.

Bring milk, butter, and cinnamon stick to a slow simmer in a large saucepan. Add rice, cover, and simmer 20 minutes. Remove from heat and allow to stand 10 minutes. Remove cinnamon stick and cool briefly.

2.

Combine remaining ingredients in a large bowl and blend thoroughly. Add rice and pour into a large 5-quart casserole, generously buttered.

3.

Bake at 350° until most of the liquid has been absorbed and the top is golden around the edges.

CHOCOLATE & BEER

Out they come and one is sampled — for quality control, of course. You take a sip of beer, a bite of cookie, another sip, another bite, and before you know it, voilà!, you have discovered the joys of chocolate and beer.

From that moment on you know the two were meant for each other and you become hard pressed not to incorporate beer into any recipe that includes chocolate.

Of course, the notion of combining chocolate and beer can be a bit overwhelming; after all, they are at opposite ends of the flavor scale. Nonetheless, opposites do attract. If you are not convinced, sample this oddly delicious combination at least once before passing final judgment.

Your earliest experience of this combination is usually an innocent one. Perhaps you are sipping a lovely English porter when the timer goes off and the chocolate chip cookies are done.

CHOCOLATE MARBLE CHEESECAKE

Makes 1 10-inch cheesecake

Cheesecake with beer in it? Just wait until you try a piece of this luscious phenomenon of creamy cheesecake swirled with a scandalous mixture of chocolate and sweet stout.

CRUST

1 1/2 cups unbleached flour
1/2 cup sugar
1 teaspoon salt
5 tablespoons chilled butter or margarine, cut into pieces
1 extra-large egg
1/2 teaspoon almond extract
1 teaspoon vanilla extract

FILLING

1 3/4 pounds cream cheese (3 1/2 8-ounce packages)
2 cups sugar
2 teaspoons vanilla
6 extra-large eggs
1 1/3 cups heavy cream
1 cup Dutch-process dark cocoa powder
1/3 cup vegetable oil
1/2 cup sweet stout
1 teaspoon almond extract

1.

In a medium mixing bowl or food processor, mix the flour, sugar, and salt. Cut in butter or margarine until crumbs are the size of large peas.

2.

In a separate bowl, mix egg, almond, and vanilla extract. Sprinkle the liquid into the flour mixture, stirring just until combined and no trace of flour is left. It should be crumbly but hold together when pressed lightly.

3.

Lightly butter or grease 10-inch springform pan. Press crust onto the sides and bottom of the pan forming a thin, uniform crust.

4.

Repeat the process, covering the bottom. Use a small cookie cutter to flute the top edge. Refrigerate.

1.

Heat oven to 325°. Beat cream cheese, sugar, and vanilla until very light and sugar crystals are dissolved.

2.

Add eggs all at once and beat on low just until blended, being sure to scrape the sides and bottom of the bowl. ▼

3.

Add heavy cream and stir just until blended. Set a scant 2 cups of batter aside. Pour half the remaining plain batter into the prepared springform pan.

4.

Stir the cocoa powder with vegetable oil until smooth. Whisk in the beer and almond extract.

5.

Stirring constantly, slowly add the 2 cups of reserved batter to the chocolate.

6.

Pour half the chocolate mixture over the plain cheesecake mixture in the pan using a zigzag motion. Gently spoon the remaining plain batter over the first marbled layer.

7.

Zigzag the remaining chocolate batter over top. Draw a sharp knife through the mixture in a zigzag motion without disturbing the crust to marbleize.

8.

Place in preheated oven and bake at 325° for 60 to 70 minutes or until the center appears nearly set. Turn oven off, prop door open, and allow cheesecake to cool completely.

9.

Remove sides of springform pan carefully, running a knife around the edge first, if necessary. Chill.

NOTES

❧ Always have eggs and cream cheese at room temperature.

❧ The cream cheese must be beaten until smooth before adding sugar.

❧ Sugar must be completely dissolved before adding the other ingredients or cheesecake will have a granular quality.

❧ Most cracks in the top of cheesecake occur from baking in a too-hot oven or rushing the cooling process.

CHOCOLATE STOUT CAKE

The most memorable chocolate cake you can imagine. The richness of cocoa and the robust flavor of stout are blended into a moist cake that can be eaten unadorned or enhanced with the lavish chocolate frosting (recipe follows).

Makes 1 8-inch
2-layer cake

1/4 cup cocoa powder (to dust the baking pans)
2 sticks butter or margarine
1 cup stout or porter
2/3 cup (scant) Dutch-process dark cocoa powder
1 scant teaspoon salt
2 cups unbleached flour
2 cups sugar
1 1/4 teaspoon baking soda, sifted
2 extra-large eggs
1/2 cup sour cream

1.
Heat oven to 350°. Lightly dust 2 greased 8-inch springform pans with cocoa powder.

2.
In a heavy saucepan or micro-wave oven, heat butter, beer, and cocoa powder until butter melts. Cool.

3.
Sift dry ingredients together, add the beer-cocoa mixture, and beat thoroughly 1 minute on medium speed. Add eggs and sour cream and beat 2 minutes on medium.

4.
Pour batter into prepared pans and bake at 350° for 25 to 30 min-utes, or until a pick inserted into the middle comes out clean. Place pans on a wire rack, cool 10 min-utes, remove the sides, and cool completely.

5.
Use a long serrated knife to even tops of the cakes. Using a flexible spatula, spread each layer with a thin coating of chocolate frosting, stack, and cover the sides with frosting.

Diamond Jim Brady's *usual habit after eating a gargantuan dinner was to have for dessert an entire tray of French pastries followed by the leisurely consumption of two pounds of chocolates.*

UNFORGETTABLY CHOCOLATE FROSTING

1.
Place chocolate and butter into the bowl of a food processor.

2.
In a medium saucepan combine heavy cream, stout, and powdered sugar, stirring until smooth. Heat to a slow boil.

3.
While motor is running, slowly pour the hot liquid into the chocolate and butter and blend until smooth. Add liqueur and cool before spreading.

12 ounces high quality, extra-bitter chocolate, chopped, or semisweet chocolate chips
8 tablespoons butter
3/4 cup heavy cream
1/4 cup stout
3 cups powdered sugar, sifted
2 tablespoons liqueur – Amaretto, Frangelico, or Kahlua (optional)

NOTE
Do not overprocess or frosting may separate.

CHOCOLATE-BEER MOUSSE WITH RASPBERRY SAUCE

Serves 10

Intrigued by the combination of dark beer and chocolate? Then uniting them in a luscious raspberry-topped mousse is not only logical but sheer eating bliss.

16 ounces high-quality semisweet chocolate chips or extra-bitter baking chocolate, chopped
3/4 cup stout, room temperature
3 tablespoons Kahlua
8 large eggs, room temperature, separated
1 1/4 cups whipping cream, chilled
1 teaspoon vanilla extract
1/2 cup sugar
1/2 teaspoon cream of tartar
mint sprigs, to garnish

1.

Melt chocolate slowly in top of double boiler. Remove from heat, stir in stout and Kahlua until smooth.

2.

Beating thoroughly after each addition, add yolks to the chocolate mixture, two at a time. Set aside.

3.

Whip cream, vanilla, and sugar until stiff peaks form. Refrigerate while you beat egg whites.

4.

Using a clean bowl and beaters, beat egg whites with cream of tartar until stiff.

5.

Gently fold egg whites and whipped cream together. Slowly fold one-fourth of this mixture into the chocolate mixture. Fold the remaining whipped mixture into the chocolate until no traces of white or lumps are visible.

6.

Spoon into goblets and refrigerate. Serve with a tablespoon of Raspberry Sauce (recipe follows) and garnish with a sprig of mint.

RASPBERRY SAUCE

24 ounces fresh or frozen raspberries
1 cup sugar
1 1/2 cups Beaujolais wine
1 1/2 cups blackberry ale, or raspberry or blackberry porter
1 cup seedless raspberry preserves
1/2 teaspoon finely ground black pepper, freshly ground

1.
Combine all ingredients in a heavy saucepan. Bring to a slow boil and simmer until reduced by half.

2.
Strain through a fine sieve and cool.

Don't let the odd ingredients deceive you, this turns into the most full-flavored, luscious raspberry sauce ever. And yes, the black pepper does belong!

CHOCOLATE-CHOCOLATE STOUT ICE CREAM

An intensely chocolate ice cream, heightened to perfection by the addition of oatmeal stout. It is extravagant, silky, and not registered under diet desserts.

Makes a generous quart

1 cup stout (oatmeal is my favorite)
1 cup heavy cream
1 1/2 cups half-and-half
1/3 cup Lyles Golden Syrup (see Note) or honey
4 to 5 ounces extra-bitter chocolate, chopped
9 large egg yolks
2/3 to 3/4 cup sugar
3/4 cup Dutch-process cocoa powder, sifted
candy thermometer

1.

Heat beer, cream, half-and-half, and Lyles Golden Syrup until hot. Pour over the chopped baking chocolate and stir until chocolate melts. Cover and set aside.

2.

Beat egg yolks and sugar until light and fluffy. Slowly add the cocoa powder and mix until well-combined.

3.

In a thin stream, slowly add the hot beer-cream mixture to the egg mixture while beating on medium speed.

4.

Transfer to a double boiler or heavy pan and cook slowly until slightly thickened. A candy thermometer should read 170° at this stage.

5.

Pour through a fine sieve and allow to cool. Chill thoroughly.

6.

Pour the mixture into ice-cream maker and proceed with factory directions for freezing.

NOTE

Lyles Golden Syrup is a buttery caramel-flavored cane syrup made in England.

HELPFUL HINT

Straining custards through a fine sieve before cooling breaks up the coagulating properties of the eggs for a satin-smooth texture.

PORTER-N-RUM CHOCOLATE DESSERT SAUCE

Makes about 3 1/2 cups

This luscious chocolate sauce is divine on ice cream. Try it warm with fresh fruits for a dipping sauce or pack in a pretty jar for gift giving (if you can part with it, that is!) I have heard rumors it is marvelous just spooned out of a jar and devoured on its own!

8 tablespoons unsalted butter
1/4 cup vegetable oil
1 1/3 cup Dutch-process dark cocoa powder
1/3 cup rum vanilla (see Note)
2/3 cup strong porter
2 cups sugar
1/2 cup Lyles Golden Syrup (see Note) or
   corn syrup
1/2 teaspoon salt
1 1/2 teaspoons vanilla

1.

Place butter, oil, and cocoa powder in a heavy saucepan on medium low. Stir until butter has melted. Add remaining ingredients except vanilla.

2.

Bring to a boil over medium. Do not stir once the liquid begins to boil. When boiling, lower to medium-low and cook for about 10 minutes. When done the sauce should look thick and glossy and coat a spoon.

3.

Remove from heat and cool just until warm. Stir in the vanilla and finish cooling.

NOTES

❧ Rum vanilla is delicious and easy to make. Simply buy a bottle of dark rum, split a vanilla bean, and place it in the bottle. Age for at least 2 weeks; 2 months is better.

❧ Lyles Golden Syrup is a buttery caramel-flavored cane syrup made in England.

LAGERED CARAMEL SAUCE

Makes about 4 cups

This luscious alliance of Oktoberfest beer, sugar, and cream is incredible served over bread pudding or ice cream. The unique qualities of the lager temper the sweetness of the sauce while adding a sumptuous dimension of flavor.

2 1/2 cups firmly packed brown sugar
1 1/2 cups light corn syrup
6 tablespoons unsalted butter
1/2 teaspoon salt
1/3 cup Oktoberfest beer
candy thermometer
4 teaspoons vanilla extract
2 cups heavy cream

1.
In a heavy pan mix sugar, corn syrup, butter, salt, and beer over low heat, stirring constantly.

2.
When sugar is dissolved, bring mixture to a boil and cook without stirring until it reaches 235° on a candy thermometer.

3.
Remove from heat and gently stir in vanilla. Allow to cool 10 minutes, stirring occasionally.

4.
Slowly stir in cream until smooth and glossy. Store in refrigerator and warm gently before serving.

The phrase "that's a lot of cock 'n bull" comes from two pubs in an English town, The Cock and The Bull, that became notorious for filling travelers' ears with wild stories that would rapidly spread. The pub names became synonymous with the unbelievable.

RASPBERRY DESSERT SAUCE

This intensely flavored sauce can also be made with blackberries or blueberries and served over Yeasty Belgian Waffles (see page 209) for a dramatic breakfast.

Makes about 2 cups

1 1/2 pounds fresh or frozen raspberries
sugar (to taste)
zest of 1 lemon, finely chopped
1/2 cup sugar (adjust to sweetness of berries)
1/4 cup raspberry lambic
1/4 cup raspberry syrup (see Note) or seedless raspberry preserves

1.

Defrost raspberries in a colander, saving juice.

2.

When thawed and drained, press half the fruit through a food press or sieve to remove seeds. Combine the sieved pulp with reserved juices, lemon zest, and sugar.

3.

On medium-high, reduce by half. Remove from heat and cool. Stir the lambic and the raspberry syrup or preserves into the reduced juice.

NOTE

Use raspberry syrup found in Middle Eastern Markets.

Lambic is a unique Belgian wheat beer produced in a very small area around Brussels. The mash is 60 to 70 percent barley, 30 to 40 percent wheat, and is spontaneously fermented with wild yeasts and bacteria. Young lambic has a sour flavor, but when older it acquires a bittersweet flavor.

JESSIE MAHONEY'S CHOCOLATE, STOUT, & BOURBON PIE

An unpretentious combination of chocolate, eggs, stout, brown sugar, and bourbon that will send your taste buds reeling.

Makes 1
10-inch pie

1 1/2 cups dark brown sugar, lightly packed

1/4 cup flour

1/3 cup cornmeal

6 extra-large eggs

1 1/2 cups granulated sugar

2 teaspoons vanilla

3/4 cup stout

1/3 cup fine bourbon (the sipping kind)

1 cup high-quality semisweet chocolate chips

10-inch pie plate lined with unbaked sweet pie crust (see page 241)

whipped cream

1.
Stir together the brown sugar, flour, and cornmeal.

2.
Beat eggs with granulated sugar until thick and light in color.

3.
Add vanilla, stout, and bourbon to the brown sugar mixture, stirring to eliminate lumps. Fold in the beaten egg mixture and chocolate chips.

4.
Pour into crust and bake at 350° for 40 to 45 minutes, or until the center is set.

5.
Cool just until warm and serve with a dollop of whipped cream.

ZABAGLIONE

An Italian wine custard, this voluptuous dessert is made with the famous Belgian beer known as Trappist ale. My favorite way to serve Zabaglione is over fresh fruit perched atop puff pastry hearts.

8 egg yolks
2/3 cup sugar
1 tablespoon regular or vanilla sugar (see Note)
1 cup Trappist ale

1.
In a stainless-steel bowl, whisk the yolks, sugar, and vanilla sugar until lemon colored. Slowly whisk in the Trappist ale.

2.
Place bowl over a pan of simmering water and continue whisking until very smooth and fluffy. Serve immediately.

PUFF PASTRY HEARTS
1 package frozen puff pastry, thawed
Lyles Golden Syrup (see Note) or honey

1.
Unfold one piece of frozen puff pastry (thawed), cut with a large heart cookie cutter. Wrap and refreeze remaining pastry.

2.
Brush hearts with Lyles Golden Syrup or honey and bake at 350° until puffy and golden.

HELPFUL HINTS

Zabaglione should be served immediately, so have the puff pastry baked, the yolks separated, all ingredients measured, and simmering water ready beforehand.

NOTES

❧ To make vanilla sugar, store whole vanilla bean in canister of sugar for one month.

❧ Lyles Golden Syrup is a buttery caramel-flavored cane syrup made in England.

CRÈME BRULÉE

Serves 4

*S*ilky and sumptuous, this is the ultimate custard. This version is enhanced with a luscious layer of Bavarian malt and Lyles Golden Syrup. For a variation, add a layer of thinly sliced Glazed Pears.

2/3 cup Bavarian light malt syrup, unhopped (see Notes)

1/3 cup Lyles Golden Syrup (see Notes)

2 teaspoons Crème de Cacao liqueur

6 tablespoons butter

1/2 cup plus 1 tablespoon sugar

3 cups heavy cream

2 cinnamon sticks

6 large egg yolks (for a firmer custard use 7 to 8 egg yolks)

2 tablespoons cornstarch

1 1/2 teaspoons vanilla extract

2 tablespoons Crème de Cacao liqueur

SUGAR GLAZE

1/2 cup raw sugar, ground fine in a food processor, or granulated sugar

1.

Stir the malt extract, Lyles Golden Syrup, and 2 teaspoons Crème de Cacao in a bowl. Divide the mixture evenly in 6 oven-proof custard cups or 5 small au gratin dishes. Refrigerate.

2.

In a double boiler combine butter, sugar, 2 cups of cream and cinnamon sticks. Bring to a slow simmer just until the butter melts.

3.

In a large bowl beat the remaining cup of cream, yolks, and cornstarch.

4.

Whisking constantly, slowly pour the cream-yolk mixture into the hot cream in a steady stream. Continue to cook, stirring constantly, at a slow simmer until you see the first bubble pop.

5.

Remove from heat immediately and pour through a fine sieve. Add vanilla and 2 tablespoons Crème de Cacao to the strained custard and whisk thoroughly.

6.

Gently ladle custard into cups over syrup and glazed pears. Chill thoroughly.

7.

Just before serving sprinkle raw sugar evenly over the tops of each custard cup, coating thoroughly.

8.

Broil directly under the broiler or use a small propane torch to caramelize sugar. This must be done under intense heat so the custard doesn't become hot and watery. Serve immediately. ▾

1.

In a food processor, process raw sugar and candied ginger until finely ground.

2.

Heat butter and sugar over medium, stirring constantly. When sugar is partially dissolved, add the beer and sliced pears.

3.

Cook over medium heat until liquid is evaporated and pears are glossy and translucent. Remove and cool.

4.

Spoon glazed pears over syrup before topping with custard.

GLAZED PEARS
FOR CRÈME BRULÉE

2/3 cup raw sugar

2 pieces candied ginger

5 tablespoons butter

1/4 cup Oktoberfest beer

3 large Bosc pears, peeled and sliced
   (seeds and core removed)

NOTES

❀ If you don't have malt extract, use the Lagered Caramel Sauce (page 253) to spread over the bottom of the custard cups.

❀ Lyles Golden Syrup is a buttery caramel-flavored cane syrup made in England.

GINGERED PINEAPPLE SORBET

1.
To prepare simple syrup, combine beer, sugar, and cinnamon stick in a small saucepan.

2.
Simmer and stir until sugar is dissolved. Bring to a slow boil and cover for one minute. Remove lid and continue to boil 4 minutes.

3.
Remove from heat, discard cinnamon stick. Chill.

4.
Combine the simple syrup, ginger, pineapple, lime juice, and rum vanilla. Pour into ice-cream maker and proceed with factory directions for freezing.

1 cup brown ale or Bavarian dark
1 1/2 cups raw sugar, processed until fine in a food processor
1 cinnamon stick
4 large pieces candied ginger, finely minced
3 cups fresh or canned pineapple, finely processed or crushed
3 tablespoons lime or lemon juice
1 to 2 tablespoons rum vanilla (optional) (see Note)

Makes a generous quart

Pineapple, ginger, and beer – harmonious flavors that are truly made for one another. This intriguing combination freezes into a sorbet for a light dessert that complements any meal.

NOTE
To make rum vanilla, add a split vanilla bean to a bottle of rum. Age for at least 2 weeks; 2 months is better.

VARIATION
Try this with peaches or nectarines for a scrumptious alternative.

POACHED PEARS

A

An elegant dessert, these pears taste divine and are easy to make. Don't skip the homemade Crème Fraîche, it is truly sublime!

3 cups granulated sugar or 2 cups packed
brown sugar plus 1 cup granulated sugar
1 1/2 cups water
1 1/2 cups weissbier or mead
1 cinnamon stick
4 whole allspice
3 thin slices lemon
4 large Bosc pears
1/3 cup pear liqueur (see Note)
1 1/2 cups lightly sweetened Crème Fraîche
(see page 35)

1.

Combine sugar, water, and beer in a large sauté pan and bring to a boil. Lower heat to medium and add cinnamon stick, allspice, and lemon slices.

2.

Simmer for 20 minutes, covered. Remove cinnamon, allspice, and lemon, and set aside.

3.

Using a potato peeler, gently peel the pears. Split in half and use a melon baller to remove core. Arrange pear halves in a large sauté pan.

4.

Add the pear liqueur to the syrup and pour over pears. Bring to a slow simmer and poach pears until very tender, turning and basting as needed. Allow to cool in the syrup, cover, and refrigerate 6 to 8 hours.

5.

When ready to serve, drain and fill core with the lightly sweetened Crème Fraîche.

NOTES

❦ In place of liqueur, simmer 12 ounces of pear nectar until reduced to 1/3 cup.

❦ Try large firm peach halves instead of pears and use a peach lambic or other peach beer.

Prehistoric cave drawings show people taking honey for the making of mead.

GLAZED PINEAPPLE

Pineapple glazed in raw sugar and beer with a touch of ginger and vanilla can transform a dish from commonplace to show stopper. Serve in corn crêpes, stuffed into an omelet, as a topping for ice cream, or threaded on skewers with marinated meat for shish kebab.

Makes about 2 1/2 cups

5 tablespoons butter or margarine
1/3 cup raw sugar, processed in a blender until fine
3/4 cup brown or pale ale
3 20-ounce cans pineapple chunks, drained or fresh cut pineapple
1 teaspoon ground ginger or 1 tablespoon minced candied ginger
1 teaspoon vanilla

1.

In a medium skillet, warm butter along with raw sugar and ale, breaking up lumps.

2.

When bubbly, add pineapple and coat thoroughly with glaze. Add ginger and simmer on medium-low, stirring occasionally, until the liquid has evaporated and the pineapple has a glazed appearance.

3.

Stir in vanilla and set aside to cool.

PEACH MELBA SORBET

Makes 1 1/2 quarts

How could a dessert that looks so innocent taste so scandalously rich? The secret is the simple syrup made of beer, sugar, and cinnamon that enlivens the sorbet and gives it a sophisticated twist.

1 cup sparkling cider
1 cup sugar
1 cinnamon stick
1 1/2 cups fresh peach purée (see Note)
1 1/2 cups fresh raspberries or seedless low
   sugar raspberry preserves
1 tablespoon lemon or lime juice

1.
In a small saucepan combine cider, sugar, and cinnamon stick.

2.
Simmer and stir until sugar is dissolved. Bring to a slow boil and cover for 1 minute. Remove lid and continue to boil 4 minutes.

3.
Remove from heat and cool to room temperature. Add remaining ingredients and refrigerate until well-chilled.

4.
Remove cinnamon stick, pour into an ice-cream maker, and proceed with factory directions for freezing.

NOTE
To make purée, peel about 3 ripe peaches, remove pits and mash, or purée in blender until smooth.

VARIATION
Be imaginative and use seasonal fruits when abundant. Strawberries, apricots, plums, nectarines, melons, berries, and tropical fruits can be used individually or in dramatic combinations for this mouth-watering concoction.

FRESH BERRY SHERBET

1.

In a small saucepan combine beer, sugar, cinnamon stick, and lemon zest.

2.

Heat slowly, stirring until sugar is dissolved. Bring to a slow boil, covered, for one minute. Remove lid and continue to boil for 3 minutes.

3.

Remove from heat, strain, and cool to room temperature. Add remaining ingredients and chill.

4.

Pour into an ice-cream maker and proceed with factory directions.

1 cup weisse beer
1 cup sugar
1 cinnamon stick
1 tablespoon finely minced lemon zest
1 1/2 cups puréed blackberries, strained
1 1/2 cups puréed raspberries, strained
2/3 cup heavy whipping cream
1 tablespoon lemon or lime juice

Serves 4 to 6

Get that ice-cream maker out of storage and treat yourself to this simple and refreshing summer indulgence.

ELEGANT BEER-DRESSED FRUIT

1.

Soak figs overnight in ale and cider. Drain, quarter, and halve each quarter.

2.

Arrange fruit on individual plates with fig slices on top. Place a spoonful of Creamy Weissbier Dressing over all and garnish with toasted almonds and strips of orange zest.

10 large dried figs
1/2 cup nut brown ale
1/2 cup fresh cider or strong apple juice
6 cups fruit in any combination (see Note)
1 batch Creamy Weissbier Dressing (page 230)
1/2 cup toasted, sliced, or slivered almonds for garnish
orange zest for garnish (optional)

Serves 8

This lovely combination of fruits is enhanced with beer-soaked figs and a cream-cheese dressing laced with beer.

NOTE

Some favorite combinations are pears, grapes, apples, melons, white raisins, cherries, orange sections, fresh berries, peaches, or nectarines. Toss sliced fruit gently with lime juice to keep it from turning dark.

STUFFED MEAD FIGS

1.

Soak figs overnight in mead and cider.

2.

Cut off stem ends and hollow out center by removing some of the pulp.

3.

Using a pastry bag fitted with a small plain tip, fill with cream cheese whipped with honey and cinnamon. Top each fig with a whole almond.

10 dried Calimyrna figs
2/3 cup mead
1/3 cup strong cider
1 pound cream cheese (2 8-ounce packages)
1/4 cup honey
1 1/2 teaspoons cinnamon
10 toasted whole almonds

Serves 4 to 5

Few words can describe the opulent flavor of these cream-cheese-stuffed, mead-soaked figs.

PUBLICANS PLUM PUDDING

Flavors from long ago come alive in this moist, dense, rich pudding. Brandy and English barley wine lend a truly distinctive flavor. Flambéed with Grand Marnier when served, it is a unique and stunning finish to holiday meals.

1 1/2 cups cake flour
1 1/2 teaspoons cinnamon
scant teaspoon ground ginger
scant teaspoon ground cloves
scant teaspoon baking soda
1/2 teaspoon salt
3/4 cup Lyles Golden Syrup (see Note)
1/3 cup barley wine or Belgian ale
15 tablespoons butter, room temperature
3/4 cup dark brown sugar
3 extra-large eggs
1 cup currants soaked in berry brandy
2/3 cup chopped apricots soaked in peach or apricot brandy
2/3 cup chopped dates
1/2 cup flour
1/2 cup toasted walnuts
1 cup hazelnuts, toasted, skinned, and chopped
1/4 cup Lyles Golden Syrup (see Note)
1/4 cup faro, or fruit brandy such as Grand Marnier

1.

Whisk flour, spices, baking soda, and salt in a small bowl and set aside. Combine the Lyles Golden Syrup and barley wine in a separate bowl and set aside.

2.

Beat butter and sugar until very light and fluffy. Add eggs and beat 1 minute. Stir in the flour and Lyles mixture alternately in thirds. Beat 1 minute.

3.

Toss currants, apricots, and dates in 1/3 cup flour to coat. Stir fruits and nuts into batter. Divide into 2 small or 1 large generously buttered pudding or bundt molds.

4.

Place molds in a large pan filled with 2 inches hot water. Place a buttered lid over each cake (the bottom to a springform pan works well) and bake at 350°.

5.

Bake about 45 minutes for small bundts, 75 minutes for 1 large bundt, or until a pick inserted into the center comes out clean.

6.

Cool for 15 minutes before unmolding. Combine the Lyles Golden Syrup and faro. Baste pudding with the mixture, wrap, and allow to absorb. Reapply as often as necessary.

7.

When ready to serve, flambé with 1/4 cup warmed Grand Marnier.

NOTE

Lyles Golden Syrup is a buttery caramel-flavored cane syrup made in England.

STOUT & WHISKEY TRUFFLES

Makes 3 dozen

Chocolate truffles made from melted chocolate, cream, and, of course, stout make a terrific gift for the chocoholic in your life.

1/3 cup stout
3 tablespoons heavy cream
4 tablespoons sweet butter
1/2 to 2/3 cup powdered sugar (to sweeten very dark chocolate)
8 ounces quality extra-dark chocolate, chopped finely
2 tablespoons quality whiskey or Baileys Irish Cream
1/2 cup pecans, toasted at 350° for 12 minutes and chopped
2/3 cup Dutch-process cocoa powder

1.
Heat stout, heavy cream, butter, and powdered sugar until bubbles form around the edges.

2.
Remove from heat and add chocolate, stirring constantly until completely melted and smooth.

3.
Stir in the whiskey and nuts.

4
Refrigerate until firm, 2 to 4 hours. Use a melon baller or a small scoop to form the mixture into rough ball shapes.

5.
Roll in Dutch-process cocoa powder. Keep cool or refrigerate.

VARIATION

Roll truffles in , toasted nuts, lightly toasted coconut, finely crushed pralines, or dip in additional melted chocolate.

Stout is a very dark, heavy-bodied, top-fermented ale. It is often highly hopped and comes in sweet and dry versions. Dark caramel malt, chocolate, and black malts are commonly used in brewing stout. It was originally called stout porter, as it was a more robust type of porter. It's best known version is Guinness.

PECAN PRALINES

Few candies are as treasured as homemade pralines. Adding the intensity of dark bock makes them positively priceless.

baking parchment
1 1/2 sticks unsalted butter
1 cup granulated sugar
1 cup packed light brown sugar
1/2 cup heavy cream
1 teaspoon baking soda
1/2 cup buttermilk
1/2 cup light or dark bock
candy thermometer
3 cups pecan halves
2 tablespoons vanilla extract

1.

Line a large cookie sheet with parchment and butter generously. In a heavy pan melt butter over high heat and add the sugars, cream, and soda. Cook 1 minute, whisking constantly.

2.

Add buttermilk and beer. Cook, stirring frequently until 200° on a candy thermometer. Add pecans and continue cooking, stirring constantly, until 250°.

3.

Remove pan from heat and beat with a wooden spoon until the mixture cools to 220°, stir in vanilla.

4.

Quickly spoon onto buttered parchment in heaping spoonfuls. Cool and store in airtight container.

CANDY'S ULTIMATE FLAN

Serves 6 to 8

Silky smooth, creamy, and luscious, this caramelized custard dish is not the typical thin, rubbery round commonly served.

1 1/4 cups raw sugar, processed in a food processor
1/3 cup brown ale or Bavarian dark
3 cups half-and-half
3 cups heavy cream
2 thick cinnamon sticks
1 vanilla bean
4 whole eggs
8 egg yolks
1 1/2 cups sugar
1/3 cup Frangelico or Amaretto
1 8-cup round or fluted cake pan or flan mold

1.

In a heavy saucepan heat sugar and ale on medium-low, stirring only until the sugar dissolves.

2.

Turn heat to medium and cook, tipping the pan from side to side until syrup turns a golden brown (do not stir).

3.

When syrup turns the desired color (the darker the color the more burnt the flavor), quickly pour into the cake pan and swirl to cover bottom. Cool while preparing custard (syrup must be hardened before adding the custard).

4.

In a heavy saucepan heat the half-and-half, cream, cinnamon sticks, and vanilla bean to a slow boil (the edges should just begin to bubble). Remove from heat and set aside.

5.

Beat eggs and yolks until frothy, add sugar and continue beating until very light and lemon colored. Beat in the liqueur.

6.

Remove cinnamon sticks and vanilla bean from the hot cream mixture. Whisking constantly, add the egg mixture to the hot cream, pouring in a thin, steady stream. Mix thoroughly.

7.

Pour custard through a fine sieve into the prepared cake pan.

8.

Place the cake pan in a large, high-sided pan in the oven. Fill larger pan with boiling water halfway up the cake pan. Bake at 350° for 35 minutes if using a shallow mold, 45 minutes for a deep mold. It will be done if set when shaken gently.

9.

Remove custard from oven and refrigerate until chilled. Immediately before serving, unmold by dipping bottom of cake pan in hot water for about 30 seconds. Dry the mold and gently shake to loosen flan. Place serving platter on top of the pan, swiftly invert onto the platter, and remove pan.

STOUT FLOAT

For adults only, a Stout Float is a heavenly concoction that should be tried at least once in a lifetime. It starts with a chunk of rich brownie in the bottom of a glass and a generous scoop (or two) of French vanilla ice cream. Fill glass to the rim with your favorite stout. The whole is decadently downed with delight. Try this for next year's holiday libation in place of eggnog.

BROWNIES FOR STOUT FLOAT

Makes 1 9 x 14-inch pan

Although these brownies have no beer among the ingredients, they are perfect for the divine Stout Float. They are extravagant in chocolate flavor and can be the mainstay of many chocolate craving fixes.

1 cup Dutch-process dark cocoa powder
2 1/2 sticks butter or margarine
5 extra-large eggs, room temperature
2 cups sugar
1 tablespoon Kahlua or Crème de Cacao
1 1/2 teaspoons vanilla
1/2 cup unbleached flour

1.
Preheat oven to 350° and prepare pan.

2.
Place cocoa powder and butter in a heat-proof container and warm in microwave oven or on stove top just until butter melts, stirring occasionally.

3.
In a mixing bowl combine eggs, sugar, and Kahlua and beat on medium for a full 5 minutes (if using a hand mixer, beat on medium-high).

4.
Turn mixer to low and add melted butter mixture and flour. Stir just until combined and no streaks of chocolate, egg, or flour remain.

5.
Pour batter into 9 1/2 x 14-inch pan buttered and dusted with cocoa powder and bake at 350° for 25 to 30 minutes, or until a pick inserted into the center comes out clean. Allow brownies to cool in the pan.

GLAZED APPLES FOR DESSERT CRÊPES

1.

Melt butter in large skillet, toss in sugar and apples.

2.

Sauté until apples begin to wilt. Add juice, cinnamon, and cider. Continue to cook until the apples are glazed and the liquid thickens.

Makes about 3 cups

Glazed apples wrapped in rich dessert crêpes form an elegant yet simple finale to any fine meal.

1/2 stick butter
1 cup sugar
8 cooking apples, peeled, cored, and sliced
2 tablespoons frozen apple juice concentrate, undiluted
1 tablespoon cinnamon
1/4 cup still or sparkling cider

1.

Beat eggs and sugar until thick and yellow. Add melted butter, oil, soda, cinnamon, and vinegar. Beat until combined.

2.

Stir in flour and mead. Add water to make a very thin batter (the thickness of thin gravy).

3.

Pour 2 tablespoons batter onto a hot, lightly greased, 8-inch frying pan. Swirl pan quickly and cook until pale gold. Turn and briefly cook other side.

4.

Stack cooked crêpes on a platter. They can be made well in advance if you place wax paper between each layer. ▼

EASY CREPES
Makes 24 to 28

3 large eggs
1/2 cup sugar
1/4 cup melted butter
1/4 cup vegetable oil
1/4 teaspoon baking soda
1 teaspoon cinnamon
3 tablespoons balsamic vinegar
1 1/2 cups unbleached flour
1/2 cup mead

1.

Fill each crêpe with a spoonful of warm glazed apples, a teaspoon of sour cream, a sprinkle of toasted almonds, then roll or fold.

2.

Sprinkle top with powdered sugar and serve immediately.

ASSEMBLING

sour cream
toasted almonds
powdered sugar

ENCHANTED APRICOT TART

1.

Generously butter a 10-inch round loose-bottom tart pan. Place a sheet of phyllo on your work surface and quickly brush with butter. Place phyllo in tart pan and sprinkle with 1 teaspoon of the sugar mixture.

2.

Repeat with 17 more sheets of buttered phyllo, turning the pan so the sheets overlap evenly.

3.

Place the tart pan on a cookie sheet and bake at 375° for 10 to 14 minutes or until golden brown. ▼

Distinctive from crust to filling, this tart is based on crunchy, flaky phyllo leaves layered and baked.

Serves 6 to 8

TART CRUST

10-inch round tart pan
1 package phyllo leaves, halved and placed under a damp towel
3/4 pound unsalted butter, melted
1/3 cup sugar mixed with 1 teaspoon Chinese 5-spice powder (star anise, fennel, cinnamon, cloves, and pepper or ginger)

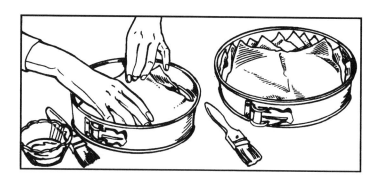

1.

Mix apricot syrup with the apricot brandy and set aside. Gently spread the warmed marmalade over the bottom of the tart crust. Top with drained apricots.

2.

Generously glaze apricots with the apricot syrup and serve immediately.

FILLING

apricot syrup (recipe follows)

2 tablespoons apricot brandy

1/2 cup orange or apricot marmalade, warmed

1 large can apricot halves, drained (or fresh halves)

1.

Combine apricots and 1/2 cup mead in food processor and purée.

2.

Simmer purèe plus all remaining ingredients slowly until very thick.

APRICOT SYRUP

5 whole canned or fresh apricots, pitted and peeled

2 cups mead

1/2 cup sugar

juice of 1 lemon

Hippocras, a drink made of mead, raisin juice, herbs and spices, is taken for medicinal purposes and is named for *Hippocrates, the father of medicine.*

IMPERIAL BAKLAVA

These nut-filled twists of phyllo dough are enhanced with a not-too-sweet syrup that is fragrant with beer and orange-blossom water.

1 cup each toasted chopped walnuts, almonds, hazelnuts, pecans
1/2 cup sesame seeds, lightly toasted
1/2 cup each white and brown sugar
2/3 teaspoon ground cardamom
2 tablespoons quality cinnamon

2 pounds phyllo sheets, thawed
2 pounds sweet butter, clarified

1 1/2 cups water
1 cup brown ale
1 1/2 cups sugar
1 cup honey
1 cup Lyles Golden Syrup or corn syrup (see Note)
3 cinnamon sticks
1/2 teaspoon whole cloves
1 tablespoon each finely grated lemon and orange zest
1/4 cup freshly squeezed lemon juice, strained
2 teaspoons rose or orange-blossom water or rose syrup (optional)

1.
For the filling, thoroughly combine first five ingredients in a bowl and set aside.

2.
Lay a sheet of phyllo on a lightly greased tray, brush top with butter.

3.
Spoon a thin strip of filling on the phyllo, roll gently, forming a long thin tube. Carefully wrap the tube into a coil.

4.
Place on a lightly greased baking sheet and cover with a damp towel until the sheet is filled.

5.
Remove towel and bake for 35 to 40 minutes at 350° until medium gold.

6.
While baklava is baking, prepare syrup. Dissolve water, ale, sugar, honey, and Lyles Golden Syrup over medium-low, add cinnamon, cloves, zest, and juice.

7.
Simmer uncovered 45 minutes. Remove from heat and stir in orange-blossom water. Cool thoroughly.

8.
When baklava is cool, pour enough syrup over the top to cover completely. Allow to stand, covered, 4 to 6 hours before serving.

NOTE
❧ Lyles Golden Syrup is a buttery caramel-flavored corn syrup made in England.

❧ Rosewater and orange-blossom water are available at most pharmacies.

SOPAPILLAS

Light as air, these flavorful pockets of fried dough are the perfect complement to a Mexican dinner or served hot as a special breakfast and smothered with honey or cinnamon sugar.

3 cups unbleached flour
1 tablespoon baking powder
1 teaspoon salt
1 1/2 teaspoons ground cinnamon
3 tablespoons margarine
1 cup warm mead or still cider
2 teaspoons vanilla extract
corn or vegetable oil for frying

1 1/2 cup honey
1/3 cup cinnamon sugar

1.
In a large bowl, combine flour, baking powder, salt, and cinnamon. Using a pastry blender, cut in margarine until crumbly.

2.
Combine mead and vanilla and stir into flour mixture, blending just to moisten. Turn onto a floured board and knead 4 to 5 minutes.

3.
Divide dough in half, wrap each piece in plastic wrap, and allow to rest 15 minutes.

4.
Heat corn or vegetable oil 5 inches deep in a heavy Dutch oven. While heating, roll half the dough on a lightly floured surface into a 10 x 10-inch square. Turn after each rolling to keep from sticking. Flour the rolling surface when necessary.

5.
Cut dough into 6 4 x 4-inch squares. Repeat with other half.

6.
When oil reaches 375°, roll each small square again until very thin (about a 6 x 6-inch square). Place squares two at a time into hot oil.

7.
When sopapillas are golden and puffy on one side, turn and fry until golden on the other side. Remove and drain on a warm pan lined with paper towels. Keep in a 200° oven until all are cooked.

8.
Drizzle with warmed honey or sprinkle with cinnamon sugar.

GERMAN'S® SWEET CHOCOLATE CAKE

Makes 1 8-inch 3-layer cake

The classic recipe everyone in the 1950s made is still unbeatable today. This recipe includes minor changes from the traditional rendition – the addition of dark bock being one of them. And though German's® Sweet Chocolate is traditional, semisweet or dark chocolate can be substituted.

CAKE

3 8-inch springform pans
2 1/2 cups cake flour, sifted
1 teaspoon baking soda, sifted
1/2 teaspoon salt
6 ounces Baker's German's® Sweet Chocolate, semisweet, or (my favorite) extra-bitter chocolate
2 sticks butter, softened
1 1/2 cups sugar
4 extra-large egg yolks
2 teaspoons vanilla extract
1/2 cup dark bock
1 cup buttermilk
1/2 cup sugar
1/4 teaspoon cream of tartar
4 extra-large egg whites, room temperature

1.
Preheat oven to 350°. Generously butter 3 8-inch springform pans and dust with cocoa powder. In a medium bowl combine flour, soda, and salt thoroughly; set aside.

2.
Melt chocolate slowly in a microwave oven or double boiler, stirring gently. Set aside to cool.

3.
Beat butter and 1 1/2 cups sugar until very light and fluffy. Beat in yolks, one at a time. Beat in vanilla and stir in the melted chocolate and beer and buttermilk.

4.
Combine 1/2 cup sugar and cream of tartar, stirring thoroughly. In a deep bowl, whip egg whites until frothy. Continue beating and slowly add sugar until stiff peaks form.

5.
Combine cake flour mixture alternately by thirds with buttermilk mixture, beating well after each addition. Repeat until completely combined.

6.
Carefully fold in one-fourth of the beaten egg whites, lightening the batter. Gently fold in remaining whites.

7.
Evenly divide batter between the 3 pans and smooth tops with a spatula. Bake at 350° for 30 minutes or until a pick inserted in the middle comes out clean.

8.
Allow cakes to cool 10 minutes in the pan before removing. ▼

1.

In a medium bowl, whisk yolks and sugar until light and fluffy. Whisk in evaporated milk, beer, powdered milk, and softened butter.

2.

Pour into a heavy 3-quart saucepan or double boiler and heat on low. Stir constantly until thick (it will cling to the spoon) about 10 to 14 minutes. Do not allow to boil or the eggs will curdle and the frosting will be ruined.

3.

Remove pan from heat and stir in chocolate gently until completely melted. Add vanilla, coconut, and pecans, blending thoroughly.

4.

Allow frosting to cool completely and refrigerate 1 hour, stirring every 20 minutes. The frosting is ready to use when it holds its shape firmly in the spoon.

5.

Wrap unfrosted sides of the cake with plastic wrap to keep them from drying out. Refrigerate until frosting is chilled.

COCONUT PECAN FROSTING

6 extra-large egg yolks
1 cup sugar
3/4 cup canned evaporated milk
1/4 cup dark bock
1/4 cup dry milk powder
12 tablespoons butter, cut in small pieces, room temperature
3 to 4 ounces German's® Sweet Chocolate, semisweet, or dark chocolate, chopped coarsely
2 teaspoons vanilla
2 cups sweetened shredded coconut, lightly toasted
1 1/2 cups lightly toasted pecans, chopped

ASSEMBLING

1.

Use a long serrated knife horizontally to even the tops of the layers. Invert the bottom layer onto the serving plate, removing the cake pan carefully so as not to tear the surface.

2.

Spread the first layer with 1/2 inch of frosting. Invert the second layer onto the frosted first layer, position, and remove cake pan, frost with 1/2 inch of frosting. Repeat with third layer, piling the remaining frosting on top.

BREAD PUDDING

1.

Beat egg yolks until light and fluffy, add brown sugar. Stir in the half-and-half, beer, Crème de Cacao, and orange zest. Set aside.

2.

Combine the torn bread, raisins, apples, nuts, and coconut. Pour in the yolk mixture and coat bread thoroughly.

3.

In a large bowl whip egg whites until frothy. Add granulated sugar and continue whipping until stiff peaks form.

4.

Gently fold the egg whites into the bread mixture until well-combined.

5.

Carefully spoon the mixture into the buttered pan kugelhopf (or 2 bundt pans). Place the baking pan in a larger pan of hot water and bake at 325° for 1 1/2 hours or until a knife inserted into the middle comes out clean.

6.

Cool 30 minutes. Run a knife around the center tube and sides of the mold. Gently shake and twist the mold until the pudding releases. Turn onto serving platter. Serve with Lagered Caramel Sauce (page 253).

10 large eggs, separated

1 cup brown sugar, firmly packed

5 to 6 cups half-and-half (using less cream gives a firmer texture)

2 cups altbier

1/4 cup Crème de Cacao

2 tablespoons orange zest, finely chopped

8 cups Italian or French bread, torn in small chunks

1 cup raisins soaked in liqueur of your choice

2 apples, peeled, cored, and chopped (optional)

2/3 cup toasted nuts, coarsely chopped (optional)

1 cup toasted coconut (optional)

3/4 to 1 cup granulated sugar

Serves 8 to 12

Bread pudding is the ultimate in simple comfort food. This recipe goes well beyond the basics by adding the richness of altbier, baking in a handsome kugelhopf mold, and serving with a luscious Lagered Caramel Sauce.

MENU PLANNER

SPRING

BREAKFAST
Savory Scones (p. 201) ♦ Marinated Skewered Fruit (p. 84) ♦ Omelets with Glazed Onions and cheese (p. 30)

LUNCH
Rustic Strata (p. 32) ♦ Grilled Tomato and Onion Salad with Southwest Feta Dressing (p. 89) ♦ Butter and Beer Cake (p. 235)

DINNER
Baked Stuffed Onions (appetizer — use small onions and halve the stuffing recipe) (p. 223) ♦ Risotto (p. 34) ♦ Fresh blanched green beans with herbed butter (p. 228) ♦ Bouillabaisse served with Tangy French Bread (p. 52) ♦ Enchanted Apricot Tarte (p. 271)

SUMMER

BREAKFAST
Corn Crêpes filled with ripe fruit, Raspberry Sauce and Crème Fraîche (p. 270) ♦ Thin grilled breakfast steaks seasoned with Homebrewed Steak Sauce (p. 214)

LUNCH
Velvet Corn Soup (p. 60) ♦ Grilled Teriyaki Fish (p. 98) served with Lo Mein ♦ Peach Melba Sorbet (p. 262)

DINNER
Southwest Stuffed Shrimp (appetizer) (p. 107) ♦ Fajitas with flour tortillas and Pico De Gallo (p. 140) ♦ Elegant Beer-dressed Fruit (p. 264)

FALL

BREAKFAST
Welsh Benedict (p. 36) ♦ Ripe pear slices adorned with Caramel Sauce (p. 253)

LUNCH
Multicolored Vegetable Chili (p. 44) ♦ Carrot and Jicama Salad (p. 90) ♦ Marvelous Corn Muffins (p. 202) ♦ Stuffed Mead Figs (p. 264)

DINNER
Potato Soup (appetizer) (p. 48) ♦ Homemade Ale and Egg Dinner Rolls (p 189) ♦ Stuffed Game Hens (p. 170) ♦ Spinach Salad with Eureka Dressing (p. 224) ♦ German's® Sweet Chocolate Cake (p. 275)

WINTER

BREAKFAST
Yeasty Belgium Waffles with Beer Syrup (p. 209) ♦ Homemade Sausage Patties (p. 154) ♦ Sectioned citrus plate with Eureka Dressing (p. 229)

LUNCH
French Onion Soup (p. 51) ♦ Smoked Meat Salad with Spiced Pecans (p. 73) ♦ Stout Float with Brownies (p. 269)

DINNER
Curried Corn (p. 81) ♦ Apple and Onion-filled Squash (p. 79) ♦ Crisp green salad with Mustard Dressing (p. 217) ♦ Swedish Rye Dinner Rolls (p. 186) ♦ Impeccable Pork Roast (p. 143) ♦ Poached Pears with Chocolate Porter Sauce and Crème Fraîche (p. 252)

ELEGANT HOLIDAY & ETHNIC MEALS

SPARKLING CHRISTMAS FEAST
Brie in Puff Pastry (appetizer) (p. 37) ♦ Beer-glazed Carrots (p. 80) ♦ Green beans with Herbed Butter and toasted slivered almonds (p. 228) ♦ Märzen Glazed New Potatoes (p. 227) ♦ Portered Roast Beast (p. 122) ♦ Black Russian Rye Dinner Rolls (p. 190) ♦ Publicans Plum Pudding with Caramel Sauce (p. 265)

NEW YEARS PARTY HORS D'OEUVRES
Steak Bundles (p. 121) ♦ Marinated and Skewered Shrimp (p. 102) ♦ Crudites and Tangy French Bread dipped in Hot Beer and Cheese Sauce (p. 184) ♦ Vibrant Antipasto Salad (p. 71) ♦ Almond Chicken Salad with Curried Bread Rolls (p. 92) ♦ Petite diamonds of Imperial Baklava (p. 273) ♦ Stout and Whiskey Truffles (p. 266)

VALENTINES DAY ROMANTIC SUPPER
Scallops Escabèche (appetizer) (p. 109) ♦ Honey Bran Bread Dinner Twists (p. 185) ♦ The Perfect Beef Steak (p. 115) ♦ Grilled Eggplant with Red Pepper Sauce (p. 76) ♦ Chocolate Mousse with Raspberry Sauce (p. 245)

EASTER
Shrimp or Crawfish Bisque (p. 58) ♦ Medley of Glazed Carrots and Parsnips (p. 80) ♦ Lightly steamed asparagus with Mustard Sauce (p. 217) ♦ Herbed French Bread and parsleyed rice ♦ Stuffed Leg of Lamb with Two Sauces (p. 133) ♦ Spring berries bathed in Zabaglione (p. 256)

FOURTH OF JULY PICNIC
Tropical Fruit Salad with Tamarind Dressing (p. 85) ♦ Stuffed Breads (p. 194) or ♦ Barbequed Pork Speedies on Tangy French Bread (p. 155) ♦ Boston Baked Beer-Beans (p. 53) ♦ Pecan Pralines (p. 267)

THANKSGIVING

The Ultimate Potato Soup (appetizer) (p. 48) ♦ Honey Wheat Walnut Rolls (p. 188) ♦ Boiled New Potatoes with Herbed Butter (p. 228) ♦ Crisp greens and grilled red onion with Antipasto Salad Dressing (p. 71) ♦ Perfectly Roasted Chicken (p. 161) (or substitute a small turkey) ♦ Chocolate Stout and Bourbon Pie (p. 255), Sweet Potato Pie (p. 241) or Apple Crisp (p. 239)

COMPANY'S COMING BUT TIME IS SHORT?

Simply Prepare the Day Ahead ♦ Chilled Blueberry Bisque (appetizer) (p. 64) ♦ Beef Beer-Buignonne served with fresh linguini (p. 120) ♦ Salad of bitter greens with Fresh Croutons and Raspberry Dressing (p. 230) ♦ Chocolate Stout Cake (p. 247)

SOUTHWEST/CASUAL

Caldo de Queso (p. 54) ♦ Crudites served with Southwest Feta Dressing (p. 89) ♦ Chicken/Turkey Fajitas (p. 168) or Enchiladas ♦ Spanish Rice (p. 226) ♦ Sopapillas (p. 274)

SOUTHWEST/LESS CASUAL

Albondigas Soup (appetizer) (p. 59) ♦ Succulent pineapple slices garnished with Spicy Fruit Salsa (p. 221) ♦ Stuffed Steak à la Candy (p. 118) ♦ Al dente fettuccini crowned with Cheese Sauce with a Twist (p. 215) ♦ The Ultimate Flan (p. 268)

SOUTHWEST BUFFET, A MAKE-YOUR-OWN PARTY

Caldo de Queso (bowls, hot stock and fixings, guests assemble their own) (p. 54) ♦ Tostados with Frijoles Borrachos (tostado shells, frijoles, and fixings) (p. 55) ♦ Candy's Version - Tacos (tortillas, meat, and fixings) (p. 135) ♦ Spanish Rice, Pico De Gallo and Salsa Ranchero (p. 226) ♦ Corn Crêpes with glazed apples (p. 270), or pineapple and Crème Fraîche (p. 35)

ASIAN

Won-ton Soup (p. 47) ♦ Lo Mein and/or Spicy Vegetarian Stir-Fry (p. 83) ♦ Beef with Snow Peas (p. 127) or ♦ Kung Pao Chicken (p. 177) or ♦ Malaysian Chicken (p. 179) ♦ Sweet-N-Sour Pork with steamed rice (p. 148) ♦ Gingered Pineapple Sorbet (p. 259)

GLOSSARY

BALSAMIC VINEGAR

This mellow, oak-aged vinegar can add flavor and depth to foods without an overpowering vinegar essence. Find a tasty, moderately priced brand you can use lavishly without wincing at the price.

BROTH AND STOCK

There seems to be a common misunderstanding of these two ingredients. *Broth* is the flavorful liquid made by simmering bones and vegetables for a few hours. *Stock* is the result of straining broth and reducing over heat by one-third or more to intensify its essence.

BASMATI RICE

This is the most flavorful, aromatic rice one could imagine, and is available in Middle Eastern or health-food stores. The following method of cooking seems to enhance the phenomenal flavor of this delightful rice.

Place 1 cup of rice in a 3-quart saucepan. Cover with water, swish the rice, and discard the water. Repeat 7 to 8 times or until the water is clear. Cover with water and 1 teaspoon of salt. Let stand 6 to 18 hours. Drain and add 1 cup fresh water plus 1 teaspoon vegetable oil. Bring to a simmer, cover, and turn heat to low. After 10 minutes remove and let stand an additional 10 minutes. Fluff with a fork and serve.

CAMERON SMOKER

See page 26.

CHINESE 5-SPICE POWDER

A blend of cinnamon, star anise, ground fennel, cloves, and ginger or pepper, this combination is perfect for adding an exotic touch to simple dishes.

CHILIES

CAUTION. Use rubber gloves when handling chilies and never touch your eyes or face with your hands or gloves.

Chipotle

A smoked ripe jalapeno, chipotle chilies are available either canned or dried. The rich, hauntingly smoky flavor these impart to a dish is incredible. It is usually necessary to reconstitute the dried form.

Green

Fresh long, mild chilies that are roasted, peeled and used extensively in Southwestern cuisine. To choose, look for smooth-skinned, straight chilies (it's hard to roast and peel twisted chilies) that have a slight heaviness to them. I love the flavor and texture of firm-fleshed roasted chilies, so I have devised my own method of preparing them.

When roasting chilies remember the object is to char the outside without overcooking the inside. This must be done with very high heat. If roasted at lower heat they become soggy and disintegrate when peeled.

To roast chilies, rub lightly with vegetable oil and sear over a very hot grill or flame, or directly under a broiler element. When the skin bubbles and scorches lightly turn them, repeating until all sides are charred.

Tradition dictates that you cover or place in a paper bag to steam after roasting. I find that the chilies continue to cook on the inside and often end up mushy when handled in this fashion. I usually space them out on a pan and allow them to cool just until I can handle them. Peel off the scorched skin using a small serrated blade to gently scrape away stubborn areas. Open to remove seeds and veins, if desired.

Store peeled chilies in the refrigerator up to two days or freeze for up to 6 months.

Red

Dried red chilies are ground to make red chili powder, or can be soaked whole and puréed. Most common are the smooth, long, dried New Mexico or California chilies, usually found in mild or hot varieties. If available, try ancho, mulatto, negro, pasilla, guajillo, or chipotle, to name a few.

Serrano

Small, narrow chili usually sold green that ripens to a bright red. These are hot but extremely tasty, making them perfect to add to sauces and relishes that will not be cooked.

Thai

These small, thin chilies are miniature sticks of dynamite. Soak and add to stir-fry for a fiery experience, or grind and sprinkle judiciously in a recipe calling for glowing flavor.

CILANTRO

Also known as Chinese parsley or fresh coriander, this green, leafy plant is grown from coriander seeds. Its pungent, distinctive flavor is used extensively in many cuisines. To store, wrap in a paper towel and place in an open plastic bag. To use, chop coarsely or use the leaves whole — mincing too finely will dominate rather than enhance the food's flavor.

CINNAMON

Often overlooked because of familiarity, cinnamon makes such a difference when you use the fresh, quality spice rather than the stale stuff found in cans at the grocery. Try the best just once and you will never go back. See The Spice House on page 26.

CRÈME FRAÎCHE

This decadent homemade soured cream is the ultimate addition to everything from beef stroganoff to cheesecake. Use to replace sour cream in any recipe.

CROUTONS

Traditionally made by sautéing cubed bread with butter, I prefer the baked version. These are simply made by slicing fresh bread (French, Italian, curry) and brushing one side with butter melted with garlic, herbs, or shallot. Bake at 375° until golden and crisp. Cool briefly and cube using a sharp serrated knife.

CURRY POWDER

An exotic blending of turmeric, ginger, chili, garlic, cumin, coriander, cloves, pepper, fenugreek, and fennel (among others). Curry powder is a lovely way to incorporate the complex essence of the East Indies into your cooking.

DEGLAZING

This is the process of adding liquid to a hot pan to remove the concentrated essence and crusty bits of food that were cooked in it. The liquid is then used to make sauce or gravy.

DUTCH-PROCESS COCOA POWDER
European-style cocoa powder that has undergone a mild alkali process to darken and enrich the chocolate flavor.

FINES HERBES (MIXED HERBS)
A sophisticated blend of chervil, parsley, chives, and tarragon, this combination is perfect for subtly flavoring a myriad of dishes.

GORGONZOLA CHEESE
This soft, creamy, blue-veined cheese is a good choice for people who prefer mild blue cheese.

HAWAIIAN CLAY
This organic clay is available in red or white for baking food. Always wrap food in parchment, banana leaves, fresh or dried reconstituted cornhusks before coating with a thick layer of clay. The clay imparts a delectable flavor all its own (similar to Hawaiian pit cooking) and moist, succulent, mouthwatering tenderness. Hawaiian organic clay is found at or ordered through ceramic specialty stores.

HOMEMADE SOUR CREAM
See Crème Fraîche, page 35.

ITALIAN ARBORIO RICE
This short, round-grained rice is perfect for risottos and puddings because it cooks up creamy and soft. Usually found in gourmet markets or the specialty section of your grocery store.

ITALIAN PARSLEY
This flat-leafed variety of parsley is far more subtle and compatible to cooking than its curly cousin. It is becoming more readily available across the nation and is worth searching out. If unavailable, substitute only half as much curly parsley in place of Italian.

KOSHER SALT
This coarse salt is perfect for roasting meats, giving a crisp, delectable crust, and for sprinkling on salads because it will not wilt your greens. If you take a grain of kosher salt and place it on your tongue it will have a light, pleasurable saltiness without the biting harshness of table salt.

LYCHEE NUTS
These succulent fruits of the Orient have a unique sweet flavor. Usually available in the oriental section of your grocery store, they are wonderful chilled and added to salads.

LYLES GOLDEN SYRUP
This rich amalgam is a taste sensation that can only be described as the flavor of English toffee — butterscotch and caramel blended into a cane syrup base. Imported from England, it is an extraordinary addition to candy, sweet sauces, and glazes of all sorts. It is worth searching out and using for your specialty cooking, but I warn you, do not let the kids taste it. They can easily consume an entire jar of this precious syrup in one sitting!

MASA HARINA FLOUR
To make corn tortillas, corn that has been treated in the same manner as hominy is ground into a dough known as masa. The dried version is masa harina flour, usually available in the Mexican section of large grocery stores. This flour is an excellent thickening agent for Southwestern cuisine and can be the base for homemade tortillas and tamales.

MEXICAN-STYLE CHEESE

Made in the United States, usually in Wisconsin or California, Mexican-style cheeses are superbly flavored and have retained that "real cheese" essence. To substitute where not available: Queso Añejo is roughly equivalent to Muenster, Queso Oaxaca is roughly equivalent to Mozzarella, Queso Ranchero is roughly equivalent to Monterey jack and Queso Panela is roughly equivalent to fresh water-packed Mozzarella. There are many other varieties, but these are the most common.

MOLÉ PASTE

A rich concoction made from ground ancho and mulatto chilies, toasted pumpkin seeds, sesame seeds, tortillas, nuts, spices, and a minuscule amount of chocolate. It takes only a small amount of this thick paste to infuse your food with the essence of Mexico.

MUSHROOMS

Shitake

Also known as Chinese black mushrooms or Black Forest mushrooms, these dried, meaty mushrooms have a deep, woodsy flavor that is deliciously different. Dried shitakes are usually available in the oriental section of the grocery store or in most Asian groceries. The fresh domestic shitake mushrooms available in some areas are delicious but not as potent as the dried.

Dried Woods Ear

Oriental mushrooms also known poetically as clouds ears or less-than-poetically as black fungus, these flavorful dried edibles are reconstituted in water before use. The tough core-stem is always removed before chopping.

NAPA OR BOK CHOY CABBAGE

Mildly flavored cabbages used extensively in oriental cooking. Napa cabbage is delicious sliced thinly and dressed lightly.

NOPALITOS

Cooked and peeled cactus pads that are lightly pickled when canned. These flavorful strips are similar to okra and should be rinsed with cold water before using. They have a distinctive tangy, slightly acidic flavor.

NUTS

Toasting nuts before using doubles their flavor qualities. Toast by spreading on a heavy pan and baking in a 350° oven for 12 to 15 minutes or in a heavy, dry skillet on the stove until fragrant.

OLIVE OIL

For dark, rich olive oil fragrant with the essence of olives, purchase cold-pressed extra-virgin olive oil extracted from the first pressing. Try oils from around the world — Italy, Spain, Greece, and France — each has uniquely flavored oils that heighten the flavor of all they grace. And make sure your oil is a "product of" the country, not "packed in" that country. Often "pure olive oil packed in" is a lesser quality oil shipped to that country and packaged there, not grown and processed there.

PARCHMENT

This specially treated, food-safe paper is designed for wrapping food to be baked in paper, and for lining pans and baking sheets. It's also used extensively in cake decorating and candy making. Lining baking pans with parchment permits food that normally would stick to be removed easily. Use to wrap and bake fish or chicken in to retain moisture.

PESTO

This Italian combination of fresh basil leaves, garlic, olive oil, nuts, and cheese can be used to grace everything from fresh pasta to soup. My favorite variation is a cilantro pesto that imparts the flavor of the Southwest to many dishes.

PICO DE GALLO

An addictive combination of chopped onions, tomatoes, fresh chilies, garlic, spices, and herbs used as a relish for many Southwestern dishes.

PIPIAN PASTE

Similar to molé paste, this is a slightly different blend of chilies, toasted nuts, pumpkin seeds, and seasonings found in the Mexican section of the grocery store.

PUFF PASTRY

A rich, buttery dough that bakes up into hundreds of fragile layers. Although not impossible to make, it is time-consuming. Frozen puff pastry from the grocery store is a great alternative.

RED CURRY PASTE

This incredibly intense blend of Thai chili, garlic, onions, and seasonings embodies the flavor of Thai cuisine in one small can. For a simple spicy meal heat 1 teaspoon red curry paste in 2 table-spoons oil and sauté fish, vegetables, or chicken. This flavorsome condiment is found in Asian grocery stores and some large supermarkets. Store in the refrigerator in an airtight jar. This stuff is too ornery to spoil!

RED CHILI POWDER

Ground red chili powder attains its fullest flavor when toasted lightly before being used. Toasting also removes bitterness. To toast, heat a heavy skillet over medium, turn heat off and add chili pow-der, stirring constantly for about 45 to 60 seconds or until fragrant. Remove immediately because it will burn in the wink of an eye.

REDUCING LIQUIDS

Reduction of liquids is a method of concentrating flavor by evaporation. The liquid is cooked quick-ly over high heat until the desired intensity is reached.

ROUX

An equal blend of flour and butter cooked slowly before using to thicken gravies and sauces. This mixture must be cooked to eliminate that starchy quality associated with wallpaper paste. See page 22 for further explanation.

SAFFRON

The most expensive and treasured spice, saffron is the dried stigma of a type of crocus grown in Mediterranean climates. It takes the stigmas from roughly 72,000 crocuses to make 1 pound of this distinctive spice.

Saffron is sold powdered or in threads. The thread form retains its flavor much longer than powdered. Saffron in any form must be mixed with a small amount of hot liquid to dissolve it before adding to a dish. Unlike other spices, saffron does not intensify in flavor with lengthy cooking and is actually more flavorful when added for just the final 10 to 15 minutes.

SESAME OIL

Dark, toasted sesame oil adds an enticing aromatic oriental essence. If you have ever enjoyed sim-ple stir-fried vegetables at a restaurant and tried to reproduce the flavor at home with no success, this probably was the missing ingredient.

When purchasing be sure to get "100 percent pure sesame oil," not "sesame-flavored oil." Store in a cool, dark place. Pale cold-pressed sesame oil available in health-food stores is not the same. To use, add sparingly drop by drop until the desired flavor is reached. Add to barbecue sauces, rub on meats to be sautéed or grilled, and include a few drops in your salad dressings for a nutty background flavor.

SHALLOTS

If you were to take the best flavor from onion and garlic, eliminate the harsh characteristics they both possess, and place that flavor in a small onion-shaped package, you would have a shallot.

The bulbs are peeled and used like onion and garlic. Sliced, chopped, minced, or pressed like garlic, their mild enhancing qualities make them perfect for almost any savory fare. Unlike onions and garlic, it is almost impossible to have too much shallot in a dish! If you enjoy preparing Thai cuisine, note that "red onion" means shallot.

SOY SAUCE

A distinctive oriental sauce widely known and appreciated for its flavor-enhancing qualities. There are a number of varieties with differing characteristics.

Light soy sauce is delicate and only slightly salty, used in both cooking and to season food such as rice at the table. Dark soy sauce is very rich, salty, and used only for cooking. An easy way to test for light or dark sauce is to shake the bottle. If the bottle clears immediately it is light soy sauce, if it remains opaque it is dark soy sauce.

SPICES

Whole spices freshly crushed are always preferable to ground powdered spices because the essential oils evaporate rapidly once ground.

STOCK

See Broth.

SZECHWAN PEPPERCORNS

Not a real peppercorn but actually a dried berry, this citrusy aromatic spice is quite distinctive and intensifies the quality of red chilies.

TAMARINDS

Grown in tropical areas, brown tamarind pods are covered by a fragile papery shell. The sticky inner pulp has a delectable sweet-tart quality that can be quite exquisite, especially when made into a syrup with beer.

Tamarind can usually be found in the oriental section of your grocery store or Asian and East Indian specialty shops.

To use whole tamarind pods, remove the shell and soak or simmer the fruit until softened. Strain, removing seeds. Small cakes of tamarind pulp can be used by merely cutting off a section, softening, and straining.

THAI SWEET HOT SAUCE

Sold as "Sweet Hot Sauce For Chicken," this spicy, flavorsome glaze combines sweet, hot, and garlic in an unbelievable alliance. Use on everything from hot dogs and hamburgers to chicken, ribs, vegetables, and rice.

WHIPPING CREAM

After braving glares from the health-conscious I have to say that if you are going to do it, do it right. Purchase cream with the highest butterfat content possible. If you have ever chilled the bowl and beaters only to have your whipped cream deflate the moment you stopped whisking, blame it on the cream. Ultrapasteurizing lowers the butterfat content that gives the cream the ability to hold its shape. The more butterfat, the stiffer the cream.

INDEX

HOMEBREWER?

Join the thousands of American Homebrewers Association members who read **zymurgy** — the magazine for homebrewers and beer lovers.

Every issue of **zymurgy** is full of tips, techniques, new recipes, new products, equipment and ingredient reviews, beer news, technical articles — the whole world of homebrewing. PLUS, the AHA brings members the National Homebrewers Conference, the National Homebrew Competition, the Beer Judge Certification Program, the Homebrew Club Network, periodic discounts on books from Brewers Publications and much much more.

Photocopy and mail this coupon today to join the AHA or call now for credit card orders, (303) 546-6514.

- -

BOOKS for Brewers and Beer Lovers

Order Now ... Your Brew Will Thank You!

These books offered by Brewers Publications are some of the most sought after reference tools for homebrewers and professional brewers alike. Filled with tips, techniques, recipes and history, these books will help you expand your brewing horizons. Let the world's foremost brewers help you as you brew. So whatever your brewing level or interest, Brewers Publications has the information necessary for you to brew the best beer in the world — your beer.

Please send me more free information on the following: (check all that apply)

◊ Merchandise & Book Catalog
◊ American Homebrewers Association

◊ Institute for Brewing Studies
◊ Great American Beer Festival℠

Ship to:

Name

Address

City   State/Province

Zip/Postal Code   Country

Daytime Phone   (   )

Payment Method

◊ Check or Money Order Enclosed (Payable to the Association of Brewers)
◊ Visa   ◊ MasterCard

Card Number   –   –   –   Expiration Date

Name on Card   Signature

Brewers Publications, PO Box 1679, Boulder, CO 80306-1679, (303) 546-6514, FAX (303) 447-2825.

BP-O93

Examine the World of

Microbrewing
and
Pubbrewing

Travel the world of commercial, small-scale brewing; the realm of microbrewers and pubbrewers.

The New Brewer magazine guides you through this new industry. Its pages introduce you to marketing, finance, operations, equipment, recipes, interviews — in short, the whole landscape.

Subscribe to ***The New Brewer*** and become a seasoned traveler.

The *New Brewer*
THE MAGAZINE FOR MICRO- AND PUBBREWERS

BREWERS PUBLICATIONS ORDER FORM

PROFESSIONAL BREWING BOOKS

QTY.	TITLE	STOCK #	PRICE	EXT. PRICE
_____	Brewery Planner	440	80.00	_____
_____	North American Brewers Resource Directory	451	80.00	_____
_____	Principles of Brewing Science	415	29.95	_____

THE BREWERY OPERATIONS SERIES
from Micro and Pubbrewers Conferences

QTY.	TITLE	STOCK #	PRICE	EXT. PRICE
_____	Volume 4, 1987 Conference	424	25.95	_____
_____	Volume 5, 1988 Conference	428	25.95	_____
_____	Volume 6, 1989 Conference	430	25.95	_____
_____	Volume 7, 1990 Conference	433	25.95	_____
_____	Volume 8, 1991 Conference, Brewing Under Adversity	442	25.95	_____
_____	Volume 9, 1992 Conference, Quality Brewing — Share the Experience	447	25.95	_____

CLASSIC BEER STYLE SERIES

QTY.	TITLE	STOCK #	PRICE	EXT. PRICE
_____	Pale Ale	431	11.95	_____
_____	Continental Pilsener	434	11.95	_____
_____	Lambic	437	11.95	_____
_____	Vienna, Märzen, Oktoberfest	444	11.95	_____
_____	Porter	443	11.95	_____
_____	Belgian Ale	446	11.95	_____
_____	German Wheat Beer	448	11.95	_____
_____	Scotch Ale	449	11.95	_____
_____	Bock (available Spring 1994)	452	11.95	_____

BEER AND BREWING SERIES, for homebrewers and beer enthusiasts
from National Homebrewers Conferences

QTY.	TITLE	STOCK #	PRICE	EXT. PRICE
_____	Volume 8, 1988 Conference	427	21.95	_____
_____	Volume 9, 1989 Conference	429	21.95	_____
_____	Volume 10, 1990 Conference	432	21.95	_____
_____	Volume 11, 1991 Conference, Brew Free Or Die!	435	21.95	_____
_____	Volume 12, 1992 Conference, Just Brew It!	436	21.95	_____

GENERAL BEER AND BREWING INFORMATION

QTY.	TITLE	STOCK #	PRICE	EXT. PRICE
_____	Brewing Lager Beer	417	14.95	_____
_____	Brewing Mead	418	11.95	_____
_____	Dictionary of Beer and Brewing	414	19.95	_____
_____	Evaluating Beer	456	25.95	_____
_____	Great American Beer Cookbook	455	24.95	_____
_____	Winners Circle	407	11.95	_____

Call or write for a free *Beer Enthusiast* catalog today.
- U.S. funds only.
- All Brewers Publications books come with a money-back guarantee.
- **Postage & Handling:** $3 for the first book ordered, plus $1 for each book thereafter. Canadian and foreign orders please add $4 for the first book and $2 for each book thereafter. Orders cannot be shipped without appropriate P&H.

SUBTOTAL _____

Colo. Residents Add 3% Sales Tax _____

P & H * _____

TOTAL _____

Brewers Publications, PO Box 1679, Boulder, CO 80306-1679, (303) 546-6514, FAX (303) 447-2825.

BP-O93